parkrun

"Such an interesting read, offering a real insight into the impact and benefits of parkrun. Not only does David Hindley understand parkrun from a parkrunner's perspective, he also understands our organisational purpose and what drives our decision-making and our approach."

Nick Pearson, *parkrun* CEO 2015 to 2022

This is the first book to take an in-depth look at parkrun – the free, weekly, timed 5 km run on a Saturday morning – and to examine why its participants love it so much and why it has been such an astonishing success.

Author David Hindley – a self-described 'middle of the pack' parkrunner – draws on new research, including interviews with other runners, volunteers, and organisers, to shine a light on the unique combination of ingredients in parkrun's magic formula. Tracing the development of parkrun from its first event in the UK in 2004 to the global network of today, he takes a close look at themes like inclusion, volunteering, community, green space, health, and wellbeing, and unpacks the mantra of 'it's a run, not a race' that has come to define the spirit of parkrun for so many of its participants. Partly a sporting event, partly a social movement, and partly a public health intervention, parkrun perhaps offers a model for sustainable public participation in other areas of social life.

This book is compulsory behind-the-scenes reading for all parkrunners and parkrun volunteers, and anybody working in sport development, events, recreation, public health, volunteering, or community organising.

David Hindley is Principal Lecturer at Nottingham Trent University's Sport Science Department, UK. He is an enthusiastic middle-of-the-pack runner and has presented and published research related to recreational running, and parkrun specifically.

parkrun

An Organised Running Revolution

David Hindley

Routledge
Taylor & Francis Group

LONDON AND NEW YORK

Cover image: Helen Hood

First published 2022
by Routledge
4 Park Square, Milton Park, Abingdon, Oxon OX14 4RN

and by Routledge
605 Third Avenue, New York, NY 10158

Routledge is an imprint of the Taylor & Francis Group, an informa business

© 2022 David Hindley

British Library Cataloguing-in-Publication Data
A catalogue record for this book is available from the British Library

Library of Congress Cataloging-in-Publication Data
A catalog record for this book has been requested

ISBN: 978-0-367-64063-7 (hbk)
ISBN: 978-0-367-64061-3 (pbk)
ISBN: 978-1-003-12196-1 (ebk)

DOI: 10.4324/9781003121961

Typeset in Bembo
by Apex CoVantage, LLC

For Steph and Rowan

In memory of my mother and father, Pamela and
John Hindley

Contents

Acknowledgements   viii

1   Introduction: The Rise of parkrun   1

2   An Inclusive Community?   21

3   Volunteering and Reciprocity   42

4   A Panacea for Health and Wellbeing?   59

5   'A Run, Not a Race'   79

6   Becoming a (park)runner   92

7   Green Exercise   110

8   Conclusion: The Future of parkrun   129

Index   136

Acknowledgements

The book began from a series of conversations with Simon Whitmore, Senior Publisher at Routledge (and keen parkrunner) who planted the seed of an idea from which this manuscript has grown. To him I owe a debt of gratitude, along with the reviewers who deemed the initial proposal to have sufficient legs. I am indebted too to those who read, commented on, and helped improve drafts of chapters, as well as providing support throughout the process of writing this book. With that in mind, special thanks are due to Steph and Rowan, who have demonstrated incredible patience, as well as being extraordinary sources of joy and inspiration. Thank you.

Chapter 1

Introduction
The Rise of parkrun

parkrun (small *p*, one word) is a series of free, weekly, mass physical activity community events, delivered by a network of local volunteers and convened in public spaces, including municipal parks and green environments. That parkrun events are organised and orchestrated exclusively by volunteers is one of the components that differentiate parkrun from many other mass participation community events. Many of the volunteers are also parkrunners themselves, switching roles from week to week contingent on availability and local needs. I hesitate to label parkrun a running event as, although this may be how many participants associate the collective, timed 5 km (3.1 mile) activity, such a description belies its distinctiveness. In contrast to traditional running events, parkrun does not present itself as a race, nor would it be accurate to categorise all participants as runners. Indeed, there are no expectations that partakers are fast or slow, favouring an emphasis on individuals completing the distance in a time and at a pace that is comfortable for them. As such parkrun has a broad target audience, eager to encourage the participation of those who are sedentary and inactive, target cohorts for numerous public health interventions.

In some ways the name 'parkrun' could be construed as misleading. In an interview, parkrun's Global Chief Executive Officer, Nick Pearson, preferred a more nuanced depiction of parkrun as 'a social intervention masquerading as a running event.'[1] The social side of parkrun can be recognised in the way aspects of each event provide affordances for social interactions, where even fleeting encounters with strangers – a greeting, smile, or very brief conversation – can help serve basic needs, such as feeling connected and appreciated (Van Lange & Columbus, 2021). As I have written elsewhere, 'parkrun acts as a temporary public space that is conducive for incidental and casual social interaction' (Hindley, 2020, p. 94). Such a portrayal underscores the sociality of parkrun, which operates as what the sociologist Ray Oldenburg (1999) described as 'third places,' spaces where people are welcome to congregate and socially interact. By their nature, third places have the potential to act as levellers, cultivating a space which is inclusive, free of any set formal criteria of membership and exclusion. It is asserted that third places provide an important function to the community in that they are accessible, convenient, and local,

DOI: 10.4324/9781003121961-1

whereas the character of a third place is determined by its 'regulars' whose incidental interactions help to create a playful ambiance and foster a desire to return to recapture the experience (Oldenburg, 1999).

Indeed, there is growing evidence that non-elite mass participation sport events are recognised as having the potential to foster a sense of belonging and 'togetherness' in host communities (Meir & Fletcher, 2019). At the participant level, sport events are similarly acknowledged to provide opportunities for the development of social capital through the building of trust, reciprocity, and networks and, thus, may contribute to individual and community wellbeing (Son et al., 2010; Zhou & Kaplanidou, 2018). On the surface, the notion of social capital encourages us to consider the social connectedness of individuals within a wider community, and as Nicholson and Hoye (2008, p. 3) contend, 'there is an inherent logic in the idea that the more connections individuals make within their communities the better off they will be emotionally, socially, physically, and economically.' Event research is also beginning to recognise their potential for promoting temporary social connections, conviviality, and cama- raderie within the event space, creating meaningful social impact for partici- pants (Hindley, 2020; Lee et al., 2016). In a paper exploring the social capital potential of open water swimming events, authors Greenwood and Fletcher (2020) argue that such events can facilitate casual social interactions, however evidence of bridging capital was less convincing. The testimonies in their study reinforced a common finding that participants preferred to interact with people from within their already-established groups, who invariably were similar to themselves in many ways and thus were not necessarily inclusive of newcomers. Furthermore, it has been noted that sport events can act to divide and exclude those who do not possess the necessary capital to participate (Richardson & Fletcher, 2018; Spaaij & Westerbeek, 2010).

Nevertheless, parkrun originated as a running event for runners. Charting its modest inauguration to a 5 km time trial around Bushy Park in South West London in October 2004 represents well-trodden ground (see Bourne, 2014). The introductory event was remarkably low key, lo-fi (the timing tokens were hand-punched steel washers), and unofficial. There was no permission from the park and no insurance. There were 18 participants in total – 13 runners and five volunteers drawn from nearby running club, Ranelagh Harriers, as well as other local clubs. Saturday was chosen because most organised races were on a Sunday, whilst 9 a.m. was the preferred time so that the runners would be out of the way and would minimise disruption to other park users later in the day. And 5 km was the elected distance because (at the time) most participants could be finished within 30 minutes. As has been widely documented, its founder, Paul Sinton-Hewitt, was facing a number of challenges in his life, hav- ing been made redundant from his marketing job, and side-lined with a long- term injury that prohibited him from training for a marathon, and (crucially) potential isolation from the running community. Paul grew up in South Africa where in his native Johannesburg several running clubs regularly arranged time trials for participants to appraise their progress and then to socialise afterwards. The emphasis on human interaction – in effect relegating the run to secondary importance – was the precondition for the original Bushy Park time trial, that runners and volunteers would assemble later to have a coffee and converse with one another. Thus, whilst the antecedents to parkrun are often labelled as altruistic, by the founder's own admission there was also a hint of selfishness in seeking to remain connected.

The maiden event in Bushy Park brought together white, middle-class, middle-aged runners, but as Nick Pearson is keen to emphasise, the initial design was founded on egalitarian principles, where everyone taking part was valued equally. To illustrate this, back then, there was a prize for both first and last places. This desire to be inclusive is manifest in later adaptations, for example, the designated tail-walker role. This ensures that at every parkrun event a self-nominated volunteer takes on the responsibility of running or walking with the last participant to provide encouragement, as well as guaranteeing to take on the mantle of last place. Consequently, no parkrun participant need fear any perceived stigma or judgement of being the final finisher. Another characteristic feature which is indicative of parkrun's claim to be inclusive is the briefing which marks the beginning of each parkrun event. The briefing sets the scene, welcoming first-timers and visitors, and explains the course, the conditions, and points of safety. The familiar recital notably includes accolades for the team of volunteers, as well as congratulations for any milestone achievements.

Sinton-Hewitt encapsulates the philosophy of parkrun in stressing its malleability and informality:

> [P]eople do what they want to do. All we are doing here is building a playground, and if you want to come and take part, you can. People have recognised that it's free in every sense of the word – it's not just that you don't have to pay, but you're not signing your life away either, there are no terms and conditions, just the same obligations you'd have as a citizen walking down the street.'[2]

In this sense parkrun is about creating an 'ecosystem' that encourages movement, in the company of others, in the outdoors (Wellington, 2021). The events are regular, predictable, and (pandemic aside) permanent but without any requirement or compulsion to participate each week. There is an onus on people being able to take part in whatever manner suits them, whether that be through walking, jogging, running, volunteering (in a range of roles), or simply coming along to watch and socialise. Furthermore, by taking place in local parks and open spaces, this increases accessibility (McIntosh, 2021). There is also a growing body of research which has shown that carrying out physical activity in a natural environment, so-called green exercise, confers greater health and wellbeing benefits in comparison to undertaking the same exercise indoors or in a built-up environment (e.g. Donnelly & Macintyre, 2019; Shanahan et al., 2016).

It is commendable that whilst parkrun has expanded and evolved over time, at its core the democratic values of the founder endure, namely, to create opportunities for participation that are accessible, socially oriented, and welcoming to all, regardless of motivation or competence. There are competitive runners whose primary motivation may be ranking and records, but these are by no means the defining quality of the events. Joggers, walkers, pushchair pushers, those trying to keep pace with their canines, children, and grandparents comingle alongside the committed diehards, and seasoned runners bedecked in athletic club attire. Put simply, no perceptible hierarchy exists between the hares and the tortoises. Moreover, there is a resolve to minimise potential barriers to participation. There is no upper age limit, whilst at the other end, accompanied children as young as four are allowed to participate. No special clothing or equipment is necessary, no restrictions of a time-limited programme, and there are no direct costs. Furthermore, as stated framing parkrun as 'a run, not a race' invites the participation of groups who do not identify with the traditional stereotypical views of running.

Parkrun events are reliant upon a significant number of volunteers, instantly identifiable by their high-vis-jackets, who are responsible for their organisation and delivery. Volunteering opportunities at parkrun is also a means of increasing inclusivity, as people who do not wish to or are physically unable can participate by volunteering. Roles are varied and include run director, course marshals, tail runner, timekeepers, and barcode scanners. There are also volunteers who mark the route, manage the finish funnel, and lead the first-timers' briefing. Additionally, there are occasional roles such as guiding blind or partially sighted runners. And afterwards results are processed, tokens sorted, and volunteers recruited for subsequent weeks. Arguably less well known is the parkrun Ambassador Programme, a support network of volunteers who have applied for a number of different volunteer roles through a formal recruitment process. They are described as an 'essential and valuable resource to parkrun' in supporting events and assisting the small, central parkrun staff team. Their roles, including outreach and translation ambassadors, typically sit outside of the volunteering that takes place at a weekend parkrun event. It has been widely reported that volunteering at parkrun helps foster a sense of involvement, although the reciprocity of volunteering is also evident in the support and encouragement given by parkrunners to each other (Stevinson et al., 2015). The parkrun Health and Wellbeing Survey in 2018 identified that a large proportion of respondents reported that volunteering at parkrun had a positive impact on their health and wellbeing, greater than the potential benefits for parkrunners. The following top five outcomes were rated better or much better due to volunteering at parkrun: feeling part of a community (84.4 per cent), meeting new people (79 per cent), ability to help people (72.4 per cent), happiness (68.7 per cent), and an ability to fulfil moral duties (65 per cent).

That parkrun entails running, jogging, or walking a 5 km course is noteworthy, not least because it is integrally a physical challenge which requires moderate-to-vigorous effort (Wiltshire & Merchant, 2021). The distance is important in respect that it provides an accessible entry point for individuals to take part in regular physical activity. This is borne out by the earliest academic research published on parkrun by Stevinson and Hickson (2014), who report its appeal to groups that are statistically less likely to exercise. Their study of 7,308 parkrunners found that most participants were men and aged between 35 and 54 years. They also found that more than a quarter of those on registration described themselves as 'non-runners,' and a further 26 per cent categorised themselves as 'occasional runners.' Almost half of those 'non-runners' were overweight or obese, more than half were female, and 61 per cent were middle-aged or older. This led the authors to conclude that this form of physical activity was inclusive and effective at reaching historically excluded populations.

These findings were echoed in parkrun's first annual review in 2016, where it was reported that 38,038 previously inactive individuals were now running, that there were 178,812 female first-timers and that 14 per cent of parkruns were by those aged 55 and over (parkrun, 2016). In 2019, nearly 20 per cent of parkruns in the UK were completed by people who did one bout or less of exercise per week when they registered for parkrun. Meanwhile evidence suggested that individuals who are 'inactive' (less than once per week) and 'just active' (about once per week) increased their physical activity by around 75 per cent as a result of parkrun participation (Wellington, 2021). In seeking to explore potential factors which encouraged initial participation and subsequently helped to sustain attendance, Stevinson et al. (2015) identified the overarching themes of freedom and reciprocity from parkrunners' individual accounts. Their qualitative study highlighted the accessible, inclusive ethos of parkrun, the provision of achievement opportunities, and a supportive social environment, along with natural outdoor settings and an integrated volunteer system. As a potential point of departure, whilst the aforementioned studies emphasised inclusion, such claims need to be tempered by the observation made by some that the numbers of ethnic minorities and individuals from lower socio-economic groups are disproportionately low (Stevinson & Hickson, 2014; Fullagar, 2016).

★

There is a prevailing discourse of healthism associated with physical activity. The positive outcomes linked to physical activity are manifold with substantial evidence underlining the universal acceptance that being physically active is a major contributor to one's overall physical and mental wellbeing. The promotion and provision of physical activity opportunities are linked with a range of personal and societal benefits. For many, though, the reality is that we are sedentary beings, our lives characterised by inactivity. In 2018, Public Health England (PHE) analysed previously unpublished data from Sport England's *Active Lives* survey, reporting that 41 per cent of adults aged 40–60 walk less than 10 minutes continuously each month at a brisk pace.[3] The same study revealed that one in five (19.7 per cent) of 40–60-year olds are physically inactive, totalling 3 million adults. This meant participating in less than 30 minutes of moderate-intensity physical activity per week.

Interest in physical inactivity has intensified in recent times such that it has been pronounced as 'pandemic,' with estimates that 6–10 per cent of all deaths from non-communicable diseases worldwide can be attributed to inactive living (Lee, I.-M. et al., 2012). Piggin (2019) identifies one of the consequences, in the context of physical activity policy and promotion, is the articulation of a 'deficit' narrative – that more people should be doing more activity more often. He goes on to contend that the 'deficit' narrative poses a problem in making claims and reflections on the past, as well as endless comparison of physical activity rates with those of a previous era. This positioning of inactivity as a modern crisis underscores *The Miracle Pill*, which laments the disappearance of everyday physical activity from the world. 'Regular, informal, unplanned exertion' author Peter Walker (2021) writes, 'an integral part of virtually every human life since the first *Homo sapiens* hunted and foraged, was designed out of existence, and with astonishing rapidity' (p. 2). The trope that we were *born* to exercise – that partaking in physical activity for hours each day is a basic aspect of the human condition – is debunked as a myth by evolutionary biologist Daniel Lieberman (2020). He asserts,

> [F]or me, it's clear we're asking people to choose to do something that's inherently abnormal in the sense that we evolved not to do it. Humans evolved to move. We evolved to be physically active. But exercise is a special kind of physical activity.[4]

And therein lies a crucial distinction. Exercise is commonly understood as discretionary, planned physical activity for the sake of health and fitness. In other words, when we go for a run, we set aside time to exercise and do so for reasons often, but not exclusively, for health and fitness. Liberman continues:

> [U]ntil recently, nobody did that. In fact, it would be a kind of a crazy thing to do because if you're a very active hunter-gatherer, for example, or a subsistence farmer, it wouldn't make sense to spend any extra energy going for a needless five-mile jog in the morning. It doesn't help you. In fact, it actually takes away precious calories from other priorities.[5]

And yet we endure a paradoxical relationship when it comes to physical activity: it is universally understood that exercise is good for physical and mental health but prescribing and selling it rarely works. This is borne out by an abundance of data which shows that the majority of adults in high-income countries don't reach the minimum of 150 minutes per week of moderately intensive physical activity recommended by health professionals. This metric has become the standard, employed by World Health Organisation (WHO), PHE, and the US Department of Health, among others. And yet many millions of people are failing to meet the minimum recommendations. This is compounded by the way we demonise sedentary behaviours, labelling those who avoid exertion as lazy. For many, voluntary physical activity has negative connotations, afflicted by misconceptions, finger-pointing, and anxiety. Exercise simply isn't enjoyable and/or a cause of discomfort, guilt, and embarrassment.

Writing in *The Lancet*, Das and Horton (2012) opined that 'for too long the focus has been on advising individuals to take an active approach to life' (p. 189) with insufficient consideration given of social and environmental factors affecting physical activity behaviours. In recent years there has been a mounting sense of urgency around the promotion and development of physical activity interventions designed to entice non-exercisers to be more active. Comprehensive reviews of physical activity interventions testify that many interventions fail, and those that do make a difference tended to report only modest effects (Hillsdon et al., 2005; Muller-Riemenschneider et al., 2008). Discovering new strategies to encourage and enable exercise therefore necessitates a reframing of a lot of what we've got wrong about physical activity promotion, as well as overriding deep, natural instincts. Instead of shaming those who routinely fail to achieve recommended targets or feeling bad about ourselves when we struggle to maintain a new fitness regime, Lieberman advises we should find ways to make exercise both necessary and rewarding. 'Of the many ways to accomplish this, I think the best is to make exercise social,' he writes. 'If you agree to meet friends to exercise regularly, you'll be obliged to show up, you'll have fun and you'll keep other going.'[6]

To a large extent the parkrun ethos encapsulates the approaches that Lieberman is advocating: that physical activity needs to be enjoyable, social, emotionally worthwhile, and something that we willingly commit ourselves to do. This is neatly summarised by Abel and Clarke (2020):

> We are continuously told we should exercise more but if the motivation is not there to do it, we will not go. However, if going for a run means spending time with friends, maybe even meeting some strangers for a chat, then getting out and doing it becomes a lot easier. Creating the right environment for these important components is the essential feature of its success.
>
> (p. 64)

The malleability of parkrun to its participants – it is whatever you want it to be – invites a broad church of runners, joggers, walkers, and volunteers, *and* the freedom to ascribe their own meanings. This echoes Zanker and Gard's (2008) observation that physical activity can 'mean different things to one person at the same time' (p. 50). As Paul Sinton-Hewitt put it in his RSA address, parkrun may well be the most successful public health initiative of the twenty-first century, but it is successful precisely because it *isn't* a public health initiative. In contrast to some physical activity interventions, it is not an imposition. There is an inbuilt informality so that you can attend or choose not to without judgement or consequence. Parkrun attendance is therefore somewhat transient with potentially weaker social bonds than at a traditional sports club (Wiltshire & Stevinson, 2018). Similarly, parkrun strives to challenge and disrupt the traditional running model which establishes a competitive hierarchy based on performance so that those who finish first are described as first finishers rather than winners, whilst language emphasising events as runs and not races is integral to the inclusive ethos.

In a thought-provoking essay Professor of Economics Theodore Turocy suggested that we can understand parkrun's success by combining economic theory with behavioural science. He proposed that strategies designed at encouraging behaviour change are more likely to be successful if four simple principles – make it Easy, Attractive, Social, and Timely – are applied (Behavioural Insights Team, 2014). 'The design of parkrun comes straight from this playbook' (Turocy, 2016) – a framework developed by the 'The Nudge Unit,' which was set up by the UK government to investigate ways in which to use such insights to effect public policy, often at a low upfront cost. First, parkrun's one-off online registration, providing a scannable barcode that can be used at any parkrun event, alongside no participation fees, means involvement is relatively simple and hassle-free (Easy). Second is the notion that we are more likely to do something that our attention is drawn towards and where there are incentives or rewards (Attractive). In the case of parkrun, events take place in local, familiar natural environments with recognition given to participants in the form of milestone T-shirts who have completed 50, 100, 250, or 500 runs, giving a target to aspire to. Third, parkrun is explicitly social, providing opportunities for informal interaction, and the possibility of strong group bonds developing. Most events have a local cafe where participants are encouraged to socialise afterwards (Social). Fourth, parkruns are regular, held on Saturday mornings at the same time every week, so can be inbuilt into people's busy routines (Timely). Similarly, in a short opinion piece published in *Perspectives in Public Health*, authors Baber et al. (2021) consider which approaches to encouraging physical activity have achieved measurable increases in exercise and lessons we can learn from them. Parkrun is cited as one of the case study examples, providing an illustration of what they describe as 'ExercisePLUS,' where, in addition to the health benefits of physical activity, at least one additional motivator ('a sense of belonging') is provided. Furthermore, 'being accessible, welcoming and inclusive' is another factor, noting parkrun's 'ability to empower people and help them overcome perceived obstacles to physical activity.' In addition, it is observed that partnership working, a whole systems approach, personal support, and activity that is simple and doable are important factors.

★

From the humble beginnings in Bushy Park, parkrun has evolved into a global phenomenon with more than 7 million people signed up to parkrun across 23 countries. By the end of 2019, parkrun had surpassed 50 million completed runs in its then 15-year history. What is sometimes overlooked is the way parkrun has grown organically and that during the formative years the introduction of new events was a gradual process. It wasn't until January 2007 when the second venue, Wimbledon Common Time Trial (about five miles from Bushy Park), was launched, over 2 years since the inaugural running event. By that point Bushy Park had reached 155 runners after the first year and 378 by the second anniversary. During the remainder of 2007 Sinton-Hewitt obtained the first external income, £5,000 from Adidas, which was invested into developing the fledgling organisation and helped the expansion to four new venues: Banstead Woods, Leeds Hyde Park, Richmond Park, and Brighton and Hove. By the time the Mayor of London provided £130,000 to fund another 20 parkruns across the capital in 2010, the initiative was already building momentum. By 2011 for the first time there were 100 parkrun events on a single weekend; on the last weekend before lockdown, on 14 March 2020 there were 675 parkruns with a total 139,823 parkrunners and 15,097 volunteers (Jones, 2021).

The weekend reference earlier is deliberate; from April 2010 junior parkrun was conceived, a 2 km spin-off event for children aged between 4 and 14 and their families, on a Sunday morning. It was the brainchild of occupational therapist, Paul Graham. In an article for *Occupational Therapy News*, he explained: 'I felt that something new was needed for children, including those with health conditions who may not be able to complete the five-kilometre events.'[7] Mirroring its predecessor, junior parkrun also originated at Bushy Park in South West London with just nine young runners one Sunday morning. Since then, junior parkrun has spread to more than 300 locations throughout the UK. The junior offshoot is closely aligned to parkrun's existing operational model, providing a series of free, weekly, collective, timed events that are organised solely by volunteers. The 2 km distance was deemed to be sufficiently challenging to present speed work for older children, whilst representing a manageable distance for younger ones. In contrast to many school-led or club-led activities where performances are judged, the junior parkrun ethos places an emphasis on inclusion and taking part with others rather than the actual task of running. For those who do not wish to, or who are unable to do physical exercise, there are a host of volunteering opportunities. 'Kids who can't run or walk can still add meaning or value to their community and have fun,' observes Paul.[8] Like the adult version, junior parkrunners are rewarded for achieving participation milestones with wristbands available to participants who complete 11, 21, and 50 events. A certificate is awarded to those juniors who complete 100 events.

The importance of establishing robust policies and procedures has become increasingly apparent in the 'cookie cutter' approach to parkrun's upscaling. These have ensured a level of quality and standardisation, which reflects the uniqueness of parkrun, whilst permitting local events a degree of flexibility to respond to local needs (Cutforth, 2017). They cover aspects such as the timing and length of events, minimum age for participants, child supervision, volunteering, safeguarding, and risk assessment. Arguably the most significant policy decision was a commitment to maintain parkrun as 'free for everyone forever.' The free at the point of use model is possible through diversified funding streams, including commercial partnerships, public funding, donations, a clothing line (CONTRA), and the sale of parkrun-branded merchandise. Back in April 2016 the issue of cost emerged as a thorny issue when Stoke Gifford parish council in South Gloucestershire voted to charge parkrun for providing a free running event, citing the runners' impact on the park, as well as other park users such as the local football team already paying fees. The growth in parkrun's popularity meant that on some weekends 300 runners would attend and 'monopolise' the park for 2 hours, blocking paths and parking their cars. The parish council said that it would be unfair to expect local residents to pay, via their Council Tax, for the additional maintenance needed, citing a bill of £55,000 to resurface the car park and £60,000 for the upkeep of paths. The case attracted extensive media coverage both nationally and internationally, as well as garnering political attention, including support for parkrun from the then Sports Minister, Tracey Crouch. Following lengthy discussions over a period of months, a decision was finally arrived in May 2016 for Little Stoke parkrun to cease. Parkrun's global chief operating officer Tom Williams stated Stoke Gifford parish council's decision to charge for the use of the park 'went completely against our most fundamental principles,' adding that the council's revised request for parkrun to financially contribute to maintaining the park was also not possible. Williams emphasised one of the founding principles of parkrun was that the events were free and if one paid an 'unsustainable precedent' would be established.

Whilst charging fees threatens to undermine the efforts of parkrun to be accessible to all, it is worth taking a step back to question whether making an event free by implication makes it inclusive? I am by nature and profession sceptical, and whilst unarguably parkrun can be seen to represent a virtuous community that attracts individuals who are driven by different motives and forces, when scrutinised, there needs to be some caution to not overstate the assumed friendliness and accessible nature of parkrun. An illustration of this can be found in the study by Bowness et al. (2020) which used qualitative data from 7,271 parkrunners to explore what attracts and binds participants to the parkrun movement and to better understand the parkrun community. The authors observed that as parkrun has expanded, many participants have struggled to maintain their attachment to their local parkrun community with some suggesting that the rising popularity of parkrun had diminished their sense of belonging to the group. They also reported that several respondents suggested that cliques prevailed at their local parkrun, making it less likely for them to feel part of its community. Others suggested that in being a slower runner, they often felt ignored by other parkrunners who had departed before they had finished or, in some cases, had thought they were a burden, particularly in those parkrun events that involved multiple laps of the same course.

Over the years, the parkrun social mission has prompted a subtle but note-worthy change of strategy and approach (Cutforth, 2017). As well as continuing to support existing events and the ongoing demand for new events, a more tar-geted approach has been developed which involves working with partners and identifying new cohorts, in particular encouraging the participation of those traditionally that are inactive and to target socially marginalised populations. As such parkrun follows the guiding principle of *proportionate universalism* in that a balance is sought between providing events which are universally open to all, whilst also targeting those most in need (Wellington, 2021). For example, in December 2018 parkrun received £3 million investment from Sport England, which explicitly aimed to establish 200 new parkrun events in areas of social deprivation and to increase the physical activity levels of women and girls, especially from low socio-economic backgrounds. Another development of note has been the introduction of parkrun events within prison environments, providing unique physical activity and volunteering opportunities for those that are incarcerated, as well as staff. This is a collaboration between parkrun and Her Majesty's Prison and Probation Service (HMPPS), with the latter facilitating access to sites, providing guidance and expertise, and contribut-ing the start-up cost for all events activated on HMPPS sites in England and Wales. There are now 24 parkruns in custodial settings across the UK, Ireland, and Australia, each inspired by HMP Haverigg, which in November 2017 became the first prison to host a weekly parkrun event. Black Combe park-run, as the event is known, is named after a prominent hill that can be seen from the outdoor sports field where parkrun takes place. And whilst physi-cal activity programmes are not a new phenomenon within a custodial estate, anecdotally prison parkruns have contributed towards a decrease in anti-social behaviour in prison communities, as good behaviour is a key component of being allowed to take part, whilst mental health has also improved (Horton, 2018). These findings add to the growing evidence base regarding gains asso-ciated with sport and physical activity for incarcerated populations, as well as recognition of sport's potential as a vehicle for promoting rehabilitation among young offenders (Buckaloo et al., 2009; Lewis & Meek, 2012; Meek, 2013). The prominence of volunteering at parkrun – prisoners are involved in all aspects of parkrun, including marshalling, timekeeping, and processing results – and the variety of volunteer roles available presents an added dimension. This in turn provides inmates when leaving prison with a local community they are familiar with and which is a safe and positive environment to be a part of to discourage reoffending.

For some, parkrun has altered the fabric and dynamic of weekends, as well as transforming the running landscape, drawing in people from far beyond what could be construed as 'traditional' athletic groups. Parkrun's exponential growth has undoubtedly contributed to the increase in 'athletics' participation – a catch-all term for a diverse array of pursuits including track and field, cross-country running, and ultra-marathon running. Over the past decade, participation has increased with close to 7 million adults taking part in some form of the sport at least twice per month (Sport England, 2020). There are two aspects that are particularly striking about the growth in running's popularity. The first is the unstructured and informal nature of the activity with the majority of participants not being affiliated to an organised running club (England Athletics, 2013). This is evidenced by the development of initiatives such as informal running networks and emergent running groups (Spiers et al., 2015). As Jennie Price, then Chief Executive of Sport England, remarked, 'running has continued to be a powerful driving force, with welcoming, low-cost and easy-to-access options like parkrun making a big impact in the last decade' (Sport England, 2016). Parkrun represents a new kind of hybrid organisation that is distinct from traditional sports organisations in a number of ways: it is a not-for-profit that relies on diversified funding streams including donations and commercial partnerships with a small, diverse global team of paid staff given the level of impact that parkrun delivers; there are no membership fees; and growth is driven by volunteers across the country who manage weekly events. The organisation structure facilitates agility, is resource-effective, and builds on the agency of local people and communities as architects of their own health (Wellington, 2021). The expansion of parkrun can, arguably, be situated against a rising interest in registered running events (Shipway & Holloway, 2010) as well as a wider change in such events, moving away from serious competition and towards sociality, camaraderie, and experience, for example, the proliferation of themed and obstacle races such as Colour Run and Tough Mudder (Weedon, 2015), as well as an identifiable increase in charitable fundraising through mass participation events (King, 2003; Nettleton & Hardey, 2006). Debatably one of the most important features of such events is, from a public health perspective, that they are encouraging previously inactive people to exercise.

The second is that despite the 'boom' in recreational running, limited data exist on the behaviours and motivations of the people involved. Of particular note, Bell and Stephenson (2014) contend that we know relatively little about the motivations of participants in 5 km events despite their prevalence, whilst Murphy and Bauman (2007) argue that the impact of mass participation events on subsequent physical activity among participants is underexplored. Relatedly, research on the motivation of runners has primarily explored the marathon distance, examining the motivations to travel to and participate in races (e.g. Masters et al., 1993; Axelsen & Robinson, 2009). Existing scholarly literature has tended to concentrate on groups of highly committed runners (Hitchings & Latham, 2017) or what Bale (2004) labels 'serious' or competitive running. As a result, key questions, particularly with regard to the experiences of comparatively casual runners, remain largely under the radar (Cook et al., 2015).

The popularity of parkrun has, in part, been attributed to its compellingly simple, standardised, and scalable operational model. As stated, parkrun does not charge those who wish to take part and maintains that free access is 'fundamental' to engaging the least active[9] to ensure parkrun is open to everyone regardless of physical competence or income. The only requirement is a one-off online registration and unique printed barcode, which enables participants to turn up and participate at any parkrun event worldwide. Once registered, participants can opt to receive regular emails from parkrun, keeping them informed of latest developments from the parkrun community, as well as a personalised email or text after each completed parkrun. The latter communication includes their result, along with the time, finishing position, and age grading. If linked with social media, participants receive opportunities to connect with others and receive motivation for continued engagement. Each registrant is provided with online access to a history of all their runs and volunteering, enabling them to monitor and review their attendance and track progress over time. Participants can walk, jog, or run as much of the 5 km course as they wish, although only finishers enter a taped-off funnel at the end. It is here that a volunteer records their time, before another volunteer hands them a finishing token containing their position number. It is this token, along with their individual barcode, that each participant hands over to a third volunteer who scans them both with a handheld electronic reader. The method of timing may appear cumbersome in comparison to more efficient, automated systems, but it's retained for an important reason: it forces you to queue and, in doing so, gently facilitates human interaction. As Professor Steve Haake explained, 'it's the queuing element that's the really important part'[10] as it necessitates social contact whilst waiting. This has parallels with the work of sociologist Richard Sennett (2018) who commended the idea of *friction* in life: those little inefficiencies that oblige you to interact with strangers.

To an extent part of the parkrun 'family' is an online community, facilitated through social media. Alberti (2019, p. 130) suggests virtual communities share a resemblance to real-life communities in the sense that 'they offer a shared view of the world and one's place in it; they reflect back and echo the feelings and opinions one might have about the world.' They also share similarities by providing support, information, acceptance, and friendship between people who may not have met in person. This depiction of a harmonious online community presumes inclusion and belonging, obscuring the fact that inclusion in social media can be fickle and conditional. Contrariwise, individuals expressing opposing views that are regarded incompatible to that community's values may be socially ostracised or shamed online.

As it has been alluded to, part of the brilliance of parkrun stems from its capacity to transcend notions of individuality by encouraging people to help one another and connect with others around them. By avoiding monetary transactions, parkrun instead encourages (and necessitates) *social* transactions which contribute to its culture. It is a culture which makes you feel like you are doing something good which contributes to your health and improved wellbeing – but not doing it alone. There are numerous studies and reviews of studies that all point to the potentially harmful effects of social isolation and conversely that people's wellbeing is positively bolstered by social contact. This is crucial to remember in our ever more atomised society, where much of the hard infrastructure that promotes efficiency tends to discourage interaction which fosters the formation of strong ties. Humans are intensely social animals, and a sense of community is essential to our personal and collective wellbeing. The COVID-19 pandemic has served as a stark reminder of this finding. Indeed, one of the major stressors during lockdowns has been the lack of social contact due to the implementation of social distancing strategies, quarantine, and isolation procedures designed to limit the spread of the virus. This has contributed to elevated levels of loneliness and social isolation, which in turn produce physical and mental health-related repercussions (Hwang et al., 2020).

In the UK parkrun was suspended on 18 March 2020, shortly before the country was put into national lockdown – an announcement which effectively meant that parkrun was closed around the world, with events in 17 countries having already been interrupted. Research undertaken by parkrun indicates that people's mental health and feelings of social isolation and disconnect have worsened since parkrun events were suspended (Quirk et al., 2021). Happiness, life satisfaction, connections with others, physical health, and mental health were all negatively impacted, although the impact was not experienced equally. Data showed that the greatest negative impact of the COVID-19 pandemic among the sample surveyed was on people's connections with others with younger adults more detrimentally impacted. The authors emphasised how people missed the socialisation and community parkrun provided, 'perhaps more so than the physical activity itself' (Quirk et al., 2021, p. 9). This is supported by previous research that has highlighted that the community and social connections are both a major appeal and positive outcome of parkrun participation (Grunseit et al., 2020).

★

As a sociologist, I feel one of the aspects that make parkrun intriguing are the paradoxes which seemingly exist. On the one hand, there is a distinctiveness about every parkrun event in that it is defined by its locality and the community that makes it happen. On the other hand, there is a degree of structure and formality that contributes to parkrun being an analogous 'cookie cutter' experience, regardless of the setting. It is wholly individual yet facilitates contact with others. There's no competitive pressure, although measures of performance and improvement are built into the results statistics if that's what you want. As this respondent in Warhurst and Black's (2021) study remarked,

> You can't help comparing yourself to others, can you? I cannot not be competitive, I like to push myself to win, to beat other people and in the final kilometre I can completely empty the tank. It sort-of brings out the worst in me and I know that this competitiveness can be dangerous, but I can't help myself and I feel like I am letting myself down if I don't give it my all.
>
> (p. 8)

On the one hand, parkrun continues to rank individual times and finishing positions, keeping records of those who complete the fastest times and those who run 5 km under 17 minutes. On the other hand, over time and as parkrun has developed, average finishing times have decreased year on year with the increased number of inactive people and walkers taking part. In 2005, the average finish time for completing a parkrun was 22:17. In 2018, it was 32:29. Reece et al. (2019) note that in 2017, there were 64,888 instances of participants taking over 50 minutes to complete a parkrun which represents an increase of 88 per cent compared with the preceding year. It requires no formal membership or long-term commitment, and yet for some parkrun provokes a sense of evangelism, analogous to a region or a 'weird cult.' There is an ethos seeped in egalitarianism and an absence of hierarchy and judgementalism. At the same time, the celebration of commitment through the award of milestone parkrun T-shirts could be construed as overt forms of subcultural capital, symbols to validate one's identity as a parkrunner. The sociability of parkrun events, combined with notions of community building and aiding friendships, is repeatedly emphasised. Conversely, runners are able to turn up, complete the course, and depart with minimal interaction.

★

Commensurate with its expansion in popularity, parkrun regularly features in articles in local, regional, and national media, as well as being the subject of podcasts and television programmes. Nevertheless, besides some published testimonials from medical practitioners endorsing the potential health and wellbeing benefits of parkrun (e.g. Masters, 2014; McIntosh, 2021; Tobin, 2018; Watson, 2013), as well as academic commentaries (Fullagar, 2016; Pringle & Pickering, 2015), empirical research – whilst increasing in number – remains in its infancy (Grunseit et al., 2020). And yet as Cleland et al. (2019, p. 22) contend, parkrun's scalability, accessibility, and widespread appeal presents a 'research imperative' to investigate its potential for public health gain. Furthermore, learning from the achievements of parkrun and developing our understanding of why it is successful may have important implications for policymakers and practitioners working in the realms of physical activity promotion and mass participation community events (Wiltshire & Merchant, 2021). In response, there are a fledgling but emerging number of empirical studies that have been published, identifying the capacity of parkrun to engage people who traditionally are less active and experience constraints to participation. One of the first studies conducted with over 7,000 parkrunners in the UK identified the majority as not having been regular runners prior to their registration and reported benefits related to psychological wellbeing and sense of community, especially among more regular attendees (Stevinson & Hickson, 2014). Parkrun has also been identified as a site of social interaction that connects people in local places (Hindley, 2020) whereas Wiltshire and Stevinson (2018) demonstrate the potential of volunteer-led community-based sports to increase an individual's social capital (the networks of relationships that people have access to). Additionally, the organisational identity of parkrun has shifted over time, from a 'sport'-oriented focus to a strategic emphasis on creating a 'healthier and happier planet' and an inclusive 'parkrun family' (Reece et al., 2019). Such a phenomenon offers a distinctive opportunity to explore and understand the 'how, what and why' of parkrun's exponential success, as well as the associated challenges.

To this end, Chapter 2 will ask to what extent the emphasis placed on the accessible nature of parkrun – manifest in a 'free for everyone, forever' strapline on the homepage of the website and the proclamation that 'parkrun is a positive, welcoming and inclusive experience' (parkrun, 2021) – stands up to empirical scrutiny. Intertwined with claims apropos parkrun's perceived inclusivity is the portrayal of a parkrun 'community' where participants regardless of age, background, and ability are valued equally. Conceiving parkrun in this way has featured in published literature, where participants refer to the shared, communal experience of completing the physical challenge of parkrun, seeing themselves as being a part of a wider community, which will be explored. In Chapter 3, we focus on the non-committal, non-traditional approach to volunteering taken by parkrun, despite being wholly reliant on volunteers to organise and deliver the weekly event. Whilst parkrun volunteering has been referred to in research, often reporting the benefits of doing so, it has been the main focus of very few studies, which are examined here and which seek to demonstrate the very varied circumstances of parkrunners, as well as the individualised levels of motivation and purpose (Hallett et al., 2020). Chapter 4 looks at the evidence that is emerging of the health and wellbeing benefits of taking part in parkrun, which, as a result, has led to medical interest in prescribing parkrun to patients through GP referrals. In Chapter 5, the concept of slow living is drawn on as a way of thinking about some of the aspects of parkrun which celebrate the average finishing time slowing each year and the growing number of participants walking the 5 km course. Drawing on a small number of studies which have reported a sizeable number of parkrun registrants identifying themselves as non-runners, Chapter 6 discusses how individuals' subjective identities may change through participating in parkrun. Chapter 7 situates parkrun within an expanding literature base on the relationship between nature, physical activity, and health. It has been widely reported that exercising in natural environs – labelled 'green exercise' – has the potential for added psychological, physiological, and social benefits (Lahart et al., 2019), and yet, curiously, there is a paucity of research which specifically considers the relationship between parkrun and nature and to what extent exposure to nature may help maintain regular physical activity. In the final chapter, I look to bring together the themes from preceding discussions to reflect upon what originated as a community time trial has expanded into a global movement encouraging mass participation in physical activity. To conclude, Chapter 8 also explores the future sustainability of parkrun amidst its worldwide evolution, paying particular attention to the challenges caused by the coronavirus pandemic when parkrun suspended all (in excess of 2,200) of its worldwide events in March 2020.

Notes

1 https://drchatterjee.com/parkrun-celebration-community-nick-pearson/
2 https://blog.strava.com/the-parkrun-story-paul-sinton-hewitt-8943/
3 www.gov.uk/government/publications/physical-inactivity-levels-in-adults-aged-40-to-60-in-england/physical-inactivity-levels-in-adults-aged-40-to-60-in-england-2015-to-2016#walk
4 https://news.harvard.edu/gazette/story/2021/01/daniel-lieberman-busts-exercising-myths/
5 https://news.harvard.edu/gazette/story/2021/01/daniel-lieberman-busts-exercising-myths/
6 www.theguardian.com/lifeandstyle/2021/jun/06/just-dont-do-it-10-exercise-myths
7 www.rcot.co.uk/file/3115/download?token=R-b6rX-U
8 www.rcot.co.uk/file/3115/download?token=R-b6rX-U
9 www.parkrun.org.uk/blog/news/2016/04/12/parkrun-reaction-to-stoke-gifford-parish-council-decision/
10 BBC Radio 4 – The Life Scientific, Steve Haake on technology, sport and health.

References

Abel, J., & Clarke, L. (2020). *The Compassion Project: A Case for Hope & Human Kindness from the Town That Beat Loneliness*. London: Aster.

Alberti, F.B. (2019). *A Biography of Loneliness: The History of an Emotion*. Oxford: Oxford University Press.

Axelsen, M., & Robinson, R. (2009). Race around the world: Identifying a research agenda for the distance runner. *Annals of Leisure Research*, 12:2, 236–257.

Baber, M., Leach, S., Musuwo, N., Pham, H., & Rollins, K. (2021). Encouraging physical activity: What works. *Perspectives in Public Health*, 141:2, 76–78.

Bale, J. (2004). *Running Cultures: Racing in Time and Space*. London: Routledge.

Behavioural Insights Team. (2014). *EAST: Four Simple Ways to Apply Behavioural Insights*. Retrieved from www.bi.team/publications/east-four-simple-ways-to-apply-behavioural-insights/

Bell, N., & Stephenson, A.L. (2014). Variation in motivations by running ability: Using the theory of reasoned action to predict attitudes about running 5K races. *Journal of Policy Research in Tourism, Leisure and Events*, 6:3, 231–247. https://doi.org/10.1080/1940796 3.2014.933227.

Bourne, D. (2014). *Parkrun: Much More Than Just a Run in the Park*. Sheffield: Chequered Flag Publishing.

Bowness, J., Tulle, E., & McKendrick, J. (2020). Understanding the parkrun community; sacred Saturdays and organic solidarity of parkrunners. *European Journal for Sport and Society*, 18:1, 44–63. https://doi.org/10.1080/16138171.2020.1792113.

Buckaloo, B.J., Krug, K.S., & Nelson, K.B. (2009). Exercise and the low-security inmate: Changes in depression, stress, and anxiety. *The Prison Journal*, 89:3, 328–343.

Cleland, V., Nash, M., Sharman, M.J., & Claflin, S. (2019). Exploring the health-promoting potential of the 'parkrun' phenomenon: What factors are associated with higher levels of participation? *Quantitative Research*, 33:1, 13–23.

Cook, S., Shaw., & Simpson, P. (2015). Jography: Exploring meanings, experiences and spatialities of recreational road running. *Mobilities*, 1–26.

Cutforth, C. (2017). So much more than a run in the park. *The Leisure Review*, 84.

Das, P., & Horton, R. (2012). Rethinking our approach to physical activity. *The Lancet*, 380, 189–190.

Donnelly, A.A., & Macintyre, T.E. (Eds.). (2019). *Physical Activity in Natural Settings: Green and Blue Exercise*. London: Routledge.

England Athletics. (2013). *A Nation That Runs: A Recreational Running and Athletics Plan for England 2013–2017*. Birmingham, England: England Athletics.

Fullagar, S. (2016). Parkrun is an important movement and should remain free for participants. *The Conversation*. Retrieved from https://theconversation.com/parkrun-is-an-important-movement-and-should-remain-free-for-participants-58097

Greenwood, S., & Fletcher, T. (2020). Open water swimming events, social capital and sociality. *Event Management*. https://doi.org/10.3727/152599521X16106577964658.

Grunseit, A.C., Richards, J., Reece, L., Bauman, A., & Merom, D. (2020). Evidence on the reach and impact of the social physical activity phenomenon parkrun: A scoping review. *Preventative Medicine Reports*, 20, 1–8. https://doi.org/10.1016/j.pmedr.2020.101231.

Hallett, R., Gombert, K., & Hurley, M. (2020). 'Everyone should muck in': A qualitative study of parkrun volunteering and conflicting motivations. *Journal of Nonprofit and Public Sector Marketing*, 33:5, 493–515.

Hillsdon, M., Foster, C., & Thorogood, M. (2005). Interventions for promoting physical activity. *Cochrane Database Systematic Reviews*, CD003180.

Hindley, D. (2020). 'More than just a run in the park': An exploration of parkrun as a shared leisure space. *Leisure Sciences*, 42:1, 85–105.

Hitchings, R., & Latham, A. (2017). How 'social' is recreational running? Findings from a qualitative study in London and implications for public health promotion. *Health & Place*, 46, 337–343.

Horton, C. (2018). I've brought parkrun to a youth jail. It's given people here a sense of pride. *The Guardian*. Retrieved from www.theguardian.com/society/2018/nov/24/parkrun-youth-jail-sense-of-pride

Hwang, T.-J., Rabheru, K., Peisah, C., Reichman, W., & Ikeda, M. (2020). Loneliness and social isolation during the COVID-19 pandemic. *International Psychogeriatrics*, May 26, 1–4. https://doi.org/10.1017/S1041610220000988.

Jones, E. (2021). *How Parkrun Changed Our Lives*. Hebden Bridge: Gritstone Publishing.

King, S.J. (2003). Doing good by running well: Breast cancer, the race for the cure, and new technologies of ethical citizenship. In Bratich, J.Z., Packer, J., & McCarthy, C. (Eds.), *Foucault, Cultural Studies, and Governmentality* (pp. 295–316). New York: State University of New York Press.

Lahart, I., Darcy, P.M., Gidlow, C., & Giovanna, C. (2019). Known knowns: A systematic review of the effects of green exercise compared with exercising indoors. In Donnelly, A.A. & Macintyre, T.E. (Eds.), *Physical Activity in Natural Settings: Green and Blue Exercise* (pp. 36–74). London: Routledge.

Lee, I.-M., Shiroma, E.J., Lobelo, F., Puska, P., Blair, S.N., & Katzmarzyk, P.T., for the Lancet Physical Activity Series Working Group. (2012). Effects of physical inactivity on major noncommunicable diseases worldwide: An analysis of burden of disease and life expectancy. *The Lancet*, 380:9838, 219–229.

Lee, I.S., Brown, G., King, K., & Shipway, R. (2016). Social identity in serious sport event space. *Event Management*, 20:4, 491–499.

Lewis, G., & Meek, R. (2012). The role of sport in reducing reoffending among young men in prison: Assessing the evidence base. *Forensic Update*, 107, 12–18.

Lieberman, D. (2020). *Exercised: The Science of Physical Activity, Rest and Health*. London: Penguin.

Masters, K., Ogles, B., & Jolton, J. (1993). The development of an instrument to measure motivation for marathon running: The motivations of marathoners scales (MOMS). *Research Quarterly in Exercise and Sport*, 64, 134–143.

Masters, N. (2014). Parkrun eases the loneliness of the long-distance runner. *British Journal of General Practice*, 64:625, e408. https://doi.org/10.3399/bjgp14X681025.

McIntosh, T. (2021). parkrun: A panacea for health and wellbeing? *Journal of Research in Nursing*, 26:5, 472–477.

Meek, R. (2013). *Sport in Prison: Exploring the Role of Physical Activity in Correctional Settings*. Abingdon: Routledge.

Meir, D., & Fletcher, T. (2019). The transformative potential of using participatory community sport initiatives to promote social cohesion in divided community contexts. *International Review for the Sociology of Sport*, 54:2, 218–238.

Muller-Riemenschneider, F., Reinhold, T., Nocon, M., & Willich, S.N. (2008). Long-term effectiveness of interventions promoting physical activity: A systematic review. *Preventative Medicine*, 47, 354–368.

Murphy, N.M., & Bauman, A. (2007). Mass sporting and physical activity events – Are they 'bread and circuses' or public health interventions to increase population levels of physical activity? *Journal of Physical Activity and Health*, 4, 193–202.

Nettleton, S., & Hardey, M. (2006). Running away with health: The urban marathon and the construction of 'charitable bodies.' *Health: An Interdisciplinary Journal for the Social Study of Health, Illness and Medicine*, 10:4, 441–460.

Nicholson, M., & Hoye, R. (2008). *Sport and Social Capital*. London: Routledge.

Oldenburg, R. (1999). *The Great Good Place – Cafes, Coffee Shops, Bookstores, Bars, Hair Salons and Other Hangouts at the Heart of a Community*. New York: Paragon House.

Parkrun. (2016). *parkrun UK: Annual run report 2016*. Retrieved from https://issuu.com/parkrun/docs/parkrun-uk-2016-run-report

Parkrun. (2021). *Parkrun.com*. Retrieved from www.parkrun.com

Piggin, J. (2019). *The Politics of Physical Activity*. Abingdon: Routledge.

Pringle, A., & Pickering, K. (2015). Smarter running: Shaping the behavioural change interventions of the future! Letter to the editor. *Perspectives in Public Health*, 135:3, 116–117.

Quirk, H., Haake, S., Goyder, E., Bullas, A., Graney, M., & Wellington, C. (2021). Impact of the COVID-19 pandemic on the wellbeing of parkrun participants in the United Kingdom. *Research Square*. https://doi.org/10.21203/rs.3.rs-690431/v1.

Reece, L.J., Quirk, H., Wellington, C., Haake, S.J., & Wilson, F. (2019). Bright spots, physical activity investments that work: parkrun; A global initiative striving for healthier and happier communities. *British Journal of Sports Medicine*, 53:6, 326–327.

Richardson, K., & Fletcher, T. (2018). Community sport development events, social capital and social mobility: A case study of Premier League Kicks and young black and minoritized ethnic males in England. *Soccer & Society*, 21:1, 79–95.

Sennett, R. (2018). *Building and Dwelling: Ethics for the City*. London: Penguin Books.

Shanahan, D.F., Franco, L., Lin, B.B., Gaston, K.J., & Fuller, R.A. (2016). The benefits of natural environments for physical activity. *Sports Medicine*, 46:7, 989–995. https://doi.org/10.1007/s40279-016-0502-4.

Shipway, R., & Holloway, I. (2010). Running free: Embracing a healthy lifestyle through distance running. *Perspectives in Public Health*, 130:6, 270–276.

Son, J., Yarnal, C., & Kerstetter, D. (2010). Engendering social capital through a leisure club for middle-aged and older women: Implications for individual and community health and well-being. *Leisure Studies*, 29:1, 67–83.

Spaaij, R., & Westerbeek, H. (2010). Sport business and social capital: A contradiction in terms? *Sport in Society*, 13:9, 1356–1373.

Spiers, A., Harris, S., Charlton, A., & Smale, P. (2015). The governance and history of running, the decision to run and trends in running participation. In Scheerder, J. & Breedveld, K. (Eds.), *Running Across Europe: The Rise and Size of one of the Largest Sport Markets* (pp. 81–104). Basingstoke: Palgrave Macmillan.

Sport England. (2016). *Stats Show Upsurge in People Doing Sport*. Retrieved from http://funding.sportengland.org/news-and-features/news/2016/june/09/active-people-10/

Sport England. (2020). *Active Lives Adult Survey November 2018/19 Report*. Retrieved from https://sportengland-production-files.s3.eu-west-2.amazonaws.com/s3fs-public/2020-04/Active%20Lives%20Adult%20November%2018-19%20Report.pdf?VersionId=BhkAy2K28pd9bDEz_NuisHl2ppuqJtpZ

Stevinson, C., & Hickson, M. (2014). Exploring the public health potential of a mass community participation event. *Journal of Public Health*, 36:2, 268–274.

Stevinson, C., Wiltshire, G., & Hickson, M. (2015). Facilitating participation in health-enhancing physical activity: A qualitative study of parkrun. *International Journal of Behavioural Medicine*, 22, 170–177.

Tobin, S. (2018). Prescribing parkrun. *British Journal of General Practice*, 68:677, e588. https://doi.org/10.3399/bjgp18X700133.

Turocy, T. (2016). The behavioural economics of parkrun. *UAE ECO Blog*. Retrieved from https://ueaeconomics.wordpress.com/2016/04/22/the-behavioural-economics-of-parkrun/

Van Lange, P.A.M., & Columbus, S. (2021). Vitamin S: Why is social contact, even with strangers, so important to well-being? *Current Directions in Psychological Science*, 30:3, 267–273.

Walker, P. (2021). *The Miracle Pill: Why a Sedentary World Is Getting It All Wrong*. London: Simon & Schuster.

Warhurst, R., & Black, K. (2021). Lost and found: parkrun, work and identity. *Qualitative Research in Sport, Exercise and Health*. https://doi.org/10.1080/2159676X.2021.1924244.

Watson, M.J. (2013). Encouraging participation in health initiatives: Parkrun. *International Journal of Therapy and Rehabilitation*, 20:6, 277.

Weedon, G. (2015). Camaraderie reincorporated: Tough mudder and the extended distribution of the social. *Journal of Sport and Social Issues*, 39:6, 431–454.

Wellington, C. (2021). *Parkrun – Supplementary Written Evidence (NPS0139)*. Retrieved from https://committees.parliament.uk/writtenevidence/22941/default/

Wiltshire, G., & Merchant, S. (2021). What can we learn about nature, physical activity, and health from parkrun? In Brymer, E., Rogerson, M., & Barton, J. (Eds.), *Nature and Health: Physical Activity in Nature* (pp. 208–222). London: Routledge.

Wiltshire, G., & Stevinson, C. (2018). Exploring the role of social capital in community-based physical activity: Qualitative insights from parkrun. *Qualitative Research in Sport, Exercise and Health*, 10:1, 47–62.

Zanker, C., & Gard, M. (2008). Fatness, fitness, and the moral universe of sport and physical activity. *Sociology of Sport Journal*, 25:1, 48–65.

Zhou, R., & Kaplanidou, K. (2018). Building social capital from sport event participation: An exploration of the social impacts of participatory sport events on the community. *Sport Management Review*, 21:5, 491–503.

Chapter 2

An Inclusive Community?

In this chapter I discuss one of the central narratives of parkrun, that of community. Indeed, the notion of community has featured prominently in both media accounts and academic research of parkrun, often in relation to its perceived ability to cultivate a sense of belonging, as well as underlining the locality of events. Likewise, parkrun promotes itself as a movement and a family, often accompanied with a welcoming storyline that accentuates the community-building function of parkrun in facilitating social connections and supportive relationships. Aditya Chakrabortty (2018) cites one parkrunner, Karen Weir, who epitomises this sentiment: '[I]t is the new church . . . the idea of the community has broken down. People don't go to church anymore. But here, you come together with a load of people – and you feel embedded in the local area.' Intertwined in this framing of parkrun as a community is the underscoring, often uncritically, of the inclusiveness of parkrun and the claim that it is 'for everyone,' supported by early research which suggested that parkrun was able to attract participants from a diversity of backgrounds, including those harder to engage in physical activity such as older adults, those overweight or obese, and those with poorer health. This forms a supplementary focus for this chapter, asking to what extent the dominant self-representations of parkrun as egalitarian – in short, anyone can take part, whether as a walker, jogger, runner, or volunteer – stand up to scrutiny. This line of inquiry is particularly pertinent given the aspiration to increase the number of parkrun events in socially deprived neighbourhoods (Sport England, 2018).

The depiction of parkrun as a 'new religion' alluded to earlier is explored in the opening chapter to Eileen Jones' book, *How Parkrun Changed Our Lives* (2021), where she compares the parkrun community to that of a church congregation. She writes:

> From diverse backgrounds and different neighbourhoods, parkrunners congregate together, and escape from the daily routine. We welcome, and are welcomed by, strangers. We great old friends in a communion of common bond. We experience and rejoice in a familiar ritual with its own liturgy and litany, and we go away feeling better about ourselves.
>
> (p. 7)

DOI: 10.4324/9781003121961-2

A secular parallel is similarly identified in a paper published in the *European Journal for Sport and Society*, whose authors Bowness et al. (2020) argue that parkrun 'can be understood as a piacular celebration: a positive ceremony that stands to symbolise the leaving behind of negative histories' (p. 14). They go on to suggest that for some 'parkrun provides a weekly ritual' where the celebrations may be personal, with individuals celebrating their leaving behind of the past (e.g. narrated stories of weight loss or health improvement) or social, referring to the renewal of community at a time when communities are widely regarded to have dwindled. The article explores what attracts and binds participants, and to what extent parkrun represents a community that normalises physical activity. Drawing on the social theories of Emile Durkheim, the authors propose that adopting a Durkheimian framework on solidarity, morality, and collective effervescence can further our understanding of the parkrun community.

To examine the parkrun community, Bowness et al. (2020) surveyed a subset of parkrun participants, that is Strava users who had linked their two accounts. The online survey was one of the largest of its type with 7,271 respondents completing the questionnaire. For the paper, grossing-up weights were used to adjust the survey population by age and gender to match the total population it represents (parkrunners registered with Strava). The survey included several open-ended questions, and it is the qualitative responses which are the primary source of data cited in their paper. The analysis is categorised into three themes derived from Durkheim's writings, namely solidarity, morality, and collective effervescence in parkrun as constituents of community. The authors conclude that parkrun can indeed be understood as community, evidenced by the findings that many respondents feel attachment to their local parkrun, as well as identifying with the ethos of parkrun. This was summarised by one of their participants who said:

> As I have a 'home' parkrun, and a parkrun shirt with the 'home' course's name on it, I feel a strong link to my local parkrun. When I visit other parkruns, I feel like I'm representing my local course and inevitably I compare the other course to my 'home' course and find them wanting! I can always find a way to rationalise why my 'home' course is better – the venue is prettier; it's better because it's quicker; it's better because it's tougher (and therefore slower); the marshals are friendlier; the runners are friendlier to the marshals . . . and so on.
>
> (p. 10)

For many, a feeling of attachment to a local parkrun was manifest as the face of community in parkrun, fuelled by recognition of being part of something bigger than oneself and by connecting with others who are like-minded. A participant in their study observed,

> My 'local' parkrun is six miles away, and the core attendees live locally, and many are members of a local running club. I know no-one in this local

area so do not really feel part of the 'local' parkrun community however I
do feel part of the wider parkrun 'global' community.

(p. 10)

This sense of identifying with the parkrun community was widespread,
although there was a suggestion that participants perceived that the inclusivity
and 'feel' of the parkrun community had altered as events expanded over time.
According to Bowness et al. (2020), 'as parkrun has grown, many participants
have struggled to maintain their attachment to their local parkrun community. Many participants suggested that the growing popularity of parkrun had
diminished their sense of belonging to the group' (p. 18). With regard to the
motives for participation, whilst varied, the study found that they tended to
relate to individual and social anxieties about the body and its appropriate
management, for example, desire to lose weight and a deterrent on behaviours
that were situated as undesirable. Survey respondents also framed parkrun as
beneficial to relationships between individuals, their families, and communities with many engaging in parkrun to support a partner or as a familial activity. In identifying with their parkrun community, respondents often referred
to the ethos and values of parkrun. These included participating to compete
against the self, as well as how parkrun events brought members of the local
community together, generating a supportive 'community feel.' One of their
participants noted:

My parkrun is a very inclusive, friendly community. Random strangers
have helped me when I started running and was very slow, they are friends
now. They have actively encouraged my daughter (under 11) who was
very slow but has cut about 10 minutes off her 5k time – she likes to go
regularly because she feels welcome and appreciated and encouraged. We
try to give back by volunteering, and people show their appreciation for
this as well.

(p. 16)

The prevailing discourse of parkrun is one of accessibility and social inclusion,
underlined by the commitment that parkrun is open to anyone, whilst also
targeting those most in need. 'It's a non-elitist, unifying thing . . . which stems
from its non-competitive nature,' writes Ben Smith in *The Guardian*'s Running
Blog.[1] The WHO (2018) in its *Global Action Plan on Physical Activity 2018–2030*
cited parkrun as an example of 'free, universally accessible, whole-of-community
events that provide opportunities to be active in local public spaces and which
aim to cultivate positive experiences and build competencies, particularly in
the least active.' I shall return to these proclamations of inclusion, access, and
belonging throughout the chapter, not to undermine parkrun's undoubted success in attracting a diversity of participants, including those harder to engage
in physical activity such as women, those obese or overweight, and those with

poorer health (Wiltshire & Merchant, 2021), but rather, to ask critical questions, particularly of those things that appear self-evident or irrefutable.

★

The word 'community' is derived from the Anglo-Norman and Middle French *communite*, which comes from the Latin *communitas*, meaning, primarily 'public spirit.' The *idea* of community, which may in part account for its enduring appeal, is related to notions of belonging and the search or a longing for meaning, solidarity, and collective identities (Delanty, 2008). This idyllic image, categorised by dense networks of personal ties, is seductive and yet appears to bear little resemblance to contemporary cities where weak ties prevail over strong ties and social interaction among residents is characterised more by instrumentality than altruism (Sampson, 2004). As such, the term 'community' evokes a romanticised lost era, often associated with a fracturing of trust and cooperation in people's everyday interactions (Williams, 2008). In modern parlance the concept of community has become more nuanced and complex with seemingly ever-increasing numbers of communities that in the words of Chocano (2018) are 'less and less about being from someplace and more about being like someone.'

In a seminal 1986 article titled 'Sense of community: A definition and theory,' psychologists McMillan and Chavis (1986) delineated four basic elements of community. The first of these, membership, refers to a feeling of belonging or of sharing a sense of personal relatedness. The second is influence, a sense of mattering, of making a difference to a group and of the group mattering to its members. The third is reinforcement, which relates to the integration and fulfilment of needs. This is the feeling that members' needs will be met by the resources received through their membership in the group. The final element is shared emotional connection or the belief that members have shared or will share history, common places, time together, and similar experiences. Additionally, McMillan and Chavis establish an important distinction between two types of community that have long coexisted. One is geographical – neighbourhood, town, city – the other is relational, concerned with the interconnections among people. For many, our sense of community shifts between these different modes of thinking with its meaning over time expanding to accommodate groups with shared values, interests, activities, and a general sense of connectedness. Echoing this, Muniz and O'Guinn (2001), in their synopsis of sociological literature, identify three core elements of community. The first is consciousness of kind so that members in a community feel an intrinsic connection to each other and a collective sense of difference from individuals outside the community. The second component is the presence of shared rituals and traditions, which help foster and maintain community history, culture, and behavioural norms. The third element is a sense of moral responsibility, suggesting that community members feel a shared sense of obligation to each other and to the community.

As outlined at the beginning of the chapter, parkrun has been conceived as a community, frequently employed, uncritically, as a self-evident description of people coming together with the objective of reaching out to previously less active population cohorts. In this sense, the notion of the parkrun community comprises a group of people – runners, joggers, walkers, volunteers, and spectators – who, to paraphrase Bowness et al. (2020), coalesce for a plurality of reasons and become interconnected through the facilitation of each other's activity. The comradeship and solidarity extend beyond individual, localised events with parkrunners indicating they feel part of a bigger parkrun 'family.' As this participant detailed in their account:

> To be a part of a free club that has its own kit is an amazing feeling. You can go anywhere in the country, or abroad and immediately connect with other likeminded people, even when it isn't a Saturday if you see someone wearing their 25 (volunteer), 50, 100, 250 or apricot top it connects you. Ultimately seeing someone away from home wearing an apricot top with your home parkrun is a great feeling. It allows for a conversation to be immediately struck up when the start of a running event normally results in people standing around on their own.
>
> (p. 11)

This representation of parkrun is underlined in the introduction to Dean Carter's *Lon-Done!* (2018) where he documents a personal challenge to complete all 49 (at the time of writing) parkruns located in Greater London over the course of a year. He writes:

> There is something satisfying, enriching and morale-boosting about running five kilometres with a large group of local, similarly-minded folk, all of whom are there to not only get fit but to socialise and encourage each other. They might be complete strangers, but it doesn't matter, they're there for the same reason as you. It's a feel-good congregation where you feel part of something unique, something special.
>
> (p. 8)

The notion of participants being 'in it together' and a shared sense of community was a theme identified in a qualitative explorative study conducted by Morris and Scott (2019). Relatedly, the authors identified four sub-themes: supportive environment, giving and receiving, socialising, and identity and purpose. In relation to the first of these, participants in their study reported that parkrun had a friendly welcoming atmosphere which encouraged participation and where participants were legitimately invested in one another. One of their respondents stated,

> People get cheered if they're incredibly slow or whether they're the fastest, and it's genuine, it's very genuine, it's very authentic, it's not contrived, it's not forced.
>
> (p. 118)

Other participants in their study valued opportunities to give back, supporting others as they have been supported. As this respondent reported, 'there's satisfaction in helping to keep parkrun going. It's almost like the parkrun family, it's like being a member of the family, instead of taking something out all the time' (p. 119).

Pulling on existing scholarly literature, the notion of running communities has attracted interest from the perspective of new forms of collective identity and social bonding that emanate from their organisation. Running is often caricatured using a dichotomy whereby runners either participate individually or run with others in organised settings, for example, an athletics club. Scheerder et al. (2015) draw a useful distinction with more informal groupings such as running together with family and friends, referring to these as 'light running.' In this sense, running individually and not being a member of a running club does not necessarily mean that runners lack social interaction when running. Pedersen et al. (2018) employ the notion of a 'peg' community as forming a bridge between contradictory desires and the need for the individuality and community. Viewed in this light, the runner is 'not that alone but shares a common passion for running with others which is cultivated in different ways *together*' (Pedersen et al., 2018, p. 247, original emphasis). In a qualitative study of a self-organised distance running group in China, Xie et al. (2020) reported that members had positive social interaction and support during running activities and social activities outside of running. Within the group, which had a simple and loose structure with limited rules, different levels of shared identity were manifest, which contributed to a sense of community. The authors pithily conclude, '[R]unning brings people together, positive social interaction keeps people together' (p. 204).

★

At the heart of the parkrun ethos is a determination to create opportunities for participation and in turn to minimise barriers. Promoting parkrun as 'a run, not a race' explicitly invites the involvement of groups who do not identify with traditional stereotypical views of running. Much emphasis is placed on parkrun being open to all abilities. The homepage of the website boldly proclaims, 'parkrun is a positive, welcoming, and inclusive experience where there is no time limit, and no one finishes last' along with the statement 'free for everyone forever.' No special clothing or expensive equipment is required, nor any specialised skills, training, or competences, and there are no direct costs. On the supply side, there is no need for new infrastructure, specialist personnel, or excessive bureaucracy (Wellington, 2021). The free at the point of use model ostensibly eliminates cost as a potential barrier to physical activity and reduces exclusivity on financial grounds (Wiltshire & Merchant, 2021). But as previously questioned, does making an event free necessarily ensure that it is accessible to all? As Wiltshire and Merchant (2021, p. 210) shrewdly observe, 'holding events in public parks opens up questions around geographical barriers and health inequalities as parks are more likely to be located in more affluent areas.'[2] Furthermore, whilst it is common in media coverage for parkrun be portrayed as an inclusive community, to what extent do such representations stand up to scrutiny? For example, Fullagar (2016) reported fewer parkrunners from non-white British backgrounds, even in areas of high ethnic diversity.

Early research suggested that parkrun 'may contribute to increasing physical activity and wellbeing among [parkrun] community members' (Stevinson & Hickson, 2014, p. 273). In their profiling of the parkrun community, using a cross-sectional survey of adult parkrunners in the UK, they found that most participants were men and between 35 and 54 years of age. They also reported that a sizable portion of participants had not been regular runners prior to their parkrun registration with a quarter identifying as non-runners. The latter cohort recorded the greatest improvements in objective measure of aerobic fitness. The inclusion of non-runners, older adults, women, overweight people, and those with limiting disabilities led the authors to conclude that parkrun was effective as a public health intervention in attracting some sections of the community. Conversely, 'the numbers of ethnic minorities and people from lower socioeconomic groups are disproportionately low' (Stevinson & Hickson, 2014, p. 273). The authors suggested further investigation to explore whether this was an indicator of parkrun contributing to increased health inequalities in some areas, or a reflection of the embryonic nature of parkrun, adding that participation among hard-to-reach groups may increase as parkrun continues to expand geographically.

Elsewhere, research has also examined parkrun's capacity to encourage and maintain the participation of those previously inactive. In a qualitative study by Stevinson et al. (2015), involving semi-structured interviews with adult parkrun participants, several features of the parkrun experience were identified as contributing to initial and sustained engagement. The authors grouped these under two overarching themes: freedom and reciprocity. Concerning the former, the perceived accessibility and inclusivity of events were important factors in encouraging initial and repeat attendance. A participant in their study said,

> The youngest to the oldest must have been around 60 years. I think any event that can pull people in of all ages, backgrounds and fitness levels has to be a great idea.
>
> (p. 173)

Reciprocity related to the dual opportunity for both personal benefits of taking part and to reciprocate these gains by helping others, which was achieved most directly by volunteering. This was also evident in relation to the social support, through encouragement received from other runners, and a desire to offer the same assistance to others. As this participant remarked,

> I was obviously struggling and she kind of, you know, supported me through the last lap, which was really nice. I mean I didn't know her and

people do that all the time, you know, encourage people, complete strangers, but everybody's kind of there and there is a spirit to encourage people.
(p. 173)

Additionally, the social and physical environmental context of parkrun was emphasised with participants identifying the welcoming atmosphere and opportunities for social contact as central to this, along with how being in a natural setting contributed to their enjoyment. The authors explain, '[O]ver half the participants discussed how being outdoors in the fresh air among beautiful scenery brought additional pleasure to the experience that increased the desire to return each week' (p. 174).

The individual, social, and environmental factors associated with parkrun's broad appeal were the focus of an exploratory qualitative study. In an Australian context, Sharman et al. (2018) undertook 10 semi-structured interviews with Tasmanian parkrun participants who were identified following a 2016 quantitative survey of adult parkrunners. A maximum variability sampling approach guided the purposive recruitment of participants, ensuring diversity between respondents, particularly regarding gender, education level, number of dependents living at home, height, weight, and pre-parkrun and current physical activity. All interviewees had been participating in parkrun for approximately 2 years or more. The interviews focused on reasons for parkrun participation with four themes identified: participation facilitators and barriers, physical activity gain and broader community benefit, social connections and networks, and organisational issues.

Echoing some of the themes identified in the Stevinson et al. (2015) study, participants reported several appealing and motivating characteristics of parkrun. These comprised giving and receiving social support, fitness and attendance incentives and rewards, and opportunities for socialising. For example, one of their participants commented:

> Like, I'm pretty shy, I'm not real socially out there, but I feel I could go up to anyone of the parkrun Saturday and have a chat about stuff. For me being fairly socially shy, that's pretty, I don't know, pretty good.
>
> (p. 167)

Another participant in their study reflected on the importance of incentives on promoting repeat attendance:

> I mean, my first time was a lot slower than I wanted, but then again it gave me incentive to try and better my time. I think my first time was like 36 minutes or something like that and I thought, shit, I can do better than that. . . . When you get that sort of encouragement and you get the email with your results that says, hey, you got a new PB and stuff like that, it's just all upbeat. And, because you're doing it every week or every couple of

weeks on average, that's got to be reinforcing. That's got to be saying, hey, you're doing the right thing. Keep going.

(p. 167)

Most respondents remarked upon the perceived inclusiveness of parkrun in assisting parkrun's attraction. Other sub-themes included parkrun's sense of community, the positive and supportive atmosphere, convenience in terms of time and location, low cost, and facilitation of new friendships. Commonly, participants indicated a desire to attend parkrun as regularly as possible, although barriers to participation included work commitments, inclement weather, clashes with children's sporting commitments, injury, or other conflicting social activities. Interviewees also identified that negative body image may contribute to lack of participation for women specifically or the need for social support (for example, 'sometimes people need somebody to meet them there'). One respondent observed that the name 'parkrun' may be a deterrent for some because it associates the event with running, even though many people walk:

Look, I get why they call it parkrun, I really do. But I also think it stops a lot of people from having a go. . . . I just think some people get put off by the name because they think they've got to be super-fast.

(p. 165)

Participants were generally positive about the local organisation of parkrun (at the time of the study, Tasmania had five geographically dispersed parkrun events). On the flip side, respondents raised concerns that the increasing popularity of parkrun could lead to a decline in the quality of its management or the possibility of a fee-paying model. Local council politics was also identified as a potential threat to parkrun. This emerged as a concern following the closure in 2016 of Little Stoke parkrun after it was decided to charge parkrun and a Western Australian local council subsequently proposed to follow suit. Additionally, concerns were expressed regarding parkrunners not volunteering for events, making it difficult on occasion to fill all the volunteer roles. A participant in the Sharman et al. (2018) study quipped, '[T]he reason I don't volunteer anymore is if the same people volunteer, those buggers that have never volunteered won't' (p. 168).

With regard to perceived physical activity benefits, three participants in the exploratory study reported that parkrun had led to significant increases in weekly exercise. Two participants remarked that parkrun had contributed to more running in their physical activity regimen as opposed to an overall increase in physical activity levels. No respondents reported decreases in physical activity since starting parkrun with all participants explicitly stating that they either intended to continue with parkrun or had implied this. Several participants indicated that parkrun was the reason for joining other running groups or taking part in other mass community running events. Most participants stated that they first attended parkrun because of encouragement from within their existing social network. Nine of the ten interviewees said they had in turn promoted parkrun within their social circles, most commonly among family and friends, and had successfully persuaded others to attend.

The importance of the interpersonal is evident in a study by Wiltshire and Stevinson (2018), which considered individual parkrunners' social networks to understand disparities in parkrun participation, which mirrored broader social inequalities. The paper drew upon data from 20 semi-structured interviews collected as part of their earlier and wider study on the public health potential of parkrun. The sample included 11 females and 9 males, aged between 27 and 63 years, all of whom reported that they were inactive prior to registering to parkrun. Using the conceptual lens of social capital, the authors suggested the latter to be a key resource in shaping parkrun participation. Existing social ties – family, friends, and colleagues – were routinely instrumental in initiating participation, often mobilised through incidental and mundane interactions. As this interviewee described,

> My husband thought it'd be a good idea. He runs quite a lot. He's done marathons and all sorts, and he signed me up and said, 'You're coming,' and I'd never run before, so I wouldn't have done it without him kind of encouraging me.
>
> (p. 53)

Through invitation or encouragement, newly active participants are gaining from the network of social relations that they hold prior to becoming active – a benefit that individuals without social ties to parkrun, or indeed with low social capital more generally, are less likely to possess. In addition, several participants acknowledged parkrun as an opportunity to develop one's social network – a place to create and build social capital. A participant in their study explained:

> You know, you turn up, you do the race and you sit around and drink coffee and do whatever afterwards and get to meet a whole bunch of other runners and, you know, some you know to nod to and a few of them you know reasonably well and some acquaintances that you've known over the years kind of congregate together.
>
> (p. 54)

Notwithstanding personal encouragement, Wiltshire and Stevinson (2018) noted an important aspect of social capital was the likelihood that members of a group both invested in and benefited from the volunteering labour of the group. The data highlighted that participants drew heavily on the collective group for support and camaraderie, which was proffered by volunteers as well as other runners. In the words of one participant:

> As you're going round, the marshals give encouragement and we encourage people as they're going round, give them a clap and whatever saying,

'Come on, you can do it!' and whatever. And people who are struggling we'll tag onto somebody and say, 'Come on, you can do it!' and things like that.

(p. 55)

The study also illustrated the function social capital played in acquiring cultural capital and the resultant network of relations from which they have access than they otherwise would have. In this context, Wiltshire and Stevinson (2018) referred to cultural capital as the symbolic resources of skills, competencies, and know-how. As such, parkrun provided a space in which knowledge of running performance, injury management, and health was disseminated, uniting the parkrun community through a shared understanding. For example, one participant is quoted as passing on advice about an undulating parkrun course and how best to tackle the hilly sections. The same interviewee also provided an illustration of sharing expertise on improving performance and prevention of injuries:

We have our own Facebook group as well so we're passing information. People come on asking for information like 'I've got this type of injury. What do you recommend?' or 'I want to improve my speed. What do you recommend?' and things like that.

(p. 57)

Wiltshire and Stevinson (2018) argued that their qualitative parkrun study illustrates how social processes within volunteer-led, community-based initiatives can mobilise the flow of cultural capital to the extent that it is potentially accessible to low socio-economic groups. This in turn assisted newly active parkrunners to feel comfortable and in alignment with the practice itself. That said, even with the promotion of community-based public health interventions such as parkrun, the authors stressed it is important to note that the objective probabilities of individuals engaging in these opportunities are linked to their social capital which is distributed unevenly across social gradients. In conclusion, they state that – without significant social, economic, and political change – relying on social capital to encourage physical activity is likely to disproportionately engage individuals from middle- to high-income groups and thus have a limited impact in tackling inequalities.

Much of the preceding discussion illustrates how the expanding body of published qualitative research has emphasised the perceived commonality among parkrunners and how interaction with fellow participants worked to draw people into a shared set of group norms and identities. The extent to which these inferred communities are effective in breaking down participation barriers merits further exploration. From my own research – an intrinsic case study which focused on Colwick parkrun – I expressed a cautionary tone in potentially overplaying the accessibility of parkrun (see Hindley, 2020). This was reflected in a number of participants in the study voicing their apprehension in attending the first time. In the majority of instances, respondents' participation was facilitated through existing social ties, accompanied by a friend, partner, or family member, and when probed expressed hesitations over whether as a newcomer they would have attended parkrun unaccompanied. This begs the question, why is it the case that some feel welcomed and included when others feel anxious about attending? Furthermore, what steps are parkrun as an organisation taking to address some of these preconceptions? As one attendee reflected, 'the biggest hurdle for parkrun is getting someone cold over the initial fence and into parkrun. I was a bit nervous the first time. I thought they'd be two hundred quality athletes.' Other participants conceded, '[Y]ou could feel isolated if you came on your own' and 'I was invited to attend Colwick parkrun by a friend. I probably wouldn't have gone that first time if I wasn't with a friend.' These comments suggested that despite the inclusive ethos that is overtly promoted by parkrun and through word of mouth, first-timers may still harbour reservations about attending.

Nuzzo and Steele (2020) adopt a similar, inquiring approach in a short discursive article published in the *American Journal of Health Promotion*, regarding the perceived inclusivity of parkrun. Their riposte specifically focused on assertions and inferences made by Cleland et al. (2019) that paid-entry run/ walk events, in sharp contrast with parkrun, are elitist, tending to attract more experienced runners who are 'racing.' The authors began by recognising that the weekly occurrence of parkrun events provided opportunities for regular physical activity, referencing past studies which reported a number of desirable characteristics of participation, including a sense of community, inclusiveness, and facilitating social interaction. In response, Nuzzo and Steele observed that these traits can also be found in other modes of physical activity, citing *Crossfit* as one example. They go on to refute the suggestion that paid-entry run/walk events are 'for the privileged few,' arguing that such claims undermined the merits of paid-entry events and merely served to perpetuate false information about parkrun.

First, it is argued, paid-entry events are indeed inclusive, often including hundreds or thousands of participants. To illustrate this, Nuzzo and Steele (2020) emphasised that many events offered courses of differing distances, accommodating individuals with contrasting levels of fitness and competence. Some events included family or child-specific runs, explicitly titled 'fun runs,' as well as mostly being staffed by volunteers. Second, it is noted that many participants in such events are motivated by a desire for enjoyment and to feel unity and integration with others. Third, registration to paid-entry events is similar to parkrun in not requiring any specialised skills, training, equipment, or clothing. Fourth, it is argued that Cleland et al. (2019) overstate the claim that parkrun participants do not race during parkrun. Finally, the general notion that parkrun attracted a different, less elitist demographic is scrutinised. In a number of published studies on parkrun, participants already walked or ran prior to registration. Relatedly, Nuzzo and Steele (2020) conducted a meta-analysis of finishing times, comparing 5 km parkrun events and paid-entry events in Australian cities. It is reported that the median finishing time in parkrun was substantially faster than in paid-entry events for females and males. Further, 82 per cent of paid-entry event participants finished in over 30 minutes, compared to 41 per cent in parkrun.

Perceptions on, and strategies for, increasing inclusivity of non-traditional participants and marginalised groups were the focus of a UK-based action research project conducted by Fullagar et al. (2020). The study enabled collaboration with volunteer event organisers at four parkrun sites across England, Scotland, and Northern Ireland to understand participant experiences and constraints and develop localised inclusive strategies. The project is noteworthy in utilising a modified participatory action research design (PAR) so that research participants were involved in each step of the research process to enable shared understandings to be produced. The following research questions shaped the direction of the study: first, how inclusive is parkrun of non-traditional participants or marginalised groups who are less active; second, what do parkrunners identify as important aspects of the participatory culture that sustains their engagement; and third, what actions do parkrunners identify as potentially improving the engagement of non-traditional participants to create a more inclusive parkrun culture and engage marginalised groups?

The four parkrun sites (anonymised for publication) were selected due to their proximity to the research team locations across the UK with each run director agreeing to be involved in researching strategies to support inclusive participation. Each site formed its own co-research team, including volunteers involved in organising their local parkrun, who were responsible for refining the chosen data collection methods (an online and paper-based survey). During site visits to administer the surveys, the academic team engaged in participant observation by either completing the run or observing the volunteers/parkrunners. In-depth interviews (19 in total) were completed after each event to explore the meanings of participation and perceptions of inclusiveness. Draft summary reports of the survey data (total respondents 655) were shared with the respective co-research teams, enabling the co-researchers an opportunity to reflect on issues and consider the strategies for change offered by parkrunners in their event. The action-oriented process was designed to engage the parkrun community at each site in the conversation about inclusiveness and raise awareness.

For the survey, the authors reported a fairly even gender distribution, which is similar to the gender breakdown of parkrun registrations where women make up approximately 50 per cent. 'The pattern of participation revealed largely middle-aged, white, more rather than less affluent and mostly able bodied parkrunners as the norm' (Fullagar et al., 2020, p. 7). This is in line with previously reported findings from a larger study in 2014 by Stevinson and Hickson. Next, the survey data identified common perceptions that the parkrun ethos was inclusive of diversity, which was reflected in the parkrun messaging and articulated in relation to parkrun being accessible to all because it was local, free, and welcoming. Interestingly, the research methodology opened up the perception of inclusiveness, highlighting how in the London site it was evident that the ethnic and religious backgrounds of parkrunners were not reflective of the culturally diverse neighbourhood. As one respondent identified:

> It would be good if the general atmosphere was warmer and more inclusive. The runners at London parkrun do not seem to represent the 30 per cent Bangladeshi population in the area – I don't know why this is or how it can be improved, but perhaps it suggests that many local residents feel it is 'not for them', which is at odds with parkrun's ethos as a community venture.
>
> (pp. 7–8)

Some respondents in the study felt that there was an insider/outsider dynamic created by established social networks in running groups, which were thought to exclude less sporty runners. In contrast, others commented on particular inclusive practices, for example, the support provided to visually impaired runners. The survey also found that access to local parks may be a constraint to participation, particularly for sites that were not easily reached by foot or public transport. For example, 43.7 per cent of respondents indicated that they strongly agreed that parkrun was hard to get to without using a car.

The authors distinguished three themes that encompassed the types of inclusive strategies that were put forward by respondents: first, to promote the parkrun ethos in ways that attract diverse participants; second, to develop joined-up relationships with local organisations to enable pathways to parkrun and access to parks; and third, fostering an inclusive culture that is supportive of less-confident runners from diverse backgrounds. The study also identified a number of constraining factors that impacted on the parkrun teams' ability to pursue some of their actions within the follow-up period. Notably, there was some reluctance to actively promote parkrun to attract *more* participants, despite the desire to address inequalities. Furthermore, for some parkrun sites, the challenge of how to engage with diverse communities raised additional issues regarding cross-cultural understanding, engagement with groups, and appropriate forms of promotion. The authors also noted, against a backdrop of austerity and pressures on local government budgets, the constraints on parkrun in developing inclusive events.

★

Parkrun's growth over the years has been organic and, to a greater extent, shaped by community demand as opposed to responding to need. This is acknowledged by parkrun CEO Nick Pearson who contends that if the number of parkrun events in socially deprived areas is to increase, then this will require a more proactive approach.[3] This provides the context to a cross-sectional ecological analysis of the socio-economic disparities in geographic access to parkrun events. The study, conducted by group of researchers from the University of Sheffield and Sheffield Hallam University in 2020, had two objectives: first, to evaluate whether geographic access to parkrun events is equitable across areas with different levels of deprivation; and second, to identify 200 optimal locations for future events to improve geographic access and thus maximise access, in particular for deprived communities (Schneider et al., 2020). This *Public Health* paper coincided with the Sport England allocated funding announced in December 2018 to support the creation of 200 new parkrun events across England within 3 years with the specific aim of increasing participation of individuals from lower socio-economic groups. The authors noted that the expansion of parkrun in England, as elsewhere, had been predominantly grassroots, driven by *demand* rather than *need*. Consequently, it is hypothesised that parkrun events may be primarily located in areas that are less deprived, whilst people living in more deprived communities may not have the same opportunities to participate.

The analysis was conducted on the level of Lower Layer Super Output Areas (LSOAs), which divide England into 32,844 geographic units which, on average, have a population of approximately 1,700. The researchers assessed the relationship between access, defined as the distance ('as the crow flies') to the nearest parkrun event, and socio-economic deprivation, measured using the Index of Multiple Deprivation (IMD). Additionally, the locations of public green spaces in England were retrieved from an open dataset of Ordnance Survey to conduct a simple location-allocation analysis to identify 200 locations for future parkrun events that maximise access.

The authors reported that in England in December 2018, 69 per cent of the population lived within 5 km of a parkrun event. A small negative correlation between distance and deprivation was stated, indicating that access is slightly better in more socio-economically deprived areas. Schneider and colleagues expressed a degree of surprise at their main finding, citing past research which has shown that physical activity levels and the availability of physical activity facilities generally decline with the level of deprivation (Farrell et al., 2014). Put simply, opportunities for physical activity are often lacking in areas of most need (Hillsdon et al., 2007). In contrast, parkrun events appear to be held in or near deprived areas and are free to attend, giving anyone equal access, irrespective of their socio-economic background. Nevertheless, the researchers reported that parkrun participation has a strong socio-economic gradient, which suggests that providing the opportunity to participate in parkrun events, whilst a necessary first step to enable participation, has not been sufficient to engage people living in deprived communities.

Setting up an additional 200 parkrun events in optimal locations would improve access, which would mean approximately 82 per cent of the population would live within 5 km of a parkrun event. The authors concluded that whilst creating additional events may improve geographic access, effective strategies will still be necessary to increase engagement in new and existing events by those living in socio-economically deprived areas. They also noted that studying barriers to participation in parkrun, other than geographic access, is needed to improve our understanding of the reasons why physical activity levels are lower in more deprived areas and may help to design more effective public health interventions.

In a separate paper by Smith et al. (2020), the research team sought to investigate earlier work which revealed substantial heterogeneity in parkrun participation across different communities in England. It is noted that the existing analysis only explored the relationship between participation, access, and deprivation and crucially did not consider ethnic density as a potential determinant of participation in parkrun. Indeed, existing evidence from survey data suggests that non-white British individuals in England are less likely to be physically active and to engage in sport in general (Rowe & Champion, 2000). Thus, the authors hypothesised that at community level, areas with higher ethnic diversity will have lower levels of participation in parkrun.

The researchers carried out an ecological analysis of parkrun participation in England in 2018. Data were obtained from a variety of sources for the LSOAs in England referred to in the previous study, including parkrun finisher data from each LSOA. The rest of the data included the IMD score, population, ethnic density, population density, rural–urban classification, percentage working age, and distance from LSOA centroid to the nearest parkrun. The findings showed that more deprived areas and areas with higher ethnic density had lower participation rates. The authors went on to argue that the results suggest that a small part of the negative effect on participation previously attributed to deprivation can actually be attributed to ethnic density. They concluded that whilst parkrun is already in the process of increasing the number of events geographically located in deprived areas in England to encourage participation from disadvantaged groups, the findings demonstrated that ethnic density (in addition to deprivation and access) is an important determinant of participation.

In a more recent study published in the journal *Health and Place*, Smith et al. (2021) conducted a longitudinal ecological analysis of the distance to and participation in parkrun in England from 2010 to 2019 and related socio-economic and ethic inequalities. As with the studies cited earlier, the group of academics calculated the distance to the nearest parkrun event for each English LSOA. This was done each month from January 2010 to December 2019. Trends in distance to and participation in parkrun by IMD quintile were also reported. Additionally, the Relative Index of Inequality (RII) by deprivation for participation and distance to nearest event was also used. Finally, Smith and colleagues investigated trends in LSOA-level determinants, for example, deprivation and ethnic density, of parkrun participation between 2010 and 2019, using multivariable Poisson regression models.

Utilising the comprehensive datasets provided by parkrun and the ONS, the authors were able to show that distance to the nearest event decreased from a mean of 34.1 km in 2010 to 4.6 km in 2019, whilst participation increased over the 10-year period. 'These can be considered as improvements given parkrun's intention to improve geographical access and therefore participation' (Smith et al., 2021, p. 5). Participation can be split into two distinct phases: from 2010 to 2013 participation increased super-linearly and inequality in participation fell dramatically; from 2013 to 2019 participation increased linearly, whilst inequality in participation remained stable. Thus, despite parkrun's ambitions of creating inclusive events and engaging with deprived communities, the socio-economic gradient in participation rates remained high and stable since 2013. This led the authors to conclude:

> While participation is likely to continue to increase for all socioeconomic groups, closing the gap in participation between the most and least deprived communities is likely to require changes to the organisation and delivery of events rather than just further increases in the number of events in more deprived areas.
>
> (p. 6)

Further research is therefore necessary to better understand why some communities are more engaged in parkrun than others, as well as comparison with other outdoor community-based physical activity. The findings of this study, it is noted, suggest that parkrun has different appeal and accessibility to some groups more than others. Encouragingly, there does appear to be a trend of increasing engagement from areas with higher ethnic density, which may be an indicator that parkrun is becoming more successful at engaging with culturally diverse communities.

In a more recent exploratory research paper, Haake et al. (2021) explore a hypothesis that parkrun participation is influenced by the socio-economic characteristics of both parkrunners and their 'home' park. The authors identified two parkruns, Castle and Hallam, in the city of Sheffield, located 4.5 km apart. Defined by indices of multiple deprivation, Castle parkrun is located in an economically deprived neighbourhood, whereas Hallam parkrun is in a more affluent area of the city. Parkrunners were defined by applying these same indices to the neighbourhood of 'home' registration. To explain, 'home' is the parkrun the registrant identifies with either because it is the event they are likely to participate in most frequently or because geographically it is the nearest to where they live. The results showed that the prosperous Hallam catchment area produced over five times more parkrun participants than Castle. Additionally, compared with Castle, Hallam parkrun attracted more participants from both catchment areas, and consequently, Hallam parkrun had more than seven times more participants than Castle parkrun. The authors report the headline findings as relating to 'place' inequality between the venues and between participants with differential participation linked to both the setting of the parkrun events (socio-economic, environmental, etc.) and the neighbour-hood setting of participants' registered addresses.

Evidentially, the authors claim, parkrun participation is associated with where parkrunners live and the park they use. It is suggested that in comparing the differential attraction of Castle and Hallam, socio-economic factors appear para-mount. Interestingly, they go on to propose that further consideration of the parkrun settings may add a multiplier effect. For example, comparison of the gradient at the respective events may make Castle (which has an increased gradi-ent) less attractive to those new to running, new to parkrun, or to those seeking a personal best time. Furthermore, Castle parkrun is located at the top of a hill, has limited on-street parking, and lacks a vibrant cafe for post-event socialising. Additionally, the authors speculate that the longevity of Hallam parkrun, which was inaugurated 3 years and 153 events prior to Castle, may be a contributing factor. Haake et al. (2021) conclude:

> The challenge for policymakers and decision-takers is that parkrun appears to reflect and maybe reinforce differential levels of physical activity linked to socio-economic context, contributing to greater inequities in health status.
>
> (p. 6)

As such, the findings in this study suggest that investing in parkrun events that are located in socially deprived neighbourhoods is a necessary but crucially 'not sufficient prerequisite for greater equity of participation.'

★

In this chapter I have drawn upon the emerging published literature on parkrun to discuss the dominant framing of parkrun as an inclusive community, wel-coming runners, and non-runners, both of which are valued equally. As such, one of the central components of parkrun is the perceived sense of belonging and community, that participants are 'in it together,' fostering a socially support-ive environment, which has previously been established as a key determinant of both initiation and continuation of exercise (Morgan et al., 2016; McGonigal, 2021). Indeed, as I have sought to emphasise, one of the key findings from the scholarly literature on parkrun is that it is social; events represent temporary spaces that are conducive for incidental and casual social interaction. However, as has also been alluded, the prevailing narrative of parkrun as one of social inclusion, that it is 'for everyone,' may be slightly exaggerated. There is evi-dence of the anxieties of first-timers that are more likely to attend if accompa-nied and the reliance on social capital to encourage participation which may disproportionately engage individuals from middle- to high-income groups and thus have a limited impact in tackling inequalities. Relatedly, published research has reported that whilst access to parkrun is generally good and is similar across socio-economic groups, participation is markedly higher in less-deprived areas. Thus, the emerging evidence suggests that improving access alone is unlikely to significantly increase participation from deprived areas.

Notes

1 www.theguardian.com/lifeandstyle/the-running-blog/2013/mar/11/parkrun-is-an-unusual-beautiful-sight
2 It has been shown by Ridgley et al. (2020) that more economically deprived areas have less-available good-quality greenspace.
3 www.connectsport.co.uk/news/exclusive-parkrun-ceo-warns-against-token-initiatives

References

Bowness, J., Tulle, E., & McKendrick, J. (2020). Understanding the parkrun community; sacred Saturdays and organic solidarity of parkrunners. *European Journal for Sport and Society*, 18:1, 44–63. https://doi.org/10.1080/16138171.2020.1792113.
Carter, D. (2018). *Lon-Done! Running the Greater London Parkruns*. Independently published.
Chakrabortty, A. (2018). Forget profit. It's love and fun that drive innovations like parkrun. *The Guardian*. Retrieved from www.theguardian.com/commentisfree/2018/aug/29/forget-profit-love-fun-innovation-parkrun
Chocano, C. (2018). What good is 'community' when someone else makes all the rules? *The New York Times Magazine*. Retrieved from www.nytimes.com/2018/04/17/magazine/what-good-is-community-when-someone-else-makes-all-the-rules.html
Cleland, V., Nash, M., Sharman, M.J., & Claflin, S. (2019). Exploring the health-promoting potential of the 'parkrun' phenomenon: What factors are associated with higher levels of participation?. *Quantitative Research*, 33:1, 13–23.
Delanty, G. (2008). *Community*. London: Routledge.
Farrell, L., Hollingsworth, B., Propper, C., & Shields, M.A. (2014). The socioeconomic gradient in physical inactivity: Evidence from one million adults in England. *Social Science & Medicine*, 123, 55–63.
Fullagar, S. (2016). Parkrun is an important movement and should remain free for participants. *The Conversation*. Retrieved from https://theconversation.com/parkrun-is-an-important-movement-and-should-remain-free-for-participants-58097
Fullagar, S., Petris, S., Sargent, J., Allen, S., Akhtar, M., & Ozakinci, G. (2020). Action research with parkrun UK volunteer organisers to develop inclusive strategies. *Health Promotion International*, 35, 1199–1209.
Haake, S., Heller, B., Schneider, P., Smith, R., & Green, G. (2021). The influence of neighbourhood equity on parkrunners in a British city. *Health Promotion International*, 1–8. https://doi.org/10.1093/heapro/daab138.
Hillsdon, M., Panter, J., Foster, C., & Jones, A. (2007). Equitable access to exercise facilities. *American Journal of Preventative Medicine*, 32:6, 506–508.
Hindley, D. (2020). 'More than just a run in the park': An exploration of parkrun as a shared leisure space. *Leisure Sciences*, 42:1, 85–105.
Jones, E. (2021). *How parkrun Changed Our Lives*. Hebden Bridge: Gritstone Publishing.
McGonigal, K. (2021). *The Joy of Movement: How Exercise Helps Us to Find Happiness, Hope, Connection, and Courage*. New York: Penguin Random House.

Mcmillan, D.W., & Chavis, D. (1986). Sense of community: A definition and theory. *Journal of Community Psychology*, 14:1, 6–23.

Morgan, F., Battersby, A., Weightman, A.L., Searchfield, L., Turley, R., Morgan, H., Jagroo, J., & Ellis, S. (2016). Adherence to exercise referral schemes by participants – What do providers and commissioners need to know? A systematic review of barriers and facilitators. *BMC Public Health*, 16:227. https://doi.org/10.1186/s12889-016-2882-7.

Morris, P., & Scott, H. (2019). Not just a run in the park: A qualitative exploration of parkrun and mental health. *Advances in Mental Health*, 17:2, 110–123.

Muniz, A.M., & O'Guinn, T.C. (2001). Brand community. *Journal of Consumer Research*, 27:4, 412–432.

Nuzzo, J.L., & Steele, J. (2020). Parkrun and the claim of 'elitism' in paid-entry run/walk events. *American Journal of Health Promotion*, 34:7, 806–807.

Pedersen, H., Kremmer Pedersen, L., & Thing, L.F. (2018). 'Liquid running communities' – An analysis of serious runners' communities. *European Journal for Sport and Society*, 15:3, 234–249.

Ridgley, H., et al. (2020). *Improving Access to Greenspace a New Review for 2020*. London: Public Health England. Retrieved from https://assets.publishing.service.gov.uk/government/uploads/system/uploads/attachment_data/file/904439/Improving_access_to_greenspace_2020_review.pdf

Rowe, N., & Champion, R. (2000). *Sports Participation and Ethnicity in England: National Survey*. London: Sport England.

Sampson, R.J. (2004). *Networks and Neighbourhoods: The Implications of Connectivity for Thinking about Crime in the Modern City*. Retrieved from www.demos.co.uk/files/File/networklogic-12sampson.pdf

Scheerder, J., Breedveld, K., & Borgers, J. (Eds.). (2015). *Running Across Europe – The Rise and Size of One of the Largest Sport Markets*. New York: Palgrave Macmillan.

Schneider, P.P., Smith, R.A., Bullas, A.M., Quirk, H., Bayley, T., Haake, S.J., Brennan, A., & Goyder, E. (2020). Multiple deprivation and geographic distance to community physical activity events – Achieving equitable access to parkrun in England. *Public Health*, 48–53.

Sharman, M.J., Nash, M., & Cleland, V. (2018). Health and broader community benefit of parkrun: An exploratory qualitative study. *Health Promotion Journal of Australia*, 30, 163–171.

Smith, R., Schneider, P., Bullas, A., Haake, S., Quirk, H., Cosulich, R., & Goyder, E. (2020). Does ethnic density influence community participation in mass participation physical activity events? The case of parkrun in England. *Wellcome Open Research*, 5:9.

Smith, R.A., Schneider, P.P., Cosulich, R., Quirk, H., Bullas, A.M., Haake, S.J., & Goyder, E. (2021). Socioeconomic inequalities in distance to and participation in a community-based running and walking activity: A longitudinal ecological study of parkrun 2010 to 2019. *Health and Place*, 71. https://doi.org/10.1016/j.healthplace.2021.102626.

Sport England. (2018). *Partnership with parkrun Worth £3m*. Retrieved from www.sportengland.org/news/sport-england-partner-with-parkrun-for-three-years-with-3-million-investment

Stevinson, C., & Hickson, M. (2014). Exploring the public health potential of a mass community participation event. *Journal of Public Health*, 36:2, 268–274.

Stevinson, C., Wiltshire, G., & Hickson, M. (2015). Facilitating participation in health-enhancing physical activity: A qualitative study of parkrun. *International Journal of Behavioural Medicine*, 22, 170–177.

Wellington, C. (2021). *Parkrun – supplementary written evidence (NPS0139)*. Retrieved from https://committees.parliament.uk/writtenevidence/22941/default/

Williams, A. (2008). Who needs community anyway? In Clements, D., Donald, A., Earnshaw, M., & Williams, A. (Eds.), *The Future of Community: Reports of a Death Greatly Exaggerated* (pp. 1–10). London: Pluto Press.

Wiltshire, G., & Merchant, S. (2021). What can we learn about nature, physical activity, and health from parkrun? In Brymer, E., Rogerson, M., & Barton, J. (Eds.), *Nature and Health: Physical Activity in Nature* (pp. 208–222). London: Routledge.

Wiltshire, G., & Stevinson, C. (2018). Exploring the role of social capital in community-based physical activity: Qualitative insights from parkrun. *Qualitative Research in Sport, Exercise and Health*, 10:1, 47–62.

World Health Organisation. (2018). *More Active People for a Healthier World. Global Action Plan on Physical Activity 2018–2030*. Retrieved from https://apps.who.int/iris/bitstream/handle/10665/272722/9789241514187-eng.pdf

Xie, H., Chen, Y., & Yin, R. (2020). Running together is better than running alone: A qualitative study of a self-organised distance running group in China. *Leisure Studies*, 39:2, 195–208.

Chapter 3

Volunteering and Reciprocity

In the preceding chapter I discussed the ways parkrun is commonly presented as a community with potential to generate public health and wellbeing benefits. It was noted how parkrun actively seeks to minimise barriers, evidenced by populations traditionally more difficult to engage in physical activity being meaningfully represented at parkrun events. In this chapter, our attention will turn to a related characteristic of parkrun's inclusive culture, namely volunteering, which provides ad hoc participation opportunities with lower levels of obligation than might be expected from membership of a traditional civic group. As with many community-based events, volunteering is central to parkrun's model of delivery; the weekly events are only feasible through the volunteer labour of local participants. However, as this chapter will illuminate, like many events and organisations, volunteer recruitment can from time to time present challenges despite an expectation of reciprocity and research into parkrun volunteering identifying personal gain and helping others as incentives (Stevinson et al., 2015).

Volunteering is integral to the parkrun model and its sustainability. Local events are contingent on a core team of volunteers who take on a wide range of roles with parkrunners encouraged from time to time to volunteer themselves. As Wiltshire et al. (2018) observe, 'the weekly events are managed through micro-economies of co-operativism underpinned by the volunteer labour of participants themselves who, occasionally, marshal instead of taking part in the spirit of reciprocity' (p. 4). The core teams are trained and supported during the set-up process, taking on the responsibility for coordinating the volunteer teams each week. Episodic volunteers – so named due to the short-term, limited-commitment, flexible nature – typically make up the majority of the volunteer team. They are requested to turn up at a designated time before the parkrun event. Some guidance may be provided, and the core team provide overall direction and support, but the volunteering role requires no specialist skills, knowledge, or experience, nor is there any formal contract or obligation (Renfree & West, 2021). Most volunteer roles also preclude the volunteer from participating in the event, although there are some exceptions, such as setting up, sorting out tokens after the event, and 'tail walker,' which allow participation. There is no

DOI: 10.4324/9781003121961-3

remuneration or expenses, although after 25 occasions of volunteering, volunteers qualify for a T-shirt.

One of parkrun's guiding principles for volunteering is that whilst volunteer recruitment can sometimes present difficulties despite expectations of reciprocity, there is no explicit or overt pressure for parkrunners to volunteer at events. 'We know from experience that some people will volunteer regularly while others will seldom or never volunteer. Event teams need to remember that volunteering is a choice, and everyone is welcome at parkrun whether they volunteer or not.'[1] As such, questions arise as to why people do – or perhaps more importantly do not – volunteer. This became one of the focuses of a 2020 small-scale study into reciprocal volunteering at parkrun undertaken by a group of researchers at Kingston University and St. George's University of London. The study conducted by Hallett et al. (2020a) aimed to investigate motivations and constraints and to better understand parkrunners' perceptions of parkrun events and volunteering. The authors drew upon the work of Bishop and Hoggett (1986, p. 41) and what they describe as mutual aid. This is where an organisation is 'by some of us, for all of us' rather than 'by them, for us,' although practically it is acknowledged that this separation is more of a continuum. It is noted by Bishop and Hoggett that in mutual aid people carrying out voluntary roles do not perceive themselves as volunteers. Characteristically, such groups have strong subcultures – often displaying shared interests – and offer participants the opportunity to develop their sense of value and identity through group-related performance. Whilst it is notable that parkrun shares some of the qualities of the mutual aid model put forward by Bishop and Hoggett, there are also some important differences. In contrast, there is less commitment required from parkrunners. There are no membership fees, and correspondingly there is no pressure; participation can be as regular or infrequent as desired. Nevertheless, there is a strong parkrun subculture.

Hallett et al. (2020a) employed a qualitative approach, carrying out ten semistructured interviews with participants drawn from respondents to an online survey regarding parkrun volunteering. It is noteworthy that from the sample, seven of the participants had not volunteered, although only one had not volunteered at the time of the interview. On the basis of the participant demographics two of the ten were seasoned volunteers, amassing 380 volunteering occasions between them. Following thematic analysis of the transcriptions, which combined deductive and inductive approaches, three themes were identified: 'hooked,' relating to the participants' enthusiasm towards parkrun and desire to take part frequently; 'obligation to give back' to reflect the commonly held view that parkrun participants should also volunteer; and 'reluctance to miss a run,' reflecting a conflict between the desire to run/jog/walk and the onus to volunteer, the first two themes. The three themes identified in relation to volunteering behaviour the authors argued are clearly interlinked, going on to suggest they presented an element of conflict.

The study raises questions regarding the perception of running as being preferable to volunteering. This was manifest through participants wanting to improve their times, the 'reward' of the results email which enables self-monitoring and comparison, as well as the emphasis on milestone T-shirts and additional challenges (again with an emphasis on running rather than volunteering). One participant in their study explained:

> If you couldn't run and volunteer on the same day, I don't know what I'd be doing. That would be difficult for me because I so look forward to the run in order to try and improve my time to get a PB for the particular course, so I would feel a slight sense of loss if I had to miss my run.
>
> (p. 14)

Additionally, study participants believed all parkrunners had an obligation to volunteer, and over time they developed a sense of obligation to volunteer themselves. This realisation was echoed by one of the participants who stated,

> The first thing that got me into marshalling was I was approaching my tenth run I thought, I'm taking the mickey here because these people are standing out marshalling for me, and I'm just enjoying it every Saturday.
>
> (p. 11)

Another respondent described a growing unease, implying a sense of unacceptability of *not* volunteering:

> I think because I'd done that many runs, I thought it's getting a bit embarrassing now. I felt like I should have put something back having done so many free runs, if you like, where everybody else had made it happen for me. I just thought it was time for me to have a go and put something back and do my bit really.
>
> (p. 12)

As the authors identified, this perceived sense of obligation is noteworthy as there is no explicit demand from parkrun to volunteer, and also because parkrunners are not necessarily aware of who has volunteered and who hasn't, so there is no direct judgement of the individual. Also noticeable from the data were the difficulties associated with recruiting volunteers, often reliant on a small core group of members, although it was recognised that individual differences affected reciprocity, as well as biographical elements such as childcare proving a barrier to both running and volunteering. To summarise, participation, completing milestone events, the need for volunteering for events to go ahead, and the recognition of necessary social exchange presented some difficulties in resolution among study participants. In turn, this led to a strategic approach towards volunteering whereby certain roles were avoided so that both the desire to run/jog/walk and the sense of obligation to volunteer could be fulfilled. This helps to shed a light on the individualised levels of practicality and motivation, reflecting the varied personalised circumstances of parkrunners.

Challenges associated with filling the volunteer roles were similarly underlined in a study by Sharman et al. (2018) where some participants accepted that finding sufficient volunteers occasionally proved difficult.

> One participant said that a possible barrier to volunteering was the time commitment had increased due to parkrun's inclusive nature – slower walkers/runner take longer to complete the course and volunteers have to stay longer to ensure that everyone safely completes the event.
>
> (p. 168)

Participants also expressed concern about parkrunners not fulfilling the volunteering component (e.g. three or four times per year), recognising the importance of volunteer labour which enables parkrun to remain free to participate. That said, no one in the study had experienced an event cancellation due to a lack of volunteers, whilst it was generally acknowledged that recruiting volunteers among other recreational/sporting pursuits was a common problem.

In a separate study, Hallett et al. (2020b) sought to examine non-volunteering behaviour at parkrun to explore barriers and identify how these might be overcome. As previously mentioned, event delivery is reliant on volunteers, which brings with it challenges when on occasion there are struggles to fill the volunteer roster. 'Shortages of volunteers can lead to safety issues and increase workload both before an event in order to recruit volunteers, and during an event if tasks are spread among fewer people' (p. 141). Moreover, without sufficient numbers of volunteers, despite encouragement and dependence on volunteers for delivery, the sustainability of community events such as parkrun may become an issue. This exploratory study collected data from 6,749 adult parkrunners using an online survey, including 860 respondents who had never volunteered. In addition to demographic information and views on incentives, non-volunteers were asked to rate agreement level for 18 statements about not volunteering. The principal reasons for not volunteering were preferring to run in the event and not having got round to volunteering, despite considering it. The former is noteworthy as there are weekly opportunities to run, as well as the option to log 'freedom runs' in one's personal profile (when a parkrun course is completed at a time other than the event itself). That said, these do not contribute towards an individual's total number of runs and the pursuit of milestone targets and T-shirts. In addition, 'the indicators are that there is some element of group running, which leads to its prioritisation among parkrunners' (Hallett et al., 2020b, p. 153). Analysis of the survey data identified four underpinning constructs: anxiety, self-interest, a lack of knowledge, and inertia, although most non-volunteers did not consider items relating to anxiety and a lack of knowledge to be a barrier. Additionally, there was concern over the expected level of commitment. For those describing further barriers, practicalities including work, childcare, and other commitments were presented. Disliking online interaction and disengaging due to pressure to volunteer were also noted.

The study findings provide some insights into why people do not volunteer where, as noted, in the context of parkrun there is encouragement and an imbedded expectation of volunteering activity (Hallett et al., 2020b). There are lessons to consider with regard to sustainability, particularly as parkrun expands with new events and growing participation numbers. The first is how parkrun can increase volunteering among participations when running is preferred to volunteering and the perception that volunteering is a barrier to achieving running goals. The second lesson is the importance of making signing up for volunteering a simple and easy process, particularly for those who may be less engaged with electronic communications and social media.

★

Whether volunteering at parkrun fits the mould of the 'typical' sport event or how the 'typical' sport volunteer is conceived is questioned by Renfree and West (2021) in a recent study published in the journal *Managing Sport and Leisure*. It is their contention that the flexible approach, where there is no formal requirement for a registered volunteer to attend every week, differentiates parkrun from others in that there are no formal roles for one individual and most roles tend to change on a weekly or rotational basis. The concept of parkrun, it is noted, is built on a less formal and systematic involvement of volunteering, nor does it require the same level of commitment as other fixed sport events or roles such as athletics clubs where a formal membership or fees are required. According to Renfree and West (2021), the non-committal, non-traditional approach promoted by parkrun

> has encouraged an investment by volunteers from the communities in which they sit. Individuals have found their own reason for becoming involved and committed, and indeed it could be suggested that volunteering at the event has become established as a leisure habit.
>
> (p. 3)

The authors contend that understanding the motivation and commitment of volunteers at parkrun is crucial to its sustainability and future growth. Drawing on the work of Mowday et al. (1982a) commitment is defined as the strength of an individual identification with an involvement in a particular activity or organisation, whereas research by Strigas and Jackson (2003) identified five factors that influenced sport volunteers' motivations: egoistic, purposive, leisure, external influences, and material. Egoistic emphasises motives linked to an individual's needs for social interaction, interpersonal relationships, and networking, as well as self-esteem and achievement. Purposive involves motives related to the desire of volunteers to benefit with their actions the stated aims of the sports organisation and contribute to the community. Leisure conceptualises volunteering as a leisure choice, assessing the motives of volunteers with regard to the individual's needs for a variety of leisure choices. External influences assess the extent to which volunteers are engaged in volunteering activities influenced by motives outside of their immediate control, such as family and significant others. Material involves incentives that can be considered as gains in exchange for their services; these rewards may be material goods or services or even social status that can be translated into a 'reward' that carries a material value.

Their study centres on two weekly parkrun events in Worcester – one held at Worcester Woods country park and one hosted at Worcester Pitchcroft – with the intention of identifying the practices, goals, values, and motivations that affect an individual's decision to volunteer. Participants were recruited via the respective run directors with the entire registered volunteer group for both events (*n* = 110) invited to complete an online survey. The authors reported an 84 per cent response rate (*n* = 92) of whom 47 identified as female and 45 as male. Demographic data were used as grouping variables with participants categorised by their gender, age, and reported employment status. Results demonstrated the levels of commitment from the participants were high across all subscales, whilst also demonstrating high levels of overall motivation for the more intrinsically valued motives. When breaking down the data by demographic groups, 'the underlying social motivations for why volunteers work at parkrun events are rather elusive' (p. 12). Renfree and West advise that their study findings highlight the role of community, family, and ideas of belonging as significant, implying that social aspects are a core purpose for attending. This is reflective of the ethos of parkrun which embraces the enthusiasm for the sport alongside facilitating social interaction and cultivating interpersonal relationships which in turn provide parkrun volunteers with improved self-esteem and a sense of achievement.

★

As previously alluded to, an important aspect of the inclusive philosophy underpinning parkrun events is how volunteering provides participation opportunities even for those not able to take part in the run. Additionally, there are other ways through which participants can make reciprocal contributions including providing support, advice, and encouragement to other runners, as well as donating or fundraising for their event (Stevinson et al., 2015). In a 2020 article titled 'The en/gendering of volunteering: "I've pretty much always noticed that the tail runner is always female",' researchers from Leeds Beckett University and Durham University examined the ways in which women volunteer, including a consideration of the key challenges they face and how they overcome them. For the study, which is part of a larger research project on gender in volunteering, Stride et al. (2020) undertook 24 interviews with women volunteers in three contexts, including parkrun (*n* = 11). The authors sought to explore the diversity of women volunteers' experiences, bringing to light the ways in which gender continues to influence the lived experiences and opportunities of women. One of the ways this was evident in the study was across volunteer roles with particular roles demarcated along gender lines. For example, 'there was a tendency for the Race Director post to be fulfilled by men, whilst a number of volunteers observed that a woman often took the role of tail runner' (p. 503). The authors proposed that it may be a lack of confidence, not opportunity, that can operate as a barrier to some women volunteering. Within the context of parkrun, a number of women volunteers linked avoidance of some positions due to not feeling prepared. As this respondent observed,

> I was a bit nervous about doing anything else because of not doing it before, so I thought if I start off doing the marshalling, I can't go too far wrong, and then I will hopefully progress to different roles over the weeks and months.

(p. 504)

Personal circumstances and the ways in which these operate to either challenge or enable volunteering were also evident within the data. For example, a number of women discussed how the family life cycle and age of their children impacted upon their opportunities to volunteer. In the context of parkrun, Stride et al. (2020) noted how the organisation is recognising the need to account for these circumstances: '[A] number of women commented upon the effectiveness of parkruns in facilitating their volunteering because of the flexibility, low time commitment, choice of roles, and inclusive family atmosphere' (p. 506).

In summarising, the findings from this study raise important questions for those responsible for attracting, retaining, and supporting women volunteering. As such the authors encourage organisations to be more attentive to and interested in the different life circumstances of their women volunteers. They also highlight the role organisations can play to challenge and disrupt gendered discourses and stereotypical views about who is 'suitable' for particular volunteer roles.

In a similar vein, Renfree and West (2019) conducted a study investigating potential differences in motivation and commitment between men and women volunteering at parkrun. The sample consisted of 92 volunteers with an almost equal proportion of males and females. Data was collected using an online survey comprising demographic information, an Organisational Commitment Questionnaire (Mowday et al., 1982b; MacLean & Hamm, 2007), and a volunteer motivation questionnaire (Strigas & Jackson, 2003). The results indicated that women had significantly higher levels of parkrun pride on the commitment to volunteer; significantly higher egotistical motivations to volunteer; and significantly higher leisure motivations to volunteer than men. These findings are supported by Skirstad and Hanstad (2013), who purport that women's volunteerism aids personal expression and development with less emphasis on human and social capital, collective identity, and belonging. Similarly, Hustinx and Lammertyn (2003) suggested that egoistic volunteerism is often limited in time and is episodic in character, which further supports the study findings in relation to parkrun. It may therefore be possible that parkrun with its non-traditional, non-committal approach to volunteering may increase numbers of women volunteering. Renfree and West (2019) concluded by suggesting,

> The significantly higher pride, egoistic and leisure motivations may reflect a greater desire for social approval amongst the women volunteers through perceptions of being valued within the parkrun environment. This aligns with the parkrun philosophy which creates a welcoming and indeed highly valued approach for all its volunteers which women seem to welcome significantly more than men.

As mentioned, parkrun offers a suitable case for examining volunteering practices, including reasons for and against volunteer participation. What is intriguing is its use of episodic volunteers and lack of obligation, whilst at the same time fostering a subculture with a strong sense of 'groupness' and reciprocity. Other research has proposed that participants appreciate the reciprocity associated with being a volunteer at parkrun and feel a sense of community at the events. The qualitative study by Stevinson et al. (2015) indicated that reciprocity was one of the vital components credited with sustained engagement. In addition to the direct personal benefits of taking part, it is argued that parkrun events allow for both 'giving' and gaining.' The volunteering, support, and encouragement epitomised 'giving,' whereas 'gains' related to the perceived health benefits and enhancing performance. Furthermore, the authors noted that volunteering added to many individuals' enjoyment of participation, which echoes existing research suggesting that volunteer activities are associated with wellbeing (Jenkinson et al., 2013).

The parkrun Health and Wellbeing Survey, which was carried out by Sheffield Hallam's Advanced Wellbeing Research Centre (AWRC), included a focus on volunteering at parkrun and the concomitant impact on health and wellbeing. The survey was distributed between 29 October and 3 December 2018 to all registered parkrunners over the age of 16 in the UK, resulting in 60,694 survey responses. Of particular relevance are two categories of respondent based upon how they self-identified: runners/walkers who volunteer (36.1 per cent, $n = 21{,}934$) and volunteers (1.1 per cent, $n = 681$). Respondents were asked to identify their motivations for first volunteering at parkrun. Across all survey respondents, the top five motives for their initial participation as a volunteer were to give something back to the community (57.7 per cent); as a parkrunner, I felt obliged to volunteer (46.9 per cent); to help people (27 per cent); to feel part of a community (23.8 per cent); and to fulfil a moral duty (16.2 per cent). With regard to the perceived impact of volunteering at parkrun on health and wellbeing, a large proportion of all respondents reported volunteering to have a positive impact. Intriguingly, those who volunteered at parkrun in addition to running or walking reported greater improvements across aspects of health and wellbeing due to parkrun; for example, 84 per cent of those who ran or walked and volunteered reported improvement to their happiness (compared to 79 per cent for the full cohort of respondents), feeling part of a community (84 per cent compared to 61 per cent), meeting new people (80 per cent compared to 45 per cent), and time spent with friends (55 per cent compared to 33 per cent). One explanation proffered by the authors is that those who volunteered in addition to running or walking at parkrun reported more social interactions in comparison to those who don't volunteer, in some cases double. This is echoed by one of the participants in the study by Sharman et al. (2018) who remarked,

> During volunteering, you chat to everybody. You meet more people as well doing it that way than you do actually running. And look, without volunteers, nothing happens. I enjoy doing it. And I love being around people and the socialness.

> (p. 167)

As numerous recounts of parkrun's modest beginnings have emphasised, one of founder Paul Sinton-Hewitt's impetuses to organise a time trial in Bushy Park was a way of staying connected and the commensurate benefits of this. Sacked from his marketing job, he'd also suffered a training injury that ended any hopes of doing a marathon. Feeling isolated and low, his response was 'to give something back.' What we have perhaps always known intuitively – that having a sense of purpose and giving support to others can be beneficial to our mental wellbeing – is now corroborated by an expanding body of empirical research. As Professor Adam Grant, organisational psychologist, and author of *Give and Take: Why Helping Others Drives Our Success*, observes, 'there is a lot of evidence that one of the best-anxiety medications available is generosity.' He goes on: '[T]he great thing about showing up for other people is that it doesn't have to cost a whole lot or anything at all, and it ends up being beneficial to the giver.'[2]

Volunteering is not a one-way street; our bodies and minds benefit in a variety of ways when we help others. According to a YouGov survey, conducted on behalf of the National Council for Voluntary Organisations, the vast majority reported that volunteering had been beneficial to their mental and physical health, as well as reducing loneliness (NCVO, 2019). Some research has focused on the notion of the 'helper's high,' a concept that arose in the 1980s, which refers to the positive emotions following selfless service to others and has been confirmed in numerous studies since (Dossey, 2018). Broadly speaking, volunteering helps as it is a social activity, and when you are doing things with others and groups that conviviality and connectedness is important. This felt particularly acute when rules that required us to be physically apart during the coronavirus pandemic resulted in the suspension of parkrun events. In October 2020 parkrun distributed a survey to more than 20,000 participants in England to ascertain the impact of the pandemic and associated restrictions have had on the parkrun community.[3] The responses (over 2,000) indicated that people's mental wellbeing and feelings of isolation and disconnect had worsened since parkrun events ceased. Sixty-two per cent of respondents reported that their mental health had been negatively impacted with 69 per cent stating that their happiness had been affected with similar numbers indicating a negative bearing on their life satisfaction. Seventy per cent stated that connections to their community had weakened.

The pandemic has thrown into sharp relief the importance of our critical social infrastructure – communal spaces where people are welcome to congregate – and communities are built through conversation and conviviality. Sociologist Ray Oldenburg coined the term 'third places' for these public locations that are not the home (known as the first place) or work (second place) in his book, *The Great Good Place*, in which he explored their positive contribution to democracy, neighbourhood communities, and residents' wellbeing. A core element of the social ecosystem of third places is familiarity but not intimacy so that whilst we may be conversant with individuals that assemble in these shared spaces, we aren't inescapably privy to the details of their lives. As Christensen explains, 'third places are not necessarily places where you're going to get into a really serious conversation, but there's always the potential for finding people to talk to, or at least sensing a commonality.'[4]

When I first started undertaking my own fieldwork researching parkrun, I was drawn to Oldenburg's work as a way of understanding the organic, informal social interactions among participants, as well as the perceived contribution of parkrun events to community-building. Empirical research was conducted over a 5-month period, using a mixed methods approach, most notably participant observation, semi-structured interviews, and a survey (both face to face and online). In doing so, the purpose of the data collection was to access and explore the experiences of parkrunners (runners, joggers, walkers, and volunteers) and the meanings they associated with participation, including perceived benefits and exploring the experiences of taking part in a mass community event. I adopted nearby Colwick parkrun in Nottingham as an intrinsic case study (Stake, 2005). It is important to recognise that whilst parkrun events share a degree of similarity in terms of ethos, format, and delivery, each location possesses some particularity. At the time of the study, Colwick was one of 13 parkruns located in Nottingham and the surrounding area and had an average attendance of 179 with a total number of 7,826 participants across the 312 events (parkrun, 2017).

Colwick parkrun was the first in Nottingham, having been in operation since June 2011, offering a free weekly Saturday run in Colwick Country Park, which is situated on the outskirts of the city. The park contains two large lakes, a marina, woodland, and meadows and has three main entrance points, each with public parking. The 5 km route, which includes one lap of the Main Lake and two laps of the West Lake, is on a mixture of informally surfaced paths, combined with short road and grass sections. After each event, participants are encouraged to socialise at the nearby Daleside Café. Participant observation focused on gaining a better understanding of the experiences and behaviours of those involved, whereas informal conversations were recorded using a digital recorder and notebooks to capture snippets of conversations and other descriptive field notes. Photography was also used during visits, and reviewing these images helped to refine observations.

A face-to-face and online survey of 235 participants (110 men and 125 women) was conducted. The scope of the questions was to explore the experiences of the respondents and to identify the perceived benefits of taking part in parkrun. A specific emphasis was made to elucidate on the physical and social environment of Colwick parkrun, as well as probing the participants' attitudes and motives for their attendance. A total of 19 interviews were conducted (10 men and 9 women) with additional qualitative data collected through conversations with participants on an ad hoc basis. The sample was largely opportunistic, based on access at appropriate times, with most interviews conducted in situ, scheduled in advance directly before or after each parkrun event. The interviews focused on participants' motives for attending, the physical and social environment, the perceived benefits of taking part in parkrun, and any additional positive or negative outcomes or observations. Thematic analysis of the transcribed audio recordings was undertaken to organise and code the qualitative data to identify patterns (themes) and for describing and interpreting the meaning and importance of these (Smith & Sparkes, 2016).

Four themes were identified, suggesting that participating in Colwick parkrun (a) provided a leisure space that helped foster casual conversation, (b) promoted accessibility and inclusion, (c) created a sense of belonging and community, and (d) facilitated a shared experience of exercising together which can be both supportive and engender a sense of personal improvement and competition. Taken together, these themes contributed to both initial attendance and sustained involvement. For many respondents, especially regular attendees, Colwick parkrun acted as a temporary public space, one that is conducive for incidental and casual social interaction. These informal exchanges tended to arise from the activity itself – intermittent conversations on running-related topics – as well as everyday interactions. This feeling of congeniality was facilitated by participants sharing some common interests and experiences, making it easy for individuals to converse because they spoke the same universal language. Put another way, although participants may have few, if any, similar interests, running provided a mutual frame of reference. Conversations with strangers were easily obtained because 'you immediately have something in common,' whilst for some the social interaction took on a core purpose. As one respondent remarked,

> Without you actually realising it, the social aspects are really important. I'm very happy just coming down here on my own knowing that I'll know

somebody, or even if I don't, you know it'll be a friendly place and you can engage in conversation with anyone because you are all here for the same reason.

(Interview 4, female)

This echoed the work of Wiltshire and Stevinson (2018), who argued that even loose ties with relative strangers can be highly valued. As a further point of reflection, parallels can be drawn between the findings of this study with the work of Amin and Thrift (2002), who use the term 'light' sociality to refer to groups and individuals who come together momentarily around a particular purpose and then disperse again. This may in part be explained by the informal ties that membership of parkrun affords, as well as the number of attendees (on occasion totalling more than 200), which lessens the possibility of strong group bonds developing. Nevertheless, as Hitchings and Latham (2017) have suggested, the casual sociality that may indirectly arise out of exercise should not be overlooked as it appears to represent a valued part of the participant experience.

The significance of casual, day-to-day interactions is a theme examined in Abel and Clarke's *The Compassion Project*, exploring the connection between social relationships and human health. They draw a distinction between inner and outer networks in thinking about the patterns of social relationships that shape our individual sense of the world we inhabit. The former refers to those to whom we feel most closely attached, for example, family members and friends, whereas the latter consists both of acquaintances with whom we commonly interact in a more casual, informal manner and have lighter, less-frequent contact. They note that 'among the most significant aspects of such relationships can be a sense of pleasant companionship that is generated along the way while we are busy doing something else' (Abel & Clarke, 2020, p. 114). They cite communal activities, such as those of a choir, as having particular importance, providing opportunities to foster new friendships among members as well as fulfilling the function of affirmative social relationships. In the context of parkrun, it is recognised that its overwhelming success can in part be attributed to creating an environment for spending time with familiar, like-minded individuals, as well as strangers to come together in a convivial and social space. They explain,

> The original parkrun ended by participants going somewhere for a cup of coffee. It meant from the beginning there was time to chat and develop friendships. The running is an excuse for the important bit, which is the social relationships, the love, laughter, and friendship, that happen along the way.
>
> (p. 64)

Opportunities for interactions with people outside of our close social circle, including strangers as well as weak ties – relationships involving less-frequent contact, such as those with acquaintances – are the focus of a study conducted by Sandstrom and Dunn (2014) which examined the effects of a customer initiating a conversation with a barista in a coffee shop. The authors found that people who had a social interaction (e.g. smiled, made eye contact, and had a brief conversation) experienced more positive affect than people who were efficient as possible. They concluded that, whilst the prospect of initiating a conversation with a stranger can be daunting, the results – supported by existing happiness literature – highlight the benefits of transforming instrumental conversations into more sociable encounters.

A second theme identified from the Colwick case study was the perceived inclusivity of events. Several aspects relating to accessibility were referred to by participants, including cost, convenience, community setting, and the rolling opportunity to turn up when desired, without overt commitment or pressure to attend. Respondents remarked upon the diversity of participants with regard to gender, age, background, and running ability, which in turn helped make parkrun feel welcoming to different sections of the community. This encouraged people to attend the first time and helped them feel relaxed and keen to return. As one respondent observed, '[Colwick] parkrun is friendly and non-threatening.' Others commented on how novice or slower-paced runners were made to feel included: '[D]espite not being a very good runner I was made to feel very welcome.' Other examples, such as the acceptance and provision for individuals with visual impairments, as well as inviting groups of Nordic walkers, indicate a desire on behalf of the Colwick parkrun event team to reflect and attract non-traditional populations.

A sense of community and affiliation with parkrun was another recurrent theme identified from the data. As one respondent noted, 'the parkrun community is like a village where everyone knows one another. You look out for one another and support each other.' Another mentioned, 'I attend not because it's a run, but because it's a community.' This hints at Colwick parkrun providing more than just a temporary leisure space for casual social interaction or to merely take part in running. It represents a social world, which, despite having no formal membership, provides participants with a sense of belonging to a wider social group ('the parkrun family'), a place within that environment, and the subsequent opportunity to use their attachment to the group to enhance feelings of self-worth and self-esteem (Green & Jones, 2005). What became evident from the qualitative data was the sense of belonging and identity that parkrun fosters, which blurred into other aspects of individuals' social lives. For many respondents, parkrun has become habitual, a regular form of exercise that is embedded within the weekend schedule with some commenting on how they would seek out the local parkrun when away on holiday or visiting family and friends.

The notion of a shared communal experience is also central to understanding the attraction of parkrun with some respondents acknowledging the value of the collective group for emotional support. Data point to several attendees' sustained participation because their motivation and enjoyment are maintained, and potentially increased, by exercising around others even if they do not talk with them. As this respondent noted, 'running with others is a massive motivation. . . . I don't think I would run 5 km every week if I didn't have a group like this to run with.' Another remarked, '[O]ne of the initial aspects that attracted me to parkrun was the fact that you are running with other people.' The data share similarities with Barnfield (2016), who noted that among respondents in his study, the conviviality of running with others and mixing with people of different abilities and body types were important aspects for thinking about health practice maintenance. Hitchings and Latham (2017) suggested that the presence of others affords a range of socialities that variously assist runners to remain on task, provide distractions, and offer a sense of being involved in a communal activity. The data also parallel the work of Wiltshire et al. (2018), who highlight the community aspect of parkrun, which allows participants to experience a collective sense of responsibility.

As noted previously, the conceptual lens of the third place was applied to the Colwick parkrun case study. According to Oldenburg (1999), third places are defined as accessible public spaces where people could gather voluntarily, informally, and habitually for social interaction to encourage citizen involvement and to help foster a sense of belonging. Oldenburg's portrayal of a third place infers that a number of characteristics are evident, which together help to account for their potential civic and community-building functions. They are neutral, welcoming spaces, which serve to treat all individuals as equals so that they are able to drift in and out as they please, in which none are encumbered to play the role of host (Oldenburg, 1999). Consequently, it is a different type of access than club membership, where the bonds are looser and the level of commitment is not as evident (Hawkins & Ryan, 2013). By their nature, third places can act as 'levellers,' providing an inclusive space that is accessible to all and as such does not set formal criteria of membership and exclusion (Oldenburg, 1999). Conversation is the primary activity within these shared spaces, mediating casual and informal social interaction among a diverse mix of people, expanding one's social network. Oldenburg affirms that third places serve the community best to the extent that they are accessible, convenient, and local. The character of a third place is shaped by its 'regulars,' whose incidental interactions help foster a desire to return.

Whilst the notion of a third place has been variously applied to a range of cultural and leisure contexts, it has yet to be harnessed extensively to sporting activities. One exception is Mair (2009) who provides a narrative account of curling clubs in rural Canada, emphasising their 'homely' and welcoming atmosphere, as well as the role membership plays in offering informal networks of social support. Also, of interest is Shipway (2012), whose work draws upon third-place literature to explore the social world of distance runners, demonstrating how running events offer athletes an opportunity for escape, as well as fostering a sense of camaraderie.

The case study data, to a large extent, speak to Oldenburg's dimensions of the third place. Arguably, parkrun events represent a social leveller on neutral ground where, in the main, individuals participate as equals and the regulars are welcoming, including first-timers. Sociability, especially informal conversation, features prominently. In the context of the Colwick case study, parkrun regulars – those who attend frequently and, in some cases, religiously – play a valuable role in setting the tone, mood, and manner, helping to illustrate how volunteerism, long-term commitment, and a sense of ownership underpin the event's character and foundations. Sustained attendance at Colwick parkrun moves the experience towards a social activity and a third place as opposed to merely a running event. Oldenburg and Brissett's (1982) notion of meeting a friend of a friend was identified as a sub-theme within the data with several respondents remarking on their enjoyment in these casual one-off encounters and chance meetings, as well as forging longer-lasting friendships with companion parkrunners. As such Colwick parkrun could be described as a re-bonding space. Third places are a conduit to do this.

In contrast, Oldenburg's (1999) conceptualisation of accessibility is markedly different from how the notion is explored here. His discussion on the ease of access focused on the long hours of third places and the proximity to their patrons. In the context of parkrun, accessibility is intertwined with notions of social inclusion, where the egalitarian principles of parkrun are manifest in seeking to minimise barriers to participation. An alternate interpretation relates to the weekly, community-based nature of parkrun events. An additional aspect of divergence relates to parkrun's temporality in that the illustrative examples cited in the literature tend to concern more lasting environments, which have a permanent physical presence (e.g. coffee shops, bars, libraries). In this context my attention has been focused more on the relationships and interactions between people in creating a shared leisure space, particularly the idea of community-building and conviviality, rather than on the physical infrastructure.

★

In conclusion, this chapter has sought to present insights from the fledgling research into parkrun volunteering. To clarify, whilst volunteering has been mentioned in published research on parkrun, until recently it has not been the main focus of any studies, despite a heavy reliance on the 'high-vis-heroes' for events to go ahead. This is now changing with a small number of papers exploring the motivations and commitment of volunteers at parkrun events. In many ways parkrun events are of particular interest as they do not fit the conventional sport volunteer or sport event mould (Renfree & West, 2021). The parkrun model is noteworthy in that opportunities to volunteer are ad hoc with lower levels of obligation than would ordinarily be expected from membership of a traditional community group. This flexibility extends in the way volunteer roles tend to change, so there is no formal or fixed role for one individual. Furthermore, the parkrun administration is keen to overtly challenge the conventional volunteer manual, where volunteering is often associated with sacrifice or martyrdom in that the individual is perceived to be giving something up. As we have seen in this chapter, mentions of parkrun volunteering in the published research have reported the benefits of doing so, supported by a wider body of literature on volunteering which shows volunteering in itself can confer many psychological and wellbeing benefits. And yet the findings presented here suggest there are ongoing challenges with volunteer recruitment,[5] as well as the potential for en/gendering of volunteering being evident.

Notes

1 https://volunteer.parkrun.com/principles/volunteer-roles
2 www.nytimes.com/2020/04/09/well/mind/coronavirus-resilience-psychology-anxiety-stress-volunteering.html
3 https://blog.parkrun.com/uk/2020/10/20/losing-connection-and-quality-of-life/
4 www.bloomberg.com/news/articles/2021-04-06/the-death-and-post-covid-rebirth-of-third-places
5 Anecdotally, last-minute pleas to ensure volunteer rosters are filled at my local parkrun events are not uncommon, implying such difficulties may not be isolated.

References

Abel, J., & Clarke, L. (2020). *The Compassion Project: A Case for Hope & Human Kindness from the Town That Beat Loneliness*. London: Aster.
Amin, A., & Thrift, N. (2002). *Cities: Reimagining the Urban*. Cambridge, UK: Polity.
Barnfield, A. (2016). Grasping physical exercise through recreational running and non-representational theory: A case study from Sofia, Bulgaria. *Sociology of Health & Illness*, 38:7, 1121–1136.
Bishop, J., & Hoggett, P. (1986). *Organising Around Enthusiasms: Mutual Aid in Leisure*. London: Comedia.
Dossey, L. (2018). The helper's high. *Explore: The Journal of Science & Healing*, 14:6, 393–399.
Grant, A. (2013). *Give and Take: Why Helping Others Drives Our Success*. London: Weidenfeld & Nicolson.
Green, C., & Jones, I. (2005). Serious leisure, social identity and sport tourism. *Sport in Society*, 8:2, 198–217.
Hallett, R., Gombert, K., & Hurley, M. (2020a). 'Everyone should muck in': A qualitative study of parkrun volunteering and conflicting motivations. *Journal of Nonprofit and Public Sector Marketing*, 33:5, 493–515.
Hallett, R.J., Mullan, N.K., Haake, S.J., Graney, M., & Hurley, M.V. (2020b). Community event sustainability: Why don't people volunteer? *Voluntary Sector Review*, 11:2, 137–167.
Hawkins, C.J., & Ryan, L.A.J. (2013). Festival spaces as third places. *Journal of Place Management and Development*, 6:3, 192–202.
Hitchings, R., & Latham, A. (2017). How 'social' is recreational running? Findings from a qualitative study in London and implications for public health promotion. *Health & Place*, 46, 337–343.
Hustinx, L., & Lammertyn, F. (2003). Collective and reflexive styles of volunteering: A sociological modernisation perspective. *Voluntas*, 14, 167–187.
Jenkinson, C.E., Dickens, A.P., Jones, K., *et al.* (2013). Is volunteering a public health intervention? A systematic review and meta-analysis of the health and survival of volunteers. *BMC Public Health*, 13, 773.

MacLean, J., & Hamm, S. (2007). Motivation, commitment, and intentions of volunteers at a large Canadian sporting event. *Leisure*, 31:2, 523–556.

Mair, H. (2009). Club life: Third place and shared leisure in rural Canada. *Leisure Sciences*, 31:5, 405–465.

Mowday, R.T., Porter, L., & Steers, R. (1982a). Organisational linkages: The psychology of commitment. *Journal of Vocational Behaviour*, 14:4, 224–247.

Mowday, R.T., Porter, L., & Steers, R. (1982b). *Employee-Organisation Linkages: The Psychology of Commitment, Absenteeism and Turnover*. New York: Academic Press.

NCVO. (2019). *Time Well Spent: A National Survey of the Volunteer Experience*. London: NCVO.

Oldenburg, R. (1999). *The Great Good Place – Cafes, Coffee Shops, Bookstores, Bars, Hair Salons and Other Hangouts at the Heart of a Community*. New York: Paragon House.

Oldenburg, R., & Brissett, D. (1982). The third place. *Qualitative Sociology*, 5:4, 265–284.

Parkrun, U.K. (2017). *Parkrun UK: 2016 Run Report*. Retrieved from http://blog.parkrun.com/uk/2017/04/27/parkrun-uk-2016-run-report/

Renfree, G., & West, J. (2019). Differences in men and women volunteers within a Parkrun environment. In *Women in Sport and Exercise 2019 Conference: Pushing the Boundaries, 11th – 12th June 2019, St Mary's University, Twickenham* (Unpublished). Retrieved from http://eprints.worc.ac.uk/8210/

Renfree, G., & West, J. (2021). Motivation and commitment of volunteers at parkrun events. *Managing Sport and Leisure*. https://doi.org/10.1080/23750472.2021.1986120.

Sandstrom, G.M., & Dunn, E.W. (2014). Is efficiency overrated?: Minimal social interactions lead to belonging and positive affect. *Social Psychology and Personality Science*, 5:4, 437–442.

Sharman, M.J., Nash, M., & Cleland, V. (2018). Health and broader community benefit of parkrun – An exploratory qualitative study. *Health Promotion Journal of Australia*, 30, 163–171.

Shipway, R. (2012). Distance running events and the 'third place.' In Fyall, A. & Shipway, R. (Eds.), *International Sport Events: Impacts, Experience and Identities* (pp. 208–220). London: Routledge.

Skirstad, B., & Hanstad, D.V. (2013). Gender matters in sport event volunteering. *Managing Leisure*, 18:4, 316–330.

Smith, B., & Sparkes, A.C. (Eds.). (2016). *Routledge Handbook of Qualitative Research in Sport and Exercise*. London: Routledge.

Stake, R. (2005). Qualitative case studies. In Denzin, N. & Lincoln, Y. (Eds.), *Handbook of Qualitative Research* (3rd ed., pp. 443–466). London: Sage.

Stevinson, C., Wiltshire, G., & Hickson, M. (2015). Facilitating participation in health-enhancing physical activity: A qualitative study of parkrun. International *Journal of Behavioural Medicine*, 22, 170–177.

Stride, A., Fitzgerald, H., Rankin-Wright, A., & Barnes, L. (2020). 'The en/gendering of volunteering: 'I've pretty much always noticed that the tail runner is always female.' *Sport Management Review*, 23:3, 498–508.

Strigas, A.D., & Jackson, E.N. (2003). Motivating volunteers to serve and succeed: Design and results of a pilot study that explores demographics and motivational factors in sport volunteerism. *International Sports Journal*, 7:1, 111–123.

Wiltshire, G.R., Fullagar, S., & Stevinson, C. (2018). Exploring parkrun as a social context for collective health practices: Running with and against the moral imperatives of health responsibilisation. *Sociology of Health & Illness*, 40:1, 3–17.

Wiltshire, G.R., & Stevinson, C. (2018). Exploring the role of social capital in community-based physical activity: Qualitative insights from parkrun. *Qualitative Research in Sport, Exercise and Health*, 10:1, 47–62.

Chapter 4

A Panacea for Health and Wellbeing?

The opening chapters have outlined the evolution of parkrun from its humble beginnings as a weekly time trial in Bushy Park in 2004 to a global physical activity initiative. Evidently a number of distinctive features of parkrun events differentiate it from other interventions, with the previous sections highlighting past studies which focus on parkrun in relation to community, inclusivity, and volunteering as recurrent themes. This leads us to now consider the growing evidence for parkrun in terms of its impact and implications for participants' health and wellbeing. Existing empirical studies suggest parkrun may have potential to enable opportunities not only for the positive expression of identity and continuation of healthy habits among runners but also for non-demanding, health-enhancing activity and social interaction for non-runners (Grunseit et al., 2018). Additionally, it has also been reported there are elements of parkrun that may be beneficial to mental health (Morris & Scott, 2019). This chapter will adopt a broad conception of parkrun as a health practice, incorporating and discussing the potential benefits of participation in relation to wellbeing, mental health, impact on lifestyle behaviours, and fitness. In 2018 the Royal College of General Practitioners (RCGP) launched what it described as 'a ground-breaking initiative that could see thousands of patients being "prescribed" outdoor physical activity rather than medication.'[1] This development followed the published testimonials of several GPs who voiced their support for parkrun. Subsequently, this chapter will also explore parkrun in this context of social prescribing and the shift towards delivering healthcare using services provided by the voluntary and community sector.

★

The health benefits of physical activity are numerous and well documented. Scholars from a range of disciplines have acknowledged the positive effects of activity on chronic diseases, mental wellbeing, and life expectancy (e.g. Colberg et al., 2010; Physical Activity Guidelines Advisory Committee, 2008; Pedersen & Saltin, 2015). Furthermore, the evidence base under the banner of 'green exercise,' contemplating the additional physical and psychological benefits that may be accrued by those who exercise in natural environments, is growing and,

DOI: 10.4324/9781003121961-4

when considered as a whole, seems increasingly robust (Bamberg et al., 2018). Nonetheless, for many adults of high-income countries, modern life is largely sedentary, described by Kohl et al. (2012) as a 'pandemic of physical inactivity.' Reportedly one in four women and one in five men in England are categorised as physically inactive, partaking in fewer than 30 minutes of moderate physical exercise per week (Public Health England, 2016). Such behaviours are concerning; the association between physical inactivity and both morbidity and mortality is well known (Knight, 2012). The management of long-term conditions such as diabetes, heart disease, asthma, or depression now accounts for the majority of the health service budget in the UK with over 26 million adults affected (Quirk & Haake, 2019). And yet historically strategies aimed at increasing physical activity have proved largely ineffective (Pedlar et al., 2021). Additionally, there is an economic burden with an estimated cost of insufficient physical activity totalling over £15 billion in the UK in 2015 (AMRC, 2015). In response, a great deal of medical and social scientific research has examined how individuals and communities might be encouraged to become more physically active. In their national physical activity framework, *Everybody Active, Every Day*, Public Health England acknowledged the need to engage with professionals, providers, and commissioners in health, social care, transportation, education, sport, and leisure, the voluntary, community and cultural sectors, in order to have a meaningful impact on participation levels. Emphasising the importance of making physical activity easy, fun, and affordable, the report explains, '[T]he most successful agents of change will be people from the communities themselves' (PHE, 2014, p. 13). As McIntosh (2021) remarks, 'never has looking after our physical and mental health been more important as the current Covid pandemic and associated lockdown restrictions take their toll on all of us' (p. 472). It is against this backdrop that a fledgling but emerging body of empirical research has engaged questions around the potential of parkrun as a public health intervention, and its impact on wellbeing, to which we will now turn.

One of the first studies, conducted by Stevinson and Hickson and published in the *Journal of Public Health*, utilised a national survey of participants to explore the potential for parkrun as a public health intervention. In particular, the authors were interested in the extent to which parkrun attracted new exercisers, including those from populations that traditionally are low in physical activity. A total of 7,308 adult participants, all registrants of a UK parkrun, completed an online questionnaire. This represented 46.8 per cent of the mean number of adults taking part in a weekly parkrun event during the study period. The majority identified as not having been regular runners or joggers prior to registration with 25.3 per cent describing themselves as non-runners. The latter group included the highest proportion of women, as well as those with a limiting disability or health problem, and those who were overweight or obese – all cohorts that are overrepresented in adult physical inactivity statistics. The initial non-runners recorded the greatest improvements in objective measures of aerobic fitness. Over half of all respondents reported benefits for health, weight control, and psychological wellbeing with these benefits consistently reported most frequently by those who attended most frequently.

The evidence from this study suggested that parkrun may contribute to increasing physical activity and wellbeing among community members. The perceived benefits of participation included physical, psychological, and social impacts with a notable proportion of non-runners progressing to regular vigorous exercise and improving their fitness since starting parkrun. The overall sociodemographic profile of participants meanwhile suggested that parkrun is effective as a community-based intervention in attracting some sections of the community, with women and older adults well represented, along with people that are overweight/obese and those with limiting disabilities. The authors acknowledged however that the numbers of ethnic minorities and people from lower socio-economic groups were disproportionately low.

Stevinson et al. (2015) published a follow-up paper in the *International Journal of Behavioural Medicine*. This study aimed at identifying factors contributing to initial and sustained engagement in parkrun using qualitative data. To this end, semi-structured interviews with 48 adult parkrunners were conducted. A sampling matrix based on age, gender, running experience, and geography was employed to purposively select individuals. Two prevalent themes were identified from the parkrunners' individual accounts: freedom and reciprocity. The freedom theme was important for initial attendance, as well as contributing to maintaining involvement. This referred to the flexible approach to participation, which lessened some of the traditional barriers associated with physical activity engagement. The authors noted that aspects relating to accessibility were remarked upon by almost all interviewees, including, for example, the simple set-up, that parkrun was free, the convenient location and time, and the rolling opportunity to turn up when desired without overt commitment or pressure to attend or perform. Additionally, the perceived inclusiveness of parkrun was remarked upon by participants, which made parkrun feel welcoming to all members of the community. The reciprocity theme highlighted the uniqueness of parkrun in combining opportunities for personal gain alongside helping others. All participants described their initial involvement being motivated by predicted potential benefits, typically in terms of fitness, weight, or health. Opportunities for social interaction were also identified as contributing to sustained involvement, alongside the sense of achievement fostered through improvements in performance, or regular attendance. The authors stated that all participants referred to self-improvement with regard to achieving faster times, progressing to be able to run the entire 5 km course, or achieving attendance milestones. Also, of note was the social support, which was mentioned by almost all interviewees. The encouragement from others (parkrunners, volunteers, and spectators) was influential in boosting confidence, as well as cultivating a culture where offering the same support to others was fortified. Throughout the identified themes of freedom and reciprocity, it was apparent that for many respondents parkrun was palpably different to traditional exercise opportunities such as attending a fitness centre or membership of a running club. In summing up, the authors identified several characteristics of parkrun that are core to the ease and enjoyment of participation that are worthy of consideration when looking at future health interventions. These included an accessible and inclusive set-up that reduces perceived barriers to physical activity engagement; providing achievement opportunities with self-monitoring tools that encourage self-improvement; a supportive social environment; the importance of natural outdoor settings that contribute the added value of green exercise; and finally, integrated opportunities to contribute to the intervention such as volunteering.

In a later research paper by Stevinson and Hickson (2018) they sought to investigate the sustained effects of participation in parkrun on behaviour and health. This study aimed to examine changes in self-reported physical activity, weight, and wellbeing in a cohort of new parkrun registrants over 12 months. Additionally, the scale of change was explored in sub-groups based on weight category and initial running status. Data were collected at registration (baseline), 6 months and 12 months. A total of 878 newly registered adults completed the baseline questionnaire. At 6 months, 553 were still attending parkrun, and 470 at 12 months with no statistically significant differences at baseline between survey completers and non-completers. Significant changes over time were reported for both total physical activity and vigorous-intensity activity. Significant increases in total activity and vigorous activity were observed at 6 months (76.9 and 20.8 minutes, respectively, per week). By 12 months total physical activity had declined but nevertheless remained significantly higher than baseline (39.4 minutes per week). Significant changes over time were observed for BMI with reductions observed at 6 months and partly maintained at 12 months. For both happiness and perceived stress, there were significant changes over time. Happiness scores increased significantly after 6 months and were maintained at 12 months representing a small positive effect size. Similarly, there were significant reductions in perceived stress scores within 6 months, which were maintained at 12 months. Speaking to the data, the authors observed that parkrun may compare favourably to other mass participation events due to its weekly occurrence, which may be helpful to individuals without a background in exercise to maintain physical activity. Additionally, the support offered by running as a collective was identified as important. Whilst the average improvements in all outcomes were described as 'modest,' collectively the results add weight to previous suggestions of the potential public health value of parkrun.

In 2019, two researchers based at the Faculty of Health Sciences at Staffordshire University conducted a study exploring the parkrun experiences of 20 participants who identified as having had current or past mental health difficulties. The respondents participated in one-to-one semi-structured interviews with the interview transcripts analysed using thematic analysis. Participants were asked to describe their experiences of parkrun, as well as about any impact that parkrun had on their mental health. They were also asked whether there was anything specific about parkrun that had been helpful or unhelpful to their mental health. Coding of the transcripts was used to generate themes, which were organised into three areas: 'sense of achievement,' 'it's for everyone,' and 'connecting with others.'

According to Morris and Scott (2019), respondents reported a sense of achievement and accomplishment through participation, which improved mood and increased confidence. Participants also reported benefits from setting and achieving goals; the latter were personalised – for example, attending a set number of times or improving times – which helped maintain motivation. A participant in their study remarked:

> You never start thinking right I'm gonna be near him, or keep an eye on him, and yet the run evolves . . . you start thinking I need something to motivate me, to keep going, what is it? . . . OK, I hate being overtaken by 10-year-old children and I will do everything in my power to chase them as fast as I can, knowing that I can never catch them in the last 500 metres anyway, but, I'll still have a go.
>
> (p. 116)

The study participants found parkrun to be welcoming and inclusive, whereas volunteering opportunities made the event more accessible, as individuals who are unable or do not wish to run are still able to participate. Additionally, parkrun was thought to represent a safe and familiar environment. As this respondent identified,

> There's a ritualistic element of it which I quite like. I respond well to routine, and . . . feeling comfortable within that probably helps.
>
> (p. 117)

Participants also reported a sense of genuine equality where everyone – from the fastest to the slowest runners – was valued. It was also noted that for some of the participants socialising was difficult when mental health was poor; therefore, having the choice not to have to socialise made parkrun more accessible to people with mental health difficulties. As this participant reflected, 'you just turn up, and if you're not feeling great you can just say hi to a few people and do your run and go. If you're feeling more sociable, you can be' (p. 118). Finally, interviewees described a strong sense of community with parkrun being likened to a family or a church. Respondents reported feeling encouraged and supported at parkrun, which was beneficial to their psychological wellbeing.

In summary, participants in the study universally felt parkrun benefitted their mental health. The authors stressed that whilst the interviewees noted the benefits of exercise and being outdoors, of greater significance was the sense of community and acceptance, as well as opportunities for social interaction, helping to reduce isolation. One participant in their study said, '[W]hatever the opposite of lonely is, that's parkun' (p. 118), whereas another respondent, Karen, commented:

> If you're feeling isolated, because you feel quite negative about life, or you're feeling depressed or anxious, then to go somewhere and just have someone say: 'oh hello, it's you again, I haven't seen you for a whole', it's wonderful because you feel valued.
>
> (p. 118)

The most consistent benefits described were improved confidence and self-worth. Participants felt valued for both their individual achievements and their contributions to the parkrun community.

In a study surveying 865 adult Australian parkrunners, Grunseit et al. (2018) examined overall and domain-specific subjective wellbeing. One of the aims of their project was to compare the wellbeing of parkrun participants to the general population, as well as to identify which of the perceived benefits (physical, mental, and/or social) of parkrun were associated with overall subjective wellbeing in adult participants. The online survey accompanied a weekly newsletter sent to all parkrun registrants in Australia (n = 155,189), from which the sample was drawn. The questionnaire was divided into four sections: demographic information, parkrun participation, personal wellbeing, and perceived benefits of parkrun. Wellbeing was measured using the Personal Wellbeing Index (PWI) which comprised a series of statements, providing a global index measure of broad but identifiable and evaluable aspects of life that contribute to wellbeing. Regression models tested associations between personal wellbeing and perceived benefits of parkrun.

The authors reported, first, that Australian parkrunners ranked higher than population norms on their perceived physical health, particularly among older and male parkrunners. Second, in comparison to the normative values, older parkrunners appeared to perform better than the general population across several wellbeing indicators. In contrast, the youngest parkrunners (aged 18–24 years) scored far below the age equivalent norms for the health and personal relationships sub-domains as well as for satisfaction with life as a whole. Third, Grunseit et al. (2018) found that for men it appears that parkrun has the potential to improve overall personal wellbeing by facilitating social connections in the community, whereas for women it appears it may be the mental health benefits from participation that might enable improvements in wellbeing.

The study determined, based on the survey sample, that Australian parkrunners mostly reflect the general population on personal wellbeing, except report superior satisfaction with physical health. It was noted that parkrun may facilitate positive expression of identity and continuation of healthy habits among athletes and non-demanding, health-enhancing activity and social interaction for non-athletes. The authors concluded by suggesting that future research could expand on this by examining whether parkrun may offer support at critical times in the life course when other sources of social connectedness and achievable physical activity may otherwise be lacking. Moreover, targeted promotion which highlights making connections within the community for men, and improved mental health mediated by better physical health for women, could capitalise on the gendered nature of perceived benefits of parkrun.

In a study surveying 371 adult parkrunners in Tasmania, Cleland et al. (2019) sought to better understand who participates in parkrun and why. The paper, which was published in the *American Journal of Health Promotion*, aimed to identify sociodemographic, health, behavioural, individual, social, and environmental factors associated with higher levels of participation. Data were collected using an online survey, which was promoted to Tasmanian parkrunners. From the participant sample, the authors observed that parkrun was effective at attracting a broad range of adults who are not just the 'active elite' and included those traditionally harder to engage in physical activity such as non- or irregular walkers/runners, women, those who are overweight or obese, or with injury, illness, or disability, and those with non-adult children. It was reported that those with lower levels of education indicated higher levels of relative participation, suggesting potential for engagement in this type of physical activity intervention by lower socio-economic groups. The study also demonstrated that greater relative parkrun participation was associated with higher perceived social benefits, social support from family, greater enjoyment, greater self-efficacy, and stronger intentions for parkrun. For example, approximately 30 per cent of study participants engaged in parkrun events with family and friends often or very often. It was also found that involvement in parkrun is more likely to be initiated from contact with immediate social ties, as well as providing an important means for individuals to develop their own social networks. On the flip side, it is the authors contention that parkrun potentially excludes or marginalises those individuals without strong social ties. Cleland et al. (2019) concluded that the study findings highlighted the promise of parkrun as a setting for physical activity promotion, especially given the numbers of participants from cohorts that are traditionally difficult to engage. The authors identified several benefits from 'weekend warrior' exercise, which combined with the low cost and broad appeal of parkrun underline parkrun's potential as a mass community event for public health.

The health, physical and mental wellbeing of the parkrun community was the primary focus of a major survey undertaken for parkrun in 2018 by the Advanced Wellbeing Research Centre (AWRC) at Sheffield Hallam University. The parkrun Health and Wellbeing Survey, which was carried out by Haake et al. (2019), sought to establish the impact of participating in parkrun on the health and wellbeing of UK parkrunners. The online survey, which was distributed between 29 October and 3 December 2018 to all parkrun UK registrants aged 16 and above, explored demographics, happiness and life satisfaction, physical activity level, motives for participation, health status, healthcare usage, mental wellbeing, perceived impact of parkrun, and the social opportunities it facilitates.

The survey resulted in 60,694 responses, totalling 11 million answers to 47 questions. Respondents were grouped into three categories based upon how they self-identified in the survey: runners/walkers, runners/walkers who volunteer, and volunteers. These subgroups were then divided into the following subcategories: females/males, those from deprived communities, and those who identified as physically inactive at registration. Survey respondents reported improvements to their physical and mental health, as well as positive impacts on their fitness and sense of personal achievement and happiness, and increased the amount of time they spent outdoors. Improvements were more prevalent in those who were previously inactive; for example, 81 per cent of those who were previously inactive reported improvements to their happiness (compared to 79 per cent for the full cohort of respondents). More women than men reported improvements across aspects of health and wellbeing, particularly in their sense of achievement, confidence, and the ability to be active in a safe environment. For example, 72 per cent of women compared to 56 per cent of men reported improvements in confidence since participating in parkrun. Additionally, two-thirds of respondents (65 per cent) with long-term health conditions (LTCs) such as arthritis, depression, and anxiety reported improvements in the management of their condition.

The survey also made a detailed examination of how much physical activity participants were doing in comparison to when they first registered. On average, respondents reported being more active at the time of completing the survey compared to parkrun registration with those who were initially less active reporting greater increases in physical activity. It was reported that 87.9 per cent of those who identified as inactive at registration now reported activity levels of at least once or more per week, whilst 67 per cent reported doing at least twice or more per week. With regard to motivation for initially participating in parkrun as a runner/walker, the top two motives cited were to contribute to my fitness and to improve my physical health.

In contrast to the studies cited to so far in this chapter, which have reported public health benefits among the parkrun community, a modest number of studies have found either a non-significant or a negative impact of parkrun. Linton and Valentin (2018) investigated the incidence and type of running-related injuries among novice and recreational runners, surveying 1,145 UK-based parkrunners. They found just under half ($n = 570$) were currently injured with 86 per cent continuing to train despite this. Further, the majority of these runners reported pain due to a running-related injury (91 per cent) with 89 per cent stating that their injury was directly affecting their running performance. The authors reported that runners with less than 6 months experience were 1.98 times more likely to be injured, but as running experience increases to over 2 years the incidence of injury is reduced, suggesting that newcomers to parkrun are at higher risk of injury. In a study involving 289 parkrunners in the south of England, Stevens et al. (2019) concluded, '[T]he present findings indicate that participation in parkrun alone (at most a once-weekly activity) is not associated with greater life satisfaction' (p. 226). They hypothesise that the lack of additional running or other forms of exercise besides parkrun may lie beneath the non-significant relationship observed among their participants. Relatedly, Grunseit et al. (2018) in a study involved 865 adult Australian parkrunners reported that 'parkrunners fell below the general population overall for satisfaction with current achievement, personal relationships, future security and life as a whole' (p. 5).

Moving on, a review of the existing scientific research, which focused specifically on parkrun and parkrunners, was published in the journal, *Preventive Medicine Reports*. Grunseit et al. (2020) examined 15 studies in total (dating from 2004 to December 2019), including 12 from the UK and 3 from Australia. The aim of the scoping review was to systematically map existing parkrun literature for evidence of its reach, health impact, and appeal, whilst identifying gaps for future research. It concluded: '[T]he current literature on parkrun suggests there are preliminary indications of public health success in terms of reach and impact on the health and wellbeing of participants' (p. 7). From the small evidence base, they found potential positive impacts on participants' health and wellbeing with reported improvements in, among other things, fitness, total physical activity, and mood (stress, anxiety, and depression). Encouragingly, the data suggested that the positive effects were largest for those who were less active when they registered with parkrun and that there is a dose response: namely the more frequently someone participates in parkrun events, the greater the positive impact.

According to the studies reviewed, the incorporation of a number of components within the parkrun model (including a timed element, informal social nature, location in green space, and the physical activity itself) worked well for those who had been accessed by the research conducted to date. The onus on participation rather than competition and its social aspects were seen as integral to parkrun's appeal to traditionally underrepresented cohorts in sport and physical activity, for example, older people and women and girls. The authors stressed, however, that whilst the reach and potential impact of parkrun have been noted anecdotally for some time, the empirical evidence in the scoping review – restricted to the UK and Australian contexts – remained limited. Critically, existing research focuses only on those who have benefitted from parkrun and consequently our knowledge is only partial; we know why it works for those it works for (Grunseit et al., 2020, p. 7). As such, according to the authors the largest groups absent from the reviewed research are people who do not register for parkrun, people who register for parkrun but don't actually participate, and people who participate in parkrun but whose involvement isn't sustained. Comparative studies examining those who discontinue attending parkrun could therefore be informative about failure in retention, for example. Moreover, expanding the research beyond English-speaking countries may also improve our understanding of cultural relevance and specificity of the parkrun model. Relatedly, 'as a multi-component intervention with a range of interacting parts and with multiple local adaptations, future research could examine the emergent properties of parkrun at the broader economic and cultural impact level' (p. 8).

★

In a qualitative study by Wiltshire et al. (2018) the trio of researchers were interested in examining how parkrun may be understood as a 'health practice' which allows individuals to seek health improvements in a collective social context. The authors analysed interview data from 19 parkrun participants. The diverse sample included 11 women and 8 men from 16 different parkrun locations across the UK, aged between 27 and 63 years, with the total number of parkruns completed varying from 10 to 274. The paper, which was published in the journal, *Sociology of Health & Fitness*, distinguished two themes. The first is that parkrun provided a space for 'collective bodywork' which enabled participants to enact personal body projects whilst also experiencing a sense of the collective ('all in this together'). In doing so the individualising notion of health behaviours is ameliorated. A participant in their study said,

> I don't know. It's just like when you go to the start line and you turn round and see how many people there are there and everybody sets off together, that's quite . . . yeah, it's quite exciting I guess, you know, and you feel part of a group
>
> (p. 9)

Similarly, as a health practice with multiple possibilities of meaning, it was acknowledged by some, how parkrun had enabled participants to socially interact. As this participant described,

> I mean the social aspect of doing something together with my son and my wife is . . . I mean we all run different times, so we don't run the parkrun together but, you know, you turn up, you do the race and you sit around and drink coffee and do whatever afterwards and get to meet a whole bunch of other runners and, you know, some you know to nod to and a few of them you know reasonably well and some acquaintances that you've known over the years kind of congregate together.
>
> (p. 10)

The second is how parkrun can be considered a health practice that entails a split between participants' own embodied subjectivities (for example, the wider goals of weight loss as well as improved fitness) and the subject position of being a 'parkrunner.' In this way, the analysis highlighted how parkrun allows participants to negotiate the seeming paradox of being an 'unfit runner.' This is highlighted by one of their participants, Patesh, who said:

> I was very heavy and I just didn't like the way that I looked. We had a reunion of friends from college and I didn't like the remarks people were making even though they were deserved, you know. Mind you, they

weren't in much better shape than me. But I resolved then that I needed to get right of the weight.

(p. 11)

In other instances where participants in their study spoke of how they had experienced serious medical issues, parkrun was framed as being potentially transformative. One respondent remarked:

2 years ago I was diagnosed with breast cancer and that sort of altered very much more how I felt about my diet and exercise, and although I've never been particularly overweight I've always had a tendency in my latter years to put on a bit of weight if I overeat or I don't exercise very much. So I think that was also part of this and my daughter also saying to me, you know, 'Come on mum, let's do something and let's try and enjoy it'. So that was the motivation as well, having been ill.

(p. 13)

Taken together, Wiltshire et al. (2018) put forward a sociological interpretation of how parkrun is practised through multiple relations to health. As such the paper calls for health promoters to consider how physical activity interventions could acknowledge the value of collective contexts, as well as how bodywork is performed and shaped through different social practices.

★

Whilst the perceived inclusive nature of parkrun has been reported in a number of academic studies, it is acknowledged that parkrun's growth has largely been organic and was initially promoted via word of mouth. Consequently, certain cohorts and communities have been less well represented among parkrun participants. For example, in the UK roughly 20 per cent of the population are living with a disability or LTC but research undertaken in 2014 indicated that just 4.3 per cent of surveyed parkrunners reported having a limiting disability or illness (Stevinson & Hickson, 2014). In response, the parkrun management team has sought to implement strategic approaches to specifically target underrepresented groups. One such example is the PROVE project (parkrun: running or volunteering for everyone), a 3-year initiative launched in 2016 to increase engagement in parkrun by people living with LTCs in England. The initial findings from the project evaluation were published in the journal *BMC Sports Science, Medicine and Rehabilitation*. The qualitative study conducted by Quirk and Haake (2019) aimed to understand the perceptions of parkrun and the PROVE project for people living with LTCs from the perspective of parkrun volunteer Outreach Ambassadors. To explain, the PROVE project was based on a peer support approach led by Outreach Ambassadors with no formal training requirements or qualifications but with an interest in the condition groups being targeted. For example, the volunteer may have personal, lived experience of the condition either as someone living with the LTC or as a carer for someone with the condition or as a health professional working in that particular field.

For the study Outreach Ambassadors were represented from a range of targeted condition groups. Semi-structured interviews were conducted with 15 PROVE Outreach Ambassadors representing 13 different LTCs in England. Verbatim transcriptions of the interviews were analysed thematically with 4 overarching main themes and 13 sub-themes identified that capture the perceptions of parkrun Outreach Ambassadors. The interviewees believed that parkrun was already supportive of people with LTCs but that the PROVE project enabled the support to be delivered in a more structured way across health conditions and locations. Moreover, it was noted that the Outreach Ambassadors considered that the PROVE project had the potential to create a welcoming, safe environment for people with LTCs to participate as walkers, runners, or volunteers. As this respondent in their study commented:

> I think it's the removal of competitiveness: the idea that it's not a race . . . at parkrun no-one really asks what your time is . . . so removing that pressure makes a huge difference, and that's I think why it's such an inclusive community.
>
> (p. 4)

The communities fostered by parkrun and PROVE, either in real life or online, were regarded as important for creating social networks and potentially breaking down barriers to physical activity and/or volunteering for people living with LTCs. That said, success of the PROVE initiative was believed to be dependent on being realistic about the potential to bring about change, challenging people's perceptions of parkrun, and engaging with key stakeholders and advocacy groups. For example, there was a preconception among some that parkrun was only for runners, which needed to be challenged. This was summarised by one of their participants who reflected:

> There's this perception out there that people who run have got to be runners, they've got to be running about like Dave Bedford in singlets and be super fit. But I think that view has changed over the years with the jogging generation and the growth of things like the London Marathon, the Great North Run, the Race for Life. I think parkrun can continue that without having to go down the field of becoming 'parkwalk' for instance. I think if it became 'parkwalk' it would put the runners off, and actually it did start with the runners. The clues in the name: parkrun. But we do say welcome to all. So, I would like to see that we still have people who are not afraid to come up and run, but people who aren't afraid to come and walk too.
>
> (p. 8)

The Outreach Ambassadors also identified several challenges for parkrun. For example, interviewees expressed concerns about communication barriers, the project's dependence on the work of volunteers for its delivery, and difficulties associated with demonstrating impact. One respondent in their study said:

> I don't know what an acceptable number of new parkrunners would be, if we get 10 new people, would that be an achievement or 100 or . . .? . . . If at the end of it we go, well, actually, do you know what, we know that we got 10 people with [health condition] to be more active, and we give ourselves a big pat on the back, but what I'm not sure on is what is considered a success?
>
> (p. 9)

Quirk and Haake (2019) concluded that parkrun's PROVE project 'has the potential to ensure that parkrun remains an inclusive and welcoming environment for people living with LTCs to engage in physical activity and/or volunteering' (p. 12).

★

Researchers from Sheffield Hallam University and the University of Sheffield undertook a case study on parkrun (Haake et al., 2020) drawing upon the health and wellbeing survey ($n = 60{,}694$) parkrun participants, which was referred to earlier. The survey responses linked to the respondents' parkrun registration data and postcode were used to estimate the participant's IMD. Encouragingly, the survey data showed that levels of self-reported physical activity increased following participation in parkrun, especially for those with previously low levels of activity. Nine out of ten reported feeling a sense of personal achievement and improvements to fitness and physical health since starting parkrun. Thus, it is concluded, parkrun impacts participants in a positive manner: physical activity levels of the least active increase, people feel a sense of personal achievement, and happiness increases.

What makes this case study distinctive from previous published studies is the focus on the role of technology and how this is incorporated. The authors noted that the low-level technology is actually a deliberate choice, highlighting the availability of alternative, automated systems (for example, simple wearable chip and timing mat as used in other mass participation events). Instead, the parkrun system, which is described as 'archaic and cumbersome,' is preferred as it promotes social interactions between parkrunners and volunteers, thus facilitating connections in a way that automated timing would not. This leads Haake et al. (2020) to conclude that one of the key lessons for technologists is that for sustained behaviour change, the application needs to be grounded in behaviour change theory. Parkrun demonstrates how this could be done using simple technology to incorporate at least seven behaviour change techniques.

★

Medical interest in parkrun understandably has grown. As alluded to at the beginning of this chapter, there have been a number of published testimonies from medical practitioners, including GPs, extolling the public health benefits of parkrun as a mass participation physical activity event which has the potential to engage the less active. One such testament, published in the *British Journal of General Practice*, suggested that parkrun may have positive benefits not just for healthy people but also for those with LTCs:

> I used to think that inspirational stories like these were rare and unique, but as time has gone on I've realised just how common tales like these are. It's actually the commonness and not the unusualness that's astonishing. I've seen the wonderful power of how parkrun can transform lives and I am convinced that it's the best sort of medicine I can prescribe.
>
> (Tobin, 2018, p. 588)

McIntosh (2021) likewise advocates the prescription of parkrun, stating that the resumption of events post-lockdown 'could have an important role to play in improving community health and facilitating social reconnection' (p. 472). In the UK, parkrun has been recognised by the RCGP as a viable option for patients as an alternative to medication – referred to as 'social prescribing.' This development is situated against a backdrop of voluntary and community sector organisations increasing their role in supporting primary care services with non-medical sources of support within the community (British Medical Association, 2019). This partnership, which started in June 2018, involves GP practices fostering closer links with their local parkrun event with clinicians referring their patients and carers to parkrun. Practices register online via the parkrun practice website, receiving marketing assets to display in their waiting room and other materials to share through various communication channels. In addition to encouraging patients to participate in parkrun as walkers, runners, volunteers, or spectators, staff are also encouraged to take part themselves through practice staff volunteer takeovers or participating in parkrun events alongside their patients. 'Not only is staff participation seen to be a morale boosting experience for the whole practice to be engaged in, but it also means that staff are more likely to be persuasive advocates' (Public Health England, 2020). To date more than 1,500 GP health practices have registered with the initiative with 70 per cent of parkruns linked to at least one general practice.

Empirical research investigating the implementation and evaluating the impact of this collaboration between GP practices and parkrun is in its infancy. One of the initial studies carried out by Fleming et al. (2020b) sought to examine the interaction between parkrun event teams and general practice, shedding light on the experiences and views of the provider to augment understanding of the initiative's potential to improve public health. In a paper published in the journal *Health and Social Care in the Community*, the authors identified challenges in linking and maintaining links between primary care and parkrun events, as well as providing practical guidance for successful collaboration between primary care and voluntary and community sector organisations.

An online questionnaire survey, which incorporated both tick box questions and free text comments, was distributed to event directors for all UK parkrun events ($n = 634$). The survey asked respondents about their parkrun event, the practices they were linked with and how those connections had been established, the activities being carried out by the event team and practices as part of the initiative, and any challenges they were experiencing. It also explored the awareness and perception of the initiative among event teams who were not linked with a practice.

Just over half (50.8 per cent) of the parkrun event teams completed the survey ($n = 322/634$). Over two-thirds (69.6 per cent) of the event teams were knowingly linked with one or more general practices; it is currently possible for a practice to register without informing their local event team. Most of these were linked with one (34.8 per cent) or two practices (32.1 per cent) with 11 (4.9 per cent) parkrun events linked with five or more practices. It was noted by the authors that for the parkrun event teams with links, this was generally viewed as having been a positive experience and was primarily motivated by wanting to positively impact on the health and wellbeing of their community. Of the 97 responding event teams who were not knowingly linked with a practice, the most frequent reason cited was that they had not yet been approached by a practice (69 per cent). Relatedly, challenges centred on the process of initiating contact between parkrun events and practices; the lack of time among parkrun event volunteers to promote the initiative; and the difficulty of clarifying parkrun event and practice responsibilities, including who takes the lead. As one respondent commented:

> There are different perspectives within the team as to how much this should be pushed by us as a parkrun, or whether we should wait for GP practices to approach us. Many people agree it's better if led by the PG practices – which in our experience it hasn't been. I know this isn't the case in other local parkrun events who are successfully linked.
>
> (p. 6)

Free text comments also described the challenge of knowing exactly who to contact within each practice:

> I would love to contact more GPs around [city] but I don't know how to approach this as I don't know who to contact. Usually, you can't get past the receptionist. We have been communicating about the initiative and this has brought GPs to us. We just don't know how to contact them.
>
> (p. 6)

In summary, the Fleming et al. (2020b) study demonstrated how the interaction between parkrun events and general practice is working at a local level from the perspective of the volunteers responsible for delivering the weekly parkrun events. Encouragingly, whilst at the early stage of national implementation, the study indicated a high level of engagement with two-thirds of those responding to the survey being linked to at least one practice. The main practical lessons from the study included ensuring clear pathways of communication between primary care and voluntary and community sector in order to initiate and maintain links; consideration of how activities can be most easily implemented by both parties, taking account of time and other resource pressures; and mutual understanding from both primary care and voluntary and community sector organisations as to their expected roles and involvement (Fleming et al., 2020b).

In a separate, mixed-methods study published in the *British Journal of General Practice*, Fleming et al. (2020a) investigated engagement with and delivery of the 'parkrun practice initiative' in general practice. In this study, practices' reasons for, and experiences of, becoming a parkrun practice were explored using an online survey of all registered parkrun practices at the time ($n = 780$) with 360 (39.2 per cent) completing the survey. A purposive sample of parkrun practice staff and non-registered staff from the West Midlands took part in either semi-structured interviews or a focus group with transcripts analysed thematically. The participants comprised GPs ($n = 6$), a GP trainee ($n = 1$), practice nurses ($n = 3$), a healthcare assistant ($n = 1$), and practice managers ($n = 5$).

The strongest motivation cited for becoming a parkrun practice was 'improving patient health and wellbeing' (92.8 per cent) with the authors identifying a dominant sub-theme that parkrun was perceived to give patients an opportunity to take charge of their own health, rather than being reliant on medical interventions. Additionally, respondents felt that involvement in the initiative had a positive impact on staff, in terms of both 'improving staff health and wellbeing' (72.5 per cent) and 'improving links with the community' (65.7 per cent). The data also highlighted the importance of there being a motivated parkrunner among practice staff to catalyse and encourage engagement in the initiative. Activities most commonly undertaken were 'encourage patients and carers to take part in parkrun' (79.4 per cent), 'encourage staff to register for parkrun and give it a go' (77.0 per cent), and 'display parkrun flyers/posters in waiting room' (74.0 per cent). It was reported that most (75.0 per cent) practices had staff members take up parkrun since becoming involved in the initiative. On the flip side, the main challenges reported were a lack of time (44.5 per cent) with some practices expressing concern regarding additional demands on their time occurring through involvement in the initiative. One practice manager in the study remarked,

> In terms of clinicians, probably time is the, the challenge I have. You know, we have a 10 minute appointment or a 15 minute appointment – how am I supposed to get this in as well?
>
> (p. 577)

In concluding, the authors concede that whilst the response rate to the online survey was relatively high, 'practices that took part may be those that are more committed to the initiative and therefore may not be representative of all registered practices' (Fleming et al., 2020a, p. 579). Furthermore, it is noted that the data collection was carried out during the first year of national implementation of the initiative, and it is likely that perceptions will change as the parkrun practice develops and becomes more established.

In a separate paper, Fleming and Mensah (2021) explored how registered parkrun practices are using their websites to promote parkrun events and, in doing so, identified implications for practice. The study comprised a qualitative examination of a sample of practices that completed an online survey as part of a larger study about being a parkrun practice (see Fleming et al., 2020a). This survey was sent to all 780 parkrun practices in the UK with 306 (39.2 per cent) responding. Of these, 114 (37.3 per cent) reported including a parkrun page on their website or link to the parkrun website. These practices were included in the study with each website systematically searched to identify parkrun content. A data extraction proforma was used to collate descriptive data (for example, information location and ease of finding). Findings demonstrated the variability that currently exists with websites ranging from being extensive and highly informative to having minimal amounts of text or images. Nevertheless, use of official parkrun literature provided some consistency with regard to parkrun activities and events. Additionally, content sought to address patients' concerns about participating in parkrun, for example:

> We were all really pleased to learn that parkrun is 'NOT A RACE'. There was reassurance about suitability for all abilities; for example, '[parkrun is] open to everyone, including those who are inactive or have health conditions or disability'.
>
> (p. 5)

Findings also highlighted the importance of practices becoming further embedded within their local communities and signposting patients to existing community services, as well as the importance of the accessibility of updated and timely information on practice websites, ease of access, and user-friendliness.

★

The aim of this chapter has been to collate the current parkrun literature in terms of the emerging evidence of the health and wellbeing benefits of taking part in parkrun. Studies suggest there are preliminary signs of public health gains, including improvements to physical health, overall personal wellbeing, as well as helping to reduce social isolation, anxiety, stress, and depression, and increasing self-esteem among runners and volunteers. Arguably, one of the most noteworthy observations is that the greatest physical and psychological benefits of participation are achieved by those who were previously inactive. What is more, studies also indicate that populations traditionally more difficult to engage in physical activity, including older adults, women, those who are overweight or obese, and those living with health conditions, are meaningfully represented at parkrun events. Relatedly, there is also evidence to indicate that the mutually supportive and encouraging environment, sense of belonging, and exposing people to local natural settings are key facilitators in maintaining participation. As McIntosh (2021, p. 476) succinctly summarises, 'parkrun offers a low-cost, community event which has the potential to have a huge positive impact on individuals, communities and healthcare systems.' Whilst the potential health and wellbeing benefits of participation should not be understated, Grunseit et al. (2020) highlight that current research focuses on those who have benefited from parkrun and therefore our knowledge is incomplete; attention has been on investigating why it works for those it works for and not on why others do not participate or benefit in the same way. Accordingly, there are a number of notable cohorts which are absent from the peer-reviewed research to date, including those who do not register for parkrun, those who register for parkrun but do not participate, and those who participate in parkrun but whose participation isn't maintained.

Note

1 www.rcgp.org.uk/about-us/news/2018/june/parkrun-uk-teams-up-with-rcgp-to-prescribe-active-lifestyles-to-patients-and-practice-staff.aspx

References

Academy of Medical Royal College. (2015). *Exercise: The Miracle Cure and the Role of the Doctor in Promoting It*. London: AMRC.

Bamberg, J., Hitchings, R., & Latham, A. (2018). Enriching green exercise research. *Landscape and Urban Planning*, 178, 270–275.

British Medical Association. (2019). *Social Prescribing: Making It Work for GPs and Patients*. British Medical Association.

Cleland, V., Nash, M., Sharman, M.J., & Claflin, S. (2019). Exploring the health-promoting potential of the parkrun phenomenon: What factors are associated with higher levels of participation? *American Journal of Health Promotion*, 33:1, 13–23.

Colberg, S., Sigal, R., Fernhall, B., Regensteiner, J., Blissmer, B., Rubin, R., Chasan-Taber, L., Albright, A., & Braun, B. (2010). Exercise and type 2 diabetes. *Diabetes Care*, 33:12, 147–167.

Fleming, J., Bryce, C., Parsons, J., Wellington, C., & Dale, J. (2020a). Engagement with and delivery of the 'parkrun practice initiative' in general practice: A mixed methods study. *British Journal of General Practice*, 70:697, 573–580. https://doi.org/10.3399/bjgp20X710453.

Fleming, J., & Mensah, B. (2021). Promoting parkrun to patients using the general practice website: a qualitative exploration of 'parkrun practice' websites. *British Journal of General Practice*. https://doi.org/10.3399/BJGPO.2020.110.

Fleming, J., Wellington, C., Parsons, J., & Dale, J. (2020b). Collaboration between primary care and a voluntary, community sector organization: Practical guidance from the parkrun practice initiative. *Health, and Social Care in the Community*, 1–10. https://doi.org/10.1111/hsc.13236.

Grunseit, A.C., Richards, J., & Merom, D. (2018). Running on a high: Parkrun and personal well-being. *BMC Public Health*, 18:1, Article 59, 1–11.

Grunseit, A.C., Richards, J., Reece, L., Bauman, A., & Merom, D. (2020). Evidence on the reach and impact of the social physical activity phenomenon parkrun: A scoping review. *Preventative Medicine Reports*, 20, 1–8. https://doi.org/10.1016/j.pmedr.2020.101231.

Haake, S., Bullas, A., & Quirk, H. (2019). *parkrun Health and Wellbeing Survey*. College of Health, Wellbeing and Life Sciences. Retrieved from https://awrcparkrunresearch.files.wordpress.com/2020/05/uk-health-and-wellbeing-survey-v5.1-final.pdf.

Haake, S., Quirk, H., & Bullas, A. (2020). The role of technology in promoting physical activity: A case-study of parkrun. *Proceedings*, 49:1, 80. https://doi.org/10.3390/proceedings2020049080.

Knight, J.A. (2012). Physical inactivity: Associated diseases and disorders. *Annals of Clinical and Laboratory Science*, 42:3, 320–337.

Kohl, H., Craig, C., Lambert, E., Inoue., S., Ramadan Alkandari, J., Leetongin, G., Kahlmeier, S., & Lancet Physical Activity Series Working Group. (2012). The pandemic of physical inactivity: Global action for public health. *Lancet*, 380, 294–305.

Linton, L., & Valentin, S. (2018). Running with injury: A study of UK novice and recreational runners and factors associated with running related injury. *Journal of Science and Medicine in Sport*, 21, 1221–1225.

McIntosh, T. (2021). Parkrun: A panacea for health and wellbeing? *Journal of Research in Nursing*, 26:5, 472–477.

Morris, P., & Scott, H. (2019). Not just a run in the park: A qualitative exploration of parkrun and mental health. *Advances in Mental Health*, 17:2, 110–123.

Pedersen, B.K., & Saltin, B. (2015). Exercise as medicine – Evidence for prescribing exercise as therapy in 26 different chronic diseases. *Scandinavian Journal of Medicine and Science in Sports*, 25:Suppl. 3, 1–72. https://doi.org/10.1111/sms.12581.

Pedlar, C.R., Myrissa, K., Barry, M., Khwaja, I.G., Simpkin, A.J., Newell, J., Scarrott, C., Whyte, G.P., Kipps, C., & Baggish, A.L. (2021). Medical encounters at community-based physical activity events (parkrun) in the UK. *British Journal of Sports Medicine*. https://doi.org/10.1136/bjsports-2021-104256.

Physical Activity Guidelines Advisory Committee. (2008). *Physical Activity Guidelines Advisory Committee Report*. Washington, DC: US Department of Health and Human Services.

Public Health England. (2014). *Everybody Active, Every Day: An Evidence-based Approach to Physical Activity*. London: PHE. Retrieved from https://assets.publishing.service.gov.uk/government/uploads/system/uploads/attachment_data/file/374914/Framework_13.pdf.

Public Health England. (2016). *Health Matters: Getting Every Adult Active Every Day*. London: PHE. Retrieved from www.gov.uk/government/publications/health-matters-getting-every-adult-active-every-day.

Public Health England. (2020). *The Parkrun Practice Initiative*. Retrieved from www.gov.uk/government/case-studies/the-parkrun-practice-initiative

Quirk, H., & Haake, S. (2019). How can we get more people with long-term health conditions involved in parkrun? A qualitative study evaluating parkrun's PROVE project. *BMC Sports Science, Medicine and Rehabilitation*, 11:22.

Stevens, M., Rees, T., & Polman, R. (2019). Social identification, exercise participation, and positive exercise experiences: Evidence from parkrun. *Journal of Sports Sciences*, 37:2, 221–228.

Stevinson, C., & Hickson, M. (2014). Exploring the public health potential of a mass community participation event. *Journal of Public Health*, 36:2, 268–274.

Stevinson, C., & Hickson, M. (2018). Changes in physical activity, weight and wellbeing outcomes among attendees of a weekly mass participation event: A prospective 12-month study. *Journal of Public Health*, 41:4, 807–814.

Stevinson, C., Wiltshire, G., & Hickson, M. (2015). Facilitating participation in health-enhancing physical activity: A qualitative study of parkrun. *International Journal of Behavioural Medicine*, 22, 170–177.

Tobin, S. (2018). Prescribing parkrun. *British, Journal of General Practice*, 68:677, e588. https://doi.org/10.3399/bjgp18X700133.

Wiltshire, G.R., Fullagar, S., & Stevinson, C. (2018). Exploring parkrun as a social context for collective health practices: Running with and against the moral imperatives of health responsibilisation. *Sociology of Health & Illness*, 40:1, 3–17.

Chapter 5

'A Run, Not a Race'

'Every Saturday morning at 9am sharp a little bit of anarchy breaks out across the country.' So begins Guardian columnist Aditya Chakrabortty's salutation of the global parkrun phenomenon. On the one hand, associating parkrun – a social movement predicated on egalitarian principles – with rebellion is a curious connection. And yet, on the other hand, much of the parkrun manual is deliberately designed to disrupt. There is none more so than challenging the entrenched belief that much of what defines running is a preoccupation with time and, in particular, speed. Consequently, for many runners – both new and experienced – there is a hesitancy to participate, deterred by past experiences and/or a perception that slow runners and those whose bodies don't meet the normative ideal are stigmatised and excluded from the running community. Indeed, even if athletes are willing to adopt running as a cosmetic body project, they may find that they are not welcome in exercise spaces (Sniezek, 2021).

In reflecting upon the stigmatisation of the slow runner, I am reminded of a particular incident involving a straggling runner, Annette Edwards, aged 46, who was stopped a mile and a half into the Spen 20 race. The marshal, who also happened to be Chair of Spenborough and District Athletics Club, voiced concerns that based on her current pace she wouldn't finish under 4 hours.

> I told her that while she could continue, if at the 10 mile marker she was still a long way behind the other runners and had taken over two hours to get to that point I would be asking her to withdraw from the race.
>
> (Bozen, 2015)

This prompted the veteran distance runner to retire, understandably hurt at being told that she was too slow and that the race 'wasn't for people like her' (Carter, 2015).

It is noteworthy that whilst any race organiser is entitled to establish a cut-off time, this wasn't the case in this particular instance although there was an option for slower runners to start the race earlier, unmarshalled, which two other entrants did. What is of greater interest is the subsequent discussion that this incident generated among the running community. To paraphrase, much

DOI: 10.4324/9781003121961-5

of the debate was concerned with differing expectations over what consti-
tutes a 'race' and whether this infers a certain level of competitive endeavour
as opposed to community events, such as parkrun, which embrace an inclusive ethos, welcoming all participants regardless of ability (and by implication,
speed). The tone of the more critical responses echoed the negativity directed
at individuals that are associated with the evolution of the 'slow running' movement. For example, self-proclaimed 'patron saint of the back of the pack' John
Bingham, who believes that running doesn't have to be a 'full speed ahead' kind
of affair, bemoans, 'I have had people say that I've ruined the sport of running.'
Likewise, Joe Henderson, in the forward to *Long Slow Distance* (2010), recalls a
phone conversation he had with a fervent critic who argued 'LSD was a cancer
that has hurt the sport for a long time, and you were the person that spread it.'

In this context, Smith's (1998) study of roadrunners in South Wales is instruc-
tive. To summarise, Smith proposed that the running community be categorised
into three distinct groups: athletes, runners, and joggers, with the latter characterised by a more casual and less-committed relationship to running. It is argued
that the jogger or 'fun runner' label is employed in a disparaging way to describe
a group that is principally engaged in body maintenance, as well as being distinct
from athletes and runners with regard to distance and pace. To put it crudely,
'runners run further, faster, and more often than joggers' (p. 182). Whilst this
study sensitises us to the different degrees of involvement and commitment among
the heterogeneous running community, in the context of parkrun and mass participation events, it is important to consider the relationships within and between
these groups. As noted, for some participants parkrun represents an accessible
form of slow running, whilst for others one of the attractions is competition,
whether against oneself or against others. Are there any tensions that emerge
from this potential dichotomy? How does parkrun 'manage' a broad church of
participation where different motivations coexist? In a qualitative study by Bowness et al. (2020) they found several respondents intimate that cliques existed at
their local parkrun, making it less likely for them, as outside the clique, to feel a
part of its community. Others indicated that in being a slow runner, they regularly felt ignored by many other parkrunners who had left before they finished.
The authors reported that on some occasions, participants had thought they
were a burden, particularly in those parkrun events that involved multiple laps
of the same circuit. In these cases, the collective effervescence of some in the
group may appear to be exclusionary to others. This has parallels with the work
of Fullagar et al. (2020), who reported that some respondents in their study felt
that there was an insider/outsider dynamic engendered by established social
networks; this was manifest through the wearing of club clothing and a spirit of
competitiveness, which was perceived to marginalise less-athletic runners.

Nowadays the jogger has become established as a ubiquitous urban figure
(Latham, 2015). Recreational running as an activity has risen in popularity in
both the UK[1] (England Athletics, 2017) and elsewhere (Scheerder et al., 2015).
Its popularity is exemplified by iconic events such as the Great North Run and

the London Marathon. More than 386,000 people entered the ballot to secure one of the 50,000 places in the 2018 Virgin Money London Marathon. In the same year the Simplyhealth Great North Run attracted 57,000 runners, bringing the total number of finishers since 1981 to in excess of 1 million people. In 2021, it was reported on the parkrun website that there were over 2,200 registered events across 23 countries with more than 7 million registered parkrunners. Furthermore, it is hypothesised that if the rate of growth continues, by 2024 more than 1 million parkrunners will be participating every single week (parkrun, 2021).

So how might we account for this growth, and what do we know about the behaviours and motivations of the people involved? According to Wilson (1995, p. 183), the rise in mass-participation 'fun running' may be understood as individual participants categorised as 'Olympians or lemmings: as gladiators in search of glory or slaves to the 1980s fashion for fitness and idealised body shape.' This crude interpretation however fails to consider the diverse nature of the running community and the broad range of activities that the practice of running encompasses.[2] As Hitchings and Latham (2017) acknowledged, running may be undertaken in a variety of places, involving differences in intensity, variations in duration, and may incorporate an assortment of purposes. Some runners are habitual, running on a regular basis, others more sporadically; some have an urge to compete, whilst others enjoy the solitude of running as a meditative and contemplative act; some opt for marathons, whilst others prefer shorter distances. Amidst this diversity Smith (1998) noted there exists a large group of what he describes as perennial 'also rans' for whom there is no readily apparent reason for participation, who devote an enormous amount of time to run and train yet stand no realistic chance of winning or doing well in *any* race.

At this juncture it may be useful to reflect upon Carter's (2018) contention that what is implicitly understood as 'running' is not actually running but a form of disciplined leisure, an intermediary practice located between work and home. Accordingly, he adopted the term 'racing' to describe an activity where the purpose is to try to cover a set distance in as little time as possible or an attempt to cover as much distance as possible in a set amount of time. Racing in this interpretation is imbued with specific, shared, embodied meanings, distinct from the act of running, which can be understood as a form of enskilled movement that is inherent to becoming a mindful, fully engaged human being (Carter, 2018, p. 7).

It is worth too underscoring the 'run, not a race' mantra that epitomises parkrun's inclusive ideals. In many ways this ethos is an explicit endeavour to chip away at the still commonly held assumption that the practice of running is associated with competition. As Cregan-Reid (2016, p. xv) speculates, 'I think what deters many people from trying or persisting with running is the idea of it as a competitive sport.' He attributes this in part to our school experiences of 'sport,' as well as the media popularising the idea of running as fundamentally competitive. 'I have to urge the many beginners to whom I talk,' Cregan-Reid writes, 'to "take it easy". Their innate belief is that good running is about speed' (p. xv).

As previously noted, presenting parkrun as distinctive from racing, where there are no expectations that participants are fast or slow, just a preference that they complete the distance in a time comfortable for them, invites the participation of groups who do not identify with the traditional stereotypical views of runners and members of athletic clubs. Nevertheless, it is acknowledged that more still needs to be done to challenge potential misconceptions of the nature of parkrun and consequently who may be deterred from participating. In a qualitative study by Fullagar et al. (2020, p. 1206) when respondents were asked about how parkrun could develop strategies to engage people from diverse backgrounds, typical comments included: '[P]eople may worry they are too slow or unfit to take part (as I first did), perhaps more could be done to focus on how parkrun is not a race or about a time.' Another respondent remarked, '[P]eople think you have to run but you can walk it.' Such perceptions reflect the anxieties of those who may be taking part in a sporting event for the first time: a fear of finishing coming last, of feeling excluded, and being ridiculed. Parkrun's response was to introduce the role of the 'tail runner,' which was made compulsory at junior parkrun events from 2013 and extended to include all parkruns in the UK from January 2017. It is noteworthy that over time the term 'tail runner' was subsequently deemed to becoming less accurate in that more participants – including the tail runners themselves – were walking. Furthermore, it was believed to be discouraging those who were less active, or fearful of coming last, from taking part. Resultantly, the name of the role changed from tail runner to 'tail walker.' As Chrissie Wellington, parkrun Global Head of Health and Wellbeing, explained:

> Semantics yes, but the change in role title was vitally important in reaffirming and reiterating the message that everyone is welcome at parkrun, including those who walk at our events. What might have been seen as an insignificant or tokenistic adjustment was actually a vital and visible manifestation of our efforts to promote inclusivity.[3]

The original manifestation of parkrun was described as a time trial and unreservedly this is some participants' approach, testing themselves against the clock as opposed to racing against one another. This is something which the parkrun system is set up to accommodate, providing each registrant with online access to a history of all their runs, times, and age grading, enabling them to monitor and review their progress over time. For those entrants who are competitive, parkrun semi-reluctantly acknowledges the 'first finisher' as opposed to the winner. Arguably, this is what differentiates parkrun from a sportised form of running, an activity where the primary concern is on the pursuit of faster times, and the enhancement of performance (Shipway & Jones, 2008; Vettenniemi, 2012). For many, running involves pushing one's physiological limits in terms of speed, whilst part of the experience comes from measuring times and racing against ourselves (Cidell, 2014). Clubs, mainstream running magazines, specialist shops, and 'experts' such as nutritionists and physiotherapists all provide sources of guidance and support to facilitate a runners' desire to improve performance (Nettleton & Hardey, 2006). In this context, 'becoming a runner' involves disciplining the body whereby participants subject themselves to techniques and processes concerned with regulating the body as an object of instrumental rationality (Tulle, 2007). In this way, runners enter what Shilling (2003) describes as a 'body project' to be worked at through conscious reshaping, management, and maintenance. The quest for improvement is a scientific endeavour with a Taylorisation involving statistics, records, and speeds. The commercialised running industry has developed an ideological construction of 'the runner' which is tied to technology and bodily techniques that reflect twenty-first-century capitalist values. Manufacturers' technological shoes, compression garments, supplements, strength and conditioning, foam-rolling, treadmills, synthetic running tracks, all provide opportunities to portray running as a rationalistic, technical, and mechanistic endeavour (Gibson, 2012).

As illuminated, individuals may experience running both as a fast and a slow practice concurrently. Running events can similarly be differentially experienced as fast and slow. Whilst a 'race' may be defined as an event, in its normative sense, it involves a competition between two or more entrants with 'success' – defeating an opponent or a particular performance – ascribed higher value than the sensory experience (Bale, 2011). As such, races are projects with a beginning and an end, where an effort is made to reduce the amount of time or increase the amount of space (Bale, 2011). However, as we have seen, the growth of mass participation in running events, leading to an increased diversity of runners' speeds and purposes for entering, has contributed to a pluralisation of motives away from a dominant emphasis on performance and racing.

Aside from the individual motives of those who run, and the practices employed, an overriding theme discernible from the scholarly literature on running relates to the 'prevalence of speed' (Eichberg, 1990, p. 129) as well as the conspicuous role time plays in the talk and activity of runners. According to Connor (2011), timekeeping is a distinguishing feature of running, more so than any other sport, whereas for Smith (2002, p. 352), 'times confer a particular and precise identity on a runner,' enabling objective measurement, as well as making individual performances accountable. As such quantification represents a barometer of progress, and improvement in times is closely aligned to confirmation of the status of runner (Altheide & Pfuhl, 1980). This is underlined by Abbas (2004, p. 161), who describes speed as a *necessary* mechanism of running 'because a "good runner" cannot be understood without reference to it.'

In relation to parkrun, some events incorporate volunteer 'pacers' who run at set speeds to enable participants to achieve their goal. For some parkrunners part of the attraction is being able to access accurate timing between the start and finish lines. Correspondingly, the notion of the *Personal Best* (PB) encourages participants to record and assess each run in relation to past performances (Abbas, 2004). In a study by Hallett et al. (2020), participants' experiences were shaped by wanting to improve their times with the results email, which includes a range of statistics, as being an element of becoming 'hooked.' The authors proposed that the personalised statistics functioned as a 'reward,' helping to prolong the parkrun experience through anticipation of receiving an official result later in the day. As this respondent (Bonnie) cited in the study by Wiltshire et al. (2018) reflects:

> Every time I go I am aiming to, you know, get a PB, but it's just personal goals that I have in mind. You know, everybody's there for their own reasons and yeah, I just think you turn up and I'll do my best and that's my only real reason for running.
>
> (p. 9)

It is notable therefore that times and speed are not the sole preoccupation of highly committed athletes but also prevalent among more casual recreational runners, albeit manifest in different ways. As noted, past studies examining the meanings of participation for parkrunners has identified competition as an important stimulus for sustained attendance with respondents driven by a target time or finishing position (Hindley, 2020). Hitchings and Latham (2017, p. 340) in their study of comparatively casual 'non-runner runners' in London found the respondents employed different speeds and used a variety of devices to monitor their runs. 'These runners were interested in how long, how far, and sometimes how fast, they could run.' Contrariwise, they noted that these recreational runners were relatively uninterested when it came to proper running technique and ambivalent about comparing themselves to the performance of others.

There are some for whom the notion of slowness, even within mass participation or recreational running, is envisaged as transgressive. One such critic, Buckingham (2005) highlighted what he described as a 'precipitous decline' in distance running, pointing to the slowing in average marathon finishing times. He argues that the latter 'rests at odds with the current popular discourse of the attenuated self: the vulnerable individual who needs to be protected by an overbearing state.' A secondary concern, according to Buckingham, is that running 'is being choked by charity raising and the anti-competitive ethos that goes with it.' This echoes Bale's (1994, p. 144) representation of jogging's expansion in popularity, which in his words 'seemed to de-emphasise competition and the record and instead emphasise a kind of communion with nature and the freedom of bodily experience.' In one sense, by deliberately slowing down, the ways in which the runner's body engages with the environment enables a different appreciation of their surroundings and one's senses. This chimes with Masters' (2014) testimony where he documents a twice-weekly jogging routine traversing the same route, which he attributes to nurturing a calm and meditative mental state. He likens this 'passive' approach to 'the slow movement' where one savours a carefully prepared slow meal. Correspondingly, the slow(er) runner is cognisant of the weather, their surroundings, and their natural bodily rhythms.

In parkrun, as stated, there are no expectations, no cut-off times, no awards for finishing first. Put simply, how fast an individual completes parkrun does not equate to the personal benefits that are accrued from that event. That the average finish time for completing a parkrun has increased year on year is cause for celebration, emblematic of parkrun's progress in seeking to broaden their participation base. In 2005, the average finish time for completing a parkrun was 22:17. In comparison, it was 32:29 in 2018 with 64,888 instances of people taking more than 50 minutes to complete – an increase of 88 per cent on the previous year (parkrun, 2018). Similarly, in a study by Pedlar et al. (2021) which looked at data from parkrun events at 702 UK locations over a 6-year period (2014–2019) it was noted that

> early in the study sample period were dominated by faster club runners but gradual diversification occurred over time, characterised by increasing participation among recreational and older joggers and walkers, reflected in a gradual slowing of mean 5 km completion times.
>
> (p. 3)

Nonetheless, parkrun CEO Nick Pearson proffers a cautionary tone. There are a significant number of fast parkrunners who regularly participate, whose achievements are as important as those who have overcome significant challenges and barriers. 'What we're not trying to do by broadening it out is to make it only for less-fit, less active people.' Pearson adds: '[W]e want everyone to feel welcome and equally comfortable, but there is clearly a disproportionate value to those who couldn't do it anywhere else.'[4]

★

In recent times the prefix 'slow' has been variously added to a range of phenomena, including slow living, slow cities, slow food, and slow travel. Slow has been labelled a social movement (Honore, 2005), whereas others have described it as a subculture (Rauch, 2011), represented in everyday practices of resistance to speed. Whilst being slow has traditionally been ascribed various negative connotations – sluggish, dull-witted, inefficient, signifying one's inability to 'keep up' in the competitive spheres of work and leisure – the meaning of slowness today has shifted, invoked as a credible metaphor for stepping off the treadmill, and is seeking a greater work-life balance (Fullagar et al., 2012). As Koepnick (2014, p. 1) remarked:

> Life is faster today than it has ever been before . . . but in accumulating ever more impressions, events, and stimulations we end up with ever less – less substance, less depth, less meaning, less freedom, less spontaneity.

This sentiment is captured in recent academic writing on the challenges of living in an ever-accelerating culture, arguing that technological advances and the expansion of consumer capitalism have resulted in our lives becoming increasingly more complex and immediate (Agger, 2004; Tomlinson, 2007). According to Parkins and Craig (2006), slowness is a deliberate subversion from the modern dominance of speed and as such reflects a style of living that is displaced from the norms associated with modernity. Slow living is recognised both as a specific lifestyle and as a new social movement, which is premised on a number of founding principles – to take time out of our hurried lives, avoiding rushing and encouraging people to take the time to reflect on their life and reconnect with nature (Lamb, 2019). According to Andrews (2008), slow living is more gratifying and presents the possibility of restoring meaning, authenticity, and identity to our lives.

In the public realm, the success and growth of the slow movement are evident in the popularity and media interest in Honore's (2005) social commentary, *In Praise of Slow*. Honoré argues that we are living in an era where speed has assumed greater importance than in the whole of human history. In elite performance sport, for example, athletes compete within a hundredth of a second with each other as the technologies to measure such miniscule differences in speed have been developed. Answers to once complicated and challenging queries are now a computer search engine away that can deliver responses in a nanosecond. Honoré goes on to explain how people can break free from the burden of time and the ill effects of speed, providing practical examples of how to live a slower life. Implicit in the values of slow living is a particular conception of time in which 'having time' means purposefully engaging in mindful practices, investing in reflection and deliberation (Parkins, 2004). From this perspective, slowness is more than simply a rebellion against speed and needs to be viewed more broadly than in a literal or temporal sense. As historian Montanari (1996, p. 56) argues:

> The contrast between a 'slow' and 'fast' culture . . . has very little to do with the concepts of slowness and haste. In some apparently 'slow' situations, slowness means exhaustion, uneasiness and even suffering. Vice versa, 'fast' situations are not always disagreeable. . . . Contrasting 'slow' and 'fast' is not the point. We badly need other adjectives.

Thus, there is nothing per se problematic with speed, or as Osbaldiston (2013, p. 12) rebuts 'the temporal question itself, especially in relation to clock-time, misses the point.' From this standpoint, the 'slow' is concerned with *how* we consume time with an emphasis on care, attention, and mindfulness (Parkins & Craig, 2006).

Of the manifestations of slow that exist, the Slow Food movement is arguably the best known. It emerged in Italy during the late 1980s as a response to the perceived dominance of fast-food chains, supermarkets, and agribusiness, regarded as a pernicious symptom of the 'fast life' (Petrini, 2003). Much of this resistance is based on the perception that the fast-food industry engenders an approach to food and eating which is hurried, joyless, and homogenised (Hsu, 2015). The core social and political practices underpinning the Slow Food movement have been linked to broader social movements, permeating many aspects of our contemporary lives. One example is the project of slow travel/tourism, which resists the homogenising forces of globalisation and the notion of tourism as a commodified experience of mobility and instead offers an alternative vision that celebrates the local – small-scale travel utilising transport modalities that minimise the impacts on the environment and facilitate a closer and more genuine connection with local people (Fullagar et al., 2012). The concept of slowness has also been researched in the domain of other leisure pursuits, including cycling. Connecting his ideas to a broader vision of degrowth and a critique of contemporary regimes of production and consumption which emphasise speed and efficiency, Popan (2018) advises that we need to slow down. Against this backdrop cycling is more just a cheap and efficient mode of transport but offers a way of moving that engenders a different way of living, one that is slower, more embodied, and sociable. Popan (2018, p. 89) believes 'a slower cycling re-awakens the multitude of bodily senses,' allowing a more meaningful appreciation of the surroundings and enabling 'playful interactions with other cyclists, conversations, as well as the transformations of the utilitarian space of the road into a more socially open space.'

Whilst the slow movements cited may result in productive outcomes, crucially it is the *process* which is both desired and experienced (Parkins & Craig, 2006). In focusing our attention on slow living in the context of parkrun, we can begin to expose assumptions about the everyday and to consider the merits of slow running. It is a reasonable assumption that incidental and casual interactions can be facilitated when companion parkrunners negotiate the course at a pace that is conducive for conversation (what is commonly described as the 'talk test'). From my own experiences and observations at parkrun events from the pedestrian end of the pack, social interactions with both acquaintances and complete strangers are not only possible but highly probable. A pertinent example is provided by Chrissie Wellington in her blog reflections of walking her local Ashton Court parkrun.[5] She notes how being towards the back of the field provided an entirely different perspective, affording her the opportunity to observe others, to listen to people's exchanges, and to engage in her own conversation with a father and daughter. Wellington observe 'we crossed the finish line together, with none of us achieving a PB in terms of time but having a PB in terms of experience.' She goes on: '[M]y park-walk opened my eyes to all of those varied, and wonderful, interactions . . . interactions that maybe wouldn't happen without parkrun as the glue binding them together.'

As I have sought to illustrate, slowness is more than anti-speed. Slowness is embodied in the qualities of rhythm, tempo, and pace that are produced in the sensory and affective relationship between the individual and the environment (Cresswell, 2010). Pace, in this sense, involves taking more time to be 'in the moment' – a mindset aimed at immersing oneself in the surroundings and in so doing augmenting the potential benefits of nature exposure. According to Weinstein et al. (2009), the positive effects of being in nature are contingent on the level of immersion in nature experiences, for example, whether an individual feels 'fully present' or 'distanced' from being in nature. In a study they developed instructions to immerse participants, who were shown photographs of either natural or built environments, by orienting their attention, encouraging them to notice or imagine colours, sounds, or smells associated with the surroundings. Whilst all participants received instructions, those who reported greater immersion were those who viewed nature photographs, testifying more nature relatedness, better mood, and more prosocial values and concern about the welfare of others (Weinstein et al., 2009). Similarly, Duvall (2011a, 2011b) discovered that when participants were instructed on how to be more engaged with their outdoor walking environment, they were more satisfied with the nature around them, reporting greater attention, less frustration, and more contentment. Interestingly, the bulk of these benefits were associated with how much time participants spent walking, regardless of instruction. Correspondingly, moving through a parkrun course at a leisurely pace where one is able to meaningfully connect with and appreciate the surroundings and the terrain – absorbing the various sights, sounds, and smells along the route – may extend richer benefits.

★

In this chapter I have homed in on the statistic that for 16 consecutive years, parkrun has witnessed the slowing of average completion times. As has been discussed, this is seen as an indicator of the growing number of participants who walk the courses, which in turn is reflective of the apparent growing appeal to less-able participants and those previously deemed as inactive. As I have sought to demonstrate, in a number of public realms, slow has positive connotations, for example, the slow food movement, slow travel, and slow fashion. Conversely, in running, slow is generally deemed not to be a plus but regressive. The prevailing narrative is one of improvement, which with an appropriate level of practice and commitment, one should naturally aspire to faster finishing times. As we have seen, a core aspect of parkrun is quantification – performances are timed and recorded, along with ranking individual times and finishing positions – which in turn enables self-monitoring and comparison. This points to some possible tensions between parkrun's claims for itself as inclusive and open to all whilst also overtly celebrating participants achieving a PB,[6] the maintenance of course records, as well as incorporating pacers.

Notes

1 Over the past 10 years participation in athletics and running in all its forms has grown by 72 per cent to 2.4 million with 7.1 million people having run in the last 12 months (England Athletics, 2017).

2 A number of authors have attempted to develop runner typologies as a way of capturing this diversity (Ogles & Masters, 2000; Vos et al., 2008). For example, based on a survey of motives and attitudes towards running, Vos and Scheerder (2009) segment the running market into five distinct categories: individual runners, social-competitive runners, social-community runners, health and fitness runners, and performance runners.
3 https://blog.parkrun.com/uk/2020/04/20/walking-the-talk/
4 www.connectsport.co.uk/news/exclusive-why-slower-better-parkrun
5 www.parkrun.org.uk/blog/news/2015/04/08/walking-the-talk/
6 At Colwick parkrun, for example, there is a PB bell which participants are encouraged to ring when recording a personal best, images of which are shared on social media.

References

Abbas, A. (2004). The embodiment of class, gender and age through leisure: A realist analysis of long distance running. *Leisure Studies*, 23:2, 159–175.

Agger, B. (2004). *Speeding Up Fast Capitalism: Cultures, Jobs, Families, Schools, Bodies*. Boulder: Paradigm Publishers.

Altheide, D.L. & Pfuhl, E.H. (1980). Self-accomplishment through running. *Symbolic Interaction*, 3, 127–142.

Andrews, G. (2008). *The Slow Food Story: Politics and Pleasure*. London: Pluto Press.

Bale, J. (1994). *Landscapes of Modern Sport*. Leicester: Leicester University Press.

Bale, J. (2011). Running: Running as working. In Cresswell, T., & Merriman, P. (Eds.), *Geographies of Mobilities: Practices, Spaces, Subjects* (pp. 35–50). Farnham: Ashgate.

Bowness, J., Tulle, E., & McKendrick, J. (2020). Understanding the parkrun community; sacred Saturdays and organic solidarity of parkrunners. *European Journal for Sport and Society*, 18:1, 44–63. https://doi.org/10.1080/16138171.2020.1792113.

Bozen, J. (2015). Spen 20 race organiser speaks out. *Women's Running*. Retrieved from https://womensrunninguk.co.uk/events/spen-20-race-organiser-speaks-out/

Buckingham, A. (2005). Running isn't just for fun. *Spiked*. Retrieved from www.spiked-online.com/newsite/article/1133

Carter, K. (2015). Is it ever right to pull someone out of a race for being too slow? *The Guardian*. Retrieved from www.theguardian.com/lifeandstyle/the-running-blog/2015/mar/16/running-blog-race-too-slow

Carter, T.F. (2018). *On Running and Becoming Human: An Anthropological Perspective*. New York: Palgrave Pivot.

Cidell, J. (2014). Running road races as transgressive event mobilities. *Social & Cultural Geography*, 15:5, 571–583.

Connor, S. (2011). *A Philosophy of Sport*. London: Reaktion Books.

Cregan-Reid, V. (2016). *Footnotes: How Running Makes Us Human*. London: Ebury Press.

Cresswell, T. (2010). Towards a politics of mobility. *Environment and Planning D: Society and Space*, 28:1, 17–31.

Duvall, J. (2011a). Enhancing the benefits of outdoor walking with cognitive engagement strategies. *Journal of Environmental Psychology*, 31, 27–35.

Duvall, J. (2011b). Using engagement-based strategies to alter perceptions of the walking environment. *Environment and Behaviour*, 45, 303–322.

Eichberg, H. (1990). Stronger, funnier, deadlier: Track and field on the way to the ritual of the record. In Carter, J.M. & Kruger, A. (Eds.), *Ritual and Record: Sports Records and Quantification in Pre-Modern Societies* (pp. 123–134). York: Greenwood Press.

England Athletics. (2017). *Athletics and Running: For Everyone, Forever. Strategic Plan: 2017 and Beyond*. Retrieved from www.englandathletics.org/strategicplan

Fullagar, S., Markwell, K., & Wilson, E. (Eds.). (2012). *Slow Tourism: Experiences and Mobilities*. Bristol: Channel View.

Fullagar, S., Petris, S., Sargent, J., Allen, S., Akhtar, M., & Ozakinci, G. (2020). Action research with parkrun UK volunteer organisers to develop inclusive strategies. *Health Promotion International*, 35, 1199–1209.

Gibson, K. (2012). Knight's children: Techno-science, consumerism and running shoes. *Qualitative Research in Sport, Exercise and Health*, 4:3, 341–361.

Hallett, R., Gombert, K., & Hurley, M. (2020). 'Everyone should muck in': A qualitative study of parkrun volunteering and conflicting motivations. *Journal of Nonprofit and Public Sector Marketing*. https://doi.org/10.1080/10495142.2020.1760996.

Hindley, D. (2020). 'More than just a run in the park': An exploration of parkrun as a shared leisure space. *Leisure Sciences*, 42:1, 85–105.

Hitchings, R., & Latham, A. (2017). How 'social' is recreational running? Findings from a qualitative study in London and implications for public health promotion. *Health & Place*, 46, 337–343.

Honore, C. (2005). *In Praise of Slowness: Challenging the Cult of Speed*. New York: Harper One.

Hsu, E.L. (2015). The slow food movement and time shortage: Beyond the dichotomy of fast or slow. *Journal of Sociology*, 51:3, 628–642.

Koepnick, L. (2014). *On Slowness: Toward an Aesthetic of the Contemporary*. New York: Columbia University Press.

Lamb, D. (2019). Taking it day-by-day: An exploratory study of adult perspectives on slow living in an urban setting. *Annals of Leisure Research*, 22:4, 463–483.

Latham, A. (2015). The history of a habit: Jogging as a palliative to sedentariness in 1960s America. *Cultural Geographies*, 22:1, 103–126.

Masters, N. (2014). Parkrun eases the loneliness of the long-distance runner. *British Journal of General Practice*, 64:625, e408. https://doi.org/10.3399/bjgp14X681025.

Montanari, M. (1996). Beware! *Slow*, 1:2, 56–9.

Nettleton, S., & Hardey, M. (2006). Running away with health: The urban marathon and the construction of 'charitable bodies.' *Health: An Interdisciplinary Journal for the Social Study of Health, Illness and Medicine*, 10:4, 441–460.

Ogles, B.M., & Masters, K.S. (2000). Older vs. younger adult male marathon runners. Participative motives and training habits. *Journal of Sport Behaviour*, 23:2, 130–143.

Osbaldiston, N. (Ed.). (2013). *Culture of the Slow: Social Deceleration in an Accelerated World*. Basingstoke: Palgrave.

Parkins, W. (2004). Out of time: Fast subjects and slow living. *Time & Society*, 13:2–3, 363–382.

Parkins, W., & Craig, G. (2006). *Slow Living*. Oxford: Berg.

Parkrun. (2018). *Parkrun UK: 2017 Run Report*. Retrieved from https://blog.parkrun.com/uk/2018/04/24/2017-run-report/

Parkrun. (2021). *17 Years of parkrun*. Retrieved from https://blog.parkrun.com/uk/2021/10/01/17-years-of-parkrun/

Pedlar, C.R., Myrissa, K., Barry, M., Khwaja, I.G., Simpkin, A.J., Newell, J., Scarrott, C., Whyte, G.P., Kipps, C., & Baggish, A.L. (2021). Medical encounters at community-based physical activity events (parkrun) in the UK. *British Journal of Sports Medicine*. https://doi.org/10.1136/bjsports-2021-104256.

Petrini, C. (2003). *Slow Food: The Case for Taste*. New York: Columbia University Press.

Popan, C. (2018). *Bicycle Utopias: Imaging Fast and Slow Cycling*. London: Routledge.

Rauch, J. (2011). The origin of slow media: Early diffusion of a cultural innovation through popular and press discourse, 2002–2010. *Transformations*, 20.

Scheerder, J., Breedveld, K., & Borgers, J. (2015). Who is doing a run with the running boom? The growth and governance of one of Europe's most popular sport activities. In Scheerder, J., Breedveld, K., & Borgers, J. (Eds.), *Running Across Europe: The Rise and Size of One of the Largest Sport Markets* (pp. 1–27). Basingstoke: Palgrave.

Shilling, C. 2003. *The Body and Social Theory* (2nd ed.). London: Sage.

Shipway, R., & Jones, I. (2008). The Great Suburban Everest: An 'insiders' perspective on experiences at the 2007 Flora London Marathon. *Journal of Sport and Tourism*, 13:1, 61–77.

Smith, G. (2002). Racing against time? Aspects of the temporal organisation of the runner's world. *Symbolic Interaction*, 25:3, 343–362.

Smith, S.L. (1998). Athletes, runners, and joggers: Participant-group dynamics in a sport of 'individuals.' *Sociology of Sport Journal*, 15, 174–192.

Sniezek, T. (2021). Running while fat: How women runners experience and respond to size discrimination. *Fat Studies*, 10:1, 64–77.

Tomlinson, J. (2007). *The Culture of Speed: The Coming of Immediacy*. London: Sage.

Tuelle, E. (2007). Running to run: Embodiment, structure and agency amongst veteran elite runners. *Sociology*, 41:2, 329–346.

Vettenniemi, E. (2012). Prologue: Representations of running. *The International Journal of the History of Sport*, 29:7, 967–979.

Vos, S., & Scheerder, J. (2009). Loopsport in veelvoud. Naar een typologie van loopsporters [The rich spectrum of running. Towards a typology of runners]. In Scheerder, J., & Boen, F. (Eds.), *Vlaanderen loopt! Sociaal-wetenschappelijk onderzoek naar de loopsportmarkt* [Running in Flanders. The running market from a social science approach] (SBS Series 1) (pp. 267–287). Ghent: Academia Press.

Vos, S., Scheerder, J., Boen, F., & Feys, J. (2008). A typology of runners. Implications for marketing strategies (Paper presented at the 16th Conference of the European Association for Sport Management (EASM); Heidelberg; 10–13 September 2008). In Preuβ, H. & Gemeinder, K. (Eds.), *Book of Abstracts* (pp. 321–323). Heidelberg/Bayreuth: University of Heidelberg & University of Bayreuth.

Weinstein, N., Przybylski, A.K., & Ryan, R.M. (2009). Can nature make us more caring? Effects of immersion in nature on intrinsic aspirations and generosity. *Personality and Social Psychology Bulletin*, 35:10, 1315–1329.

Wilson, K. (1995). Olympians or lemmings? The postmodernist fun run. *Leisure Studies*, 14:3, 174–185.

Wiltshire, G.R., Fullagar, S., & Stevinson, C. (2018). Exploring parkrun as a social context for collective health practices: Running with and against the moral imperatives of health responsibilisation. *Sociology of Health & Illness*, 40:1, 3–17.

Chapter 6

Becoming a (park)runner

In the previous chapter I drew upon literature relating to slow living and the 'slow movement' as a way of reflecting upon parkrun and in particular how parkrun offers a domain in which walkers, joggers, runners, and the elite can cohabit. Relatedly, part of our attention was on parkrun's stated goal of attracting participants that were not runners before parkrun. Indeed, existing studies have identified that a sizeable number of participants identify themselves as non-runners at the time of registration and then through engagement with parkrun progress to regular exercise and increasing their fitness (Stevinson & Hickson, 2014). The purpose of this chapter is to examine how individuals' subjective identities may change after participation in parkrun. To this end, I am keen to consider the extent to which parkrun represents a vehicle or pathway for individuals who prior to parkrun were not runners to become runners. Furthermore, can subjective running identity explain how parkrun impacts upon individuals' health and wellbeing? A secondary focus within the chapter will be to draw on Stebbins' (1992) work on 'serious leisure' (which denotes defining characteristics such as the need for perseverance, effort, durable benefits, unique ethos, and sense of identity), thinking about the extent to which this conceptual lens can be applied to participants' transition to becoming a (park)runner. A third, related focus will be on presenting research that examines individuals' motivations for engaging in parkrun.

★

Latham (2015) documented the widespread proliferation during the 1960s of running as a means of mass participation, exploring how jogging was framed as physical exercise suitable for inactive middle-aged men and women. In this way jogging evolved as a counter to the problem of sedentary lifestyles, providing a source of self-fulfilment and bodily expression. Qvistrom's (2017) historical account of the 'jogging wave' in Sweden in the late 1970s similarly uncovered a close association with running for fitness and self-improvement. As such, running is bound up with ideas of healthiness, held up as one way to both achieve and demonstrate this (Perrier & Bridel, 2016, p. 205). Indeed, in a qualitative study by Hitchings and Latham (2017) involving casual, non-affiliated,

DOI: 10.4324/9781003121961-6

recreational runners in London, the respondents revealed that for them running had a largely instrumental orientation in that it provided direct, individual benefits. Nash (1979) meanwhile suggested that involvement in running events can be both an eventful and rewarding experience for participants, regardless of age, gender, or ability level. In this way, running affords a dual function: it promotes a person's health and gives meaning to their lives. Furthermore, it has been found that running can benefit individuals through providing a sense of mastery and self-confidence and, relatedly, has the capability to engender a particularly strong and valued identity (Allen-Collinson & Hockey, 2007).

For Baxter (2021) attempts to characterise running are far from straightforward. He argues to begin, ostensibly, it would appear to fall within the category of leisure, broadly defined as uncoerced activity engaged in during free time that is either satisfying or fulfilling (see Stebbins, 2012). More explicitly, it could also be labelled as a sport, and yet both of these definitions feel incomplete and unsatisfactory. As Baxter (2021, p. 4) reflects:

> Certainly, running can be a competitive sport with races, medals and championships, but is a gentle jog with a friend on a Sunday morning or a session on a treadmill really a sport or something else? For some, running might be better understood as part of a project of healthy living, a beauty practice, a weight loss tool, a social activity, a way to experience the outdoors or the limits of human endurance; for others, it could be best understood as a charity fundraising device or simply as a way of getting from A to B.

As the aforementioned illustrates, running then does not necessarily bear all the traditional characteristics of competitive sport. Likewise, it may also be possible to scrutinise the extent to which running corresponds with conventional definitions of leisure.[1] Furthermore, as outlined in Chapter 1, running is manifest in the wide array of pursuits, ranging from jogging to cross-country and from treadmill to ultramarathon, each considered as discrete practice and associated with different values and sporting identities. This disparateness, the way running 'appears to flex to fulfil different needs for different groups of people' (Baxter, 2021, p. 5), is integral to exploring what underlines the popularity of parkrun today. As such parkrun events act as public leisure spaces where a wide range of identities find expression and within which participants are active in structured processes of self-definition.

A prominent theme in existing empirical studies on parkrun is the meanings attached to health and fitness by parkrunners, internalising the neoliberal discourse of 'healthism' (see Poulson, 2016) in which responsibility for achieving a healthy society is delegated from the state to individuals. For Fitzpatrick and Tinning (2014, p. 5), notions of healthism refer to the desire to improve health and the consequent drive for 'many people to monitor their bodies and stems from a concern for being healthy, eating healthily and behaving in health-enhancing way.' In this regard, the individualised record of attendance and performance is noteworthy, providing self-monitoring opportunities for personal competence challenges, for example, improving finishing times, running the entire distance, or achieving milestones of the total number of runs. Consequently, some park-runners may become engaged in self-discipline through self-surveillance by appraising and comparing their performances (Warhurst & Black, 2021). Relat-edly, the pursuit of goals, for example, amassing runs to complete celebrated milestones, may, for some, help to develop an identity as a runner, facilitated by parkrun providing the means for mastery experiences (Stevinson et al., 2015).

The term 'serious leisure' offers a conceptual framework that can be used to argue that leisure could go beyond a simple recreational or free-time activity (Lee et al. 2016), referring to 'the systematic pursuit of an amateur, hobbyist, or volunteer activity' (Stebbins, 2014, p. 4). The adjective 'serious' embodies a number of qualities such as earnestness and importance, as well as emphasising the valuable role of 'serious pursuits' in self-fulfilment and benefits to wellbeing. Whilst the term has been utilised in a range of different leisure contexts, includ-ing climbing (Dilley & Scraton, 2010) and running events (Shipway & Jones, 2008), it has yet to be applied to parkrun. Serious leisure has been defined with a number of characteristics that distinguish it from *casual* leisure, which Steb-bins (2014, p. 4) describes as 'immediately intrinsically rewarding and relatively a short-lived pleasurable activity . . . fundamentally hedonistic, pursued for its significant level of pure enjoyment or pleasure.' These are a need to *persevere* in the activity, 'sticking with it through thick and thin'; the opportunity to follow a *career* in the endeavour; significant personal *effort* using their specially acquired knowledge, training, or skill; realisation of numerous *durable benefits*, or tan-gible, salutary outcomes of such activity for its participants, which could include self-expression, feelings of accomplishment, and sense of belonging; a unique *ethos*, related to the 'social world' (Unruh, 1980) inhabited by participants with shared attitudes, practices, values, and beliefs; and a strong *identification* with their chosen pursuit, becoming the basis for a distinctive identity (Elkington & Stebbins, 2014). According to Lee et al. (2016), an emphasis has been placed on the sixth characteristic, social identification with the activity, in order to better understand the behaviours of serious leisure participants – the argument being that social identity could be the starting point, and once established the other five characteristics could serve to strengthen this. For Shipway and Jones (2008) social identities are important in that they provide the individual with a sense of belonging and a means to connect with others with commensurate oppor-tunities to enhance self-esteem. Relatedly, social identity theory has grown in prominence in terms of its utility to explore group behaviours and belonging ('we') in a variety of sport-related contexts, rather than the individual or inter-personal level ('I'). By extension, social groups provide distinctive discourses and sustain particular narratives, which are appropriated and validated by individuals through their own identity work (Stevens et al., 2019).

In the context of committed amateur runners, there is a small but grow-ing body of literature which has focused on distance running identity as an example of serious leisure, interweaving its defining characteristics in its need for perseverance, effort involved, durable benefits, unique ethos, and sense of identity (Shipway & Jones, 2007, 2008). This positions running as a practice which pulls those doing it towards a distinctive running career, a career that begins with the initiation and socialisation of the individual into the 'social world' of running (Shipway et al., 2013) and is accompanied by a maturation process involving the acquisition and mastery of technical skills, 'inside' knowledge, expertise, and associations appropriate to the continued pursuit of the activity (Altheide & Pfuhl, 1980; Wilson, 1995). In this context, becoming a serious runner involves disciplining the body whereby participants subject themselves to techniques and processes concerned with regulating the body as an object of instrumental rationality (Tulle, 2007). In this way runners enter what Shilling (2003) describes as a 'body project' to be worked at through conscious reshaping, management, and maintenance. However, questions invariably arise as to what extent these notions can be applied to recreational and/ or casual runners. In a study involving accompanied runs and interviews with recreational runners who do not belong to running clubs in London, Hitchings and Latham (2017) found the respondents viewed running as a healthy habit as opposed to a career or serious leisure pursuit, were relatively uninterested in the idea of proper running technique, and were reticent about being pulled into a more committed collective practice. Conversely, as we have seen in earlier chapters, for some, participation in parkrun is manifest in exerting a degree of control over one's leisure time, impacting on habits and routines such as what they drank the previous evening and when they went to bed. Furthermore, parkrun has been described a religion, or cult, given the sense of tribalism and evangelism that the movement evokes among some of its disciples (Jones, 2021). A phenomenon which I would argue is apposite in this context is the growth in what has been dubbed 'parkrun tourism,' with an increasing number of 'parkrun tourists' planning trips in order to tick off unusual and scenic routes (Wilson, 2019).

In a conceptual paper published in the *International Journal of Culture, Tourism and Hospitality Research*, authors McKendrick et al. (2020) reflect on the nature of parkrun tourism and the challenges this presents to the understanding of sport tourism. In doing so, four faces of parkrun tourism are presented, spanning the domestic and global; the informal and formal; the organic and institutional; and the experience and commercial product. In relation to the global, parkrun tourism is conceived as having two dimensions: first as a commercial product, with a commercial sponsor, Exodus Travel, offering tourist packages to participate in a parkrun in different countries; second as 'a fusing together of kindred spirits' where parkrunners are encouraged to holiday with Exodus Travel, benefiting from the 'community feel' and sense of 'togetherness' that participation engenders. In relation to domestic parkrun tourism, two conceptualisations are presented: one which promotes collections of sub-types of parkrun, where the focus is centred on amassing a particular type of parkrun, which includes those defined by the character of the route, quirks around hostnames, geographic location, as well as the landscapes through which they pass. The other promotes the collection of as many parkruns as possible. These 'achievements' are celebrated through inclusion on a UK 'roll of honour' for those that have attended at least 20 different parkrun events in the UK. A global equivalent is also available for those who have attended 30 events.

The authors go on to discuss the contradictions and contested terrain of sports tourism, as well as the particular challenges that parkrun tourism presents to existing understandings of sport tourism. Here it is noted that there may be tensions between the local orientation of parkrun and what tourism tends to imply. For example, parkrun is positioned as a free and ostensibly accessible, mass participation event, convened within local parks, whereas tourism necessitates expense, and commonly framed as experiences that are beyond the means of many. 'These contradictions mean the encouragement of the parkrunner as a tourist who collects experiences – extending their community beyond the familiar of the everyday – might be viewed as a contradiction to the roots of parkrun' (McKendrick et al., 2020, p. 338).

The paper develops a multidimensional framework for re-conceptualising sports tourism through parkrun tourism. In doing so it is proposed that the sports tourist may be classified according to four dimensions: motivations; whether it is event-based; whether the participant is an active sporting participant; and providing it conforms to a locational constraint, whether the visit involves an overnight stay or a day visit that is beyond the local realm. The authors conclude by discussing the empirical directions for future research, potentially raising 'a rich vein of theoretical issues for scholars of sports tourism' (p. 344).

Drawing upon previous studies there are aspects of parkrun that may influence the formation of social identity: spaces that promote the cocreation of experiences and values, liminality, and *communitas*. As Warhurst and Black (2021, p. 4) note, 'membership of a favoured community, such as parkrun, can provide a liminal, enabling, space to explore or experiment with the construction of alternative, possible and preferred identities.' In this sense, parkrun events act as public spaces where participants are able to comingle, constructing their own experiences and creating different values depending on their interaction and engagement with the atmosphere and with other people. Engagement with parkrun can engender a subculture in which individuals (including strangers) of different social backgrounds, ages, and abilities congregate around the movement's shared values, providing collective emotional support from the wider group. The encouragement of casual sociability and the sense of camaraderie and community can strengthen the feeling of belonging and recognition as a member of a social group, serving to reinforce social identity. Thus, the collective parkrun experience can increase the emotional intensity of connections among participants and affirm the social identity in relation to serious leisure.

Reflecting on my own participant experiences as a seasoned parkrunner, taking part as a runner and a volunteer (including volunteering at junior parkrun), and a researcher of parkrun, I would tentatively propose there are elements of the 'social world' that Stebbins refers. Group membership is manifest through the use of subcultural capital such as clothing and language with self-presentation of a parkrunner identity clearly evident. Whilst there is diversity in terms of those present, most notably in terms of ages and abilities, it is commonplace to observe a degree of homogeneity in the appearance of participants at an event with a sizeable number bedecked in clothing identifying them as runners, most notably milestone parkrun T-shirts demonstrating recurrent participation. The latter could be construed as a 'badge of honour,' signifying a prized level of commitment and perseverance in the form of completed parkruns.

A clear limitation in this interpretation is, obviously, the anti-elitist, non-competitive ethos of the parkrun administration, which acclaims participation at parkrun as equal; whether someone chooses to walk, jog, run or volunteer, whether fast or slow, all are welcome and are valued the same. This mitigates against the possibility of hierarchies, which whilst laudable can present practical challenges, as evidenced by Fullagar et al. (2020), who noted,

> In terms of the friendly parkrun culture, some respondents felt that there was an insider/outsider dynamic created by established social networks in running groups. Such groups were often mentioned in relation to their more visible 'sport' identity (club clothing and competitiveness) which was thought to exclude non-sporty runners.
>
> (p. 8)

★

Several existing studies on parkrun have, consciously or unconsciously, reproduced existing typologies of runners' identities in seeking to discern different categories of participants, particularly when capturing pre-registration identity (Bowness et al., 2021). Drawing on running literature, attempts at segmentation tend to focus on psychographic characteristics for example, motivations and attitudes towards running. For example, Borgers et al. (2015) in their overview of running in Flanders (Belgium) identified five distinct cohorts of runners from the heterogeneous group of people that participate. These are 'the individual runner,' 'the social-competitive runner,' the 'social-community runner,' 'the health-and-fitness runner,' and 'the performance runner.' Other typologies include Smith (1998), who identified three participant groups involved in mass non-elite road running in Britain, namely athletes, runners, and joggers/fun runners, and Shipway (2008) who categorises runners into experienced 'insiders,' 'regular' runners, 'occasional' runners, and sporting 'outsiders.' In a more recent report, Evans (2020) presented a typology of runners who use Strava based on the benefits that a person values and the extent that they run in social settings such as groups or races. His work distinguishes five clusters of runners: passionate, invested, fitness, mindful, and reluctant.

The early work of Stevinson and Hickson (2014) divided their participants according to initial running status. Less than half the sample (47.8 per cent) identified themselves as regular runners when first registering for parkrun. The remainders were either occasional runner/joggers (26.5 per cent) or non-runners (25.8 per cent). Cleland et al. (2019) similarly developed a survey tool to describe pre-registration identity. Their work found that a similar proportion (47.2 per cent) identified as regular runners, although in contrast there were more occasional runners (38.2 per cent) than walkers/non-runners (14.6 per cent). Sharman et al. (2018) in their exploratory qualitative study of factors associated with driving initial and ongoing parkrun participation employed a similar typology based on their physical activity status prior to parkrun. These were regular runner/walker ($n = 4$), occasional runner/walker ($n = 4$), and non-runner/walker ($n = 2$). In my own intrinsic case study involving Colwick parkrun, participants were asked to identify their running status as 'competitive runner,' 'recreational runner,' 'club runner,' 'regular runner,' 'occasional runner,' or 'non-runner,' as well as noting their frequency of attendance at parkrun. The largest proportion of the sample identified themselves as regular runners (59.1 per cent), and 14 per cent labelled themselves as either occasional runners or non-runners (6.8 per cent). The majority of participants were unattached to a running club with 12.3 per cent identified as club runners. From the studies cited, it would appear prior to registration that the majority of parkrun participants already identify as runners. However, as Bowness et al. (2021) perceptively discern, none of this work has captured physical activity status or athletic self-identity beyond the initial point of parkrun registration to explore dynamic changes to subjective identity over time. And yet the nature of identity is that it is situational and variable; it shifts and alters with time, context, and interaction with others, and therefore it is constantly in the process of being (re)created (Weiss, 2001).

As outlined earlier, one of the central pillars of parkrun as a community-based public health intervention is the commitment to minimise the common barriers to exercise, thus differentiating it from traditional exercise opportunities that are predicated on conventional, often discriminatory structures. As such, the parkrun administration is explicit in their messaging that events are open to all abilities with an emphasis on people being able to participate in whatever manner is comfortable to them, whether that be through walking, jogging, running, volunteering, or turning up to spectate and support. Research suggests that parkrun's claims to be welcoming to a broad church of participants are, to a reasonable degree, justifiable with numerous studies noting its perceived inclusivity, successfully eliminating some of the traditional deterrents to physical activity for novice exercisers (Stevinson & Hickson, 2014; Stevinson et al., 2015; Hindley, 2020). An early study on parkrun (Stevinson et al., 2015) reported that 'the diversity of participants in terms of age, background, and running ability, made parkrun feel equally welcoming to all members of the community' (p. 172). A respondent in their study said, '[I]t isn't just fit, sporty running obsessed people who do it, there is a whole range of people who do parkrun which I think is great and it's very inclusive' (p. 173). Another remarked,

> [I]t does not allow me to use the barrier 'Oh I'm not going to be good enough' because it's so inclusive by involving everyone, and I know there are people who are slower that finish last every week, but still go and try.
> (p. 173)

As alluded to earlier, less well-established is our understanding of how parkrun may facilitate subjectivity change, for example, whether participation by former non-runners in parkrun may lead to engagement in running outside of the event.

The subjective athletic identities of those who initially self-identified as non-runners are the subject of a paper by Bowness et al. (2021) published in the journal *International Review for the Sociology of Sport*. Their study drew upon a UK-wide survey of parkrunners to explore the transformative potential of parkrun with a focus on comparing individuals who were new to running at registration to those who self-identified as being a runner when signing up to parkrun. Furthermore, the paper sought to examine whether the parkrun experience differs according to the extent to which non-runners transition to a running identity. The study pulls upon the social theory of Pierre Bourdieu to consider the connection between social identity as subject position on the one hand and individual health behaviours and public health on the other. In focusing on identity as dynamic, social, and embodied, Bowness et al. (2021) explored how parkrun participation impacts on running subjectivity over time and how this may subsequently impact on embodied experiences and overall wellbeing. As such the authors were interested in exploring the running trajectories of those who get involved in parkrun as non-runners, as ways of thinking about individual and structural change.

The study utilised a bespoke online survey which was distributed to Strava-using UK parkrunners. The sample consisted of 8,157 participants who accessed the survey online, of whom 7,271 fully completed it. Just over a half of the respondents had taken part in 11–49 parkruns with 20.1 per cent having taken part in fewer than ten. The survey explored eight themes: four of these were for profiling purposes with the remaining four exploring issues relating to identity, wellbeing, performance, and community. The findings speak to the notion that parkrun does not only appeal to runners, and more specifically, the analysis suggested that a significant number of those who were not runners prior to registration have now adopted the subject identity of 'runner.' Most non-runners/joggers had been involved in parkrun for over 1 year and took part either weekly or fortnightly. For them parkrun has provided the opportunity to become runners by cultivating the conditions necessary for them to develop a running habitus. Moreover, this group of participants was the most likely to suggest that parkrun had aided improvements to their 5 km performance, general fitness, and motivation to exercise. Bowness et al. (2021) suggest that if individuals envisage that parkrun participation is worthwhile in terms of producing tangible capital (improved performance, weight loss, increased body satisfaction, and so on) then participation is more likely to be maintained, ultimately leading to the emergence of becoming a 'runner.' Additionally, it was reported that 48.1 per cent of non-runners had extended their participation beyond parkrun events to become involved in organised running groups. This is echoed by research carried out by Sharman et al. (2018) which found that participation at parkrun often leads to individuals joining running clubs and attending other organised running events.

The authors argued that those who frequently engaged in parkrun perceived a variety of health and performance changes that became legitimising factors for new health/sport behaviours. The data suggest that parkrun provides a platform for individuals to become runners, whilst also providing sociological insights of how behaviour change may occur. Bowness et al. (2021) purport that parkrun is not a direct cause of changes to wellbeing and health but rather acts as a conduit to broader changes to health-related behaviour. They conclude,

> parkrun acts as a 'nudging' (Mols et al., 2015) springboard for identity change, which enables those who previously were non-runners to avail themselves of the opportunities that exist beyond parkrun, somethings through the use of organised athletics clubs or community running groups.
> (p. 715)

The theme of identity was the focus of a more recent article by Warhurst and Black (2021), two associate professors based at Newcastle Business School, Northumbria University, in which they sought to examine parkrun in the broader context of runners' lives, particularly their occupations. Their qualitative inquiry focused on professional and managerial workers. Eight female and 11 male parkrunners participated in the study with the participants holding a diversity of roles including clinician, professor, landscape-architect, and pharmacist. Participants had completed between 39 and 242 parkruns and were classified as 'runners' with most doing additional running each week. Data were generated from participants through an artefact-prompted conversational method with visual and narrative findings published in the journal *Qualitative Research in Sport, Exercise and Health*.

The authors' initial research question was to understand the popularity of parkrun by examining the interplay of parkrun and paid work. The results showed that a desired sense of self was unlikely to be derived from occupations, where their work was 'increasingly controlled by senior managers and external stakeholders, lacking in meaning and increasingly individualised. The consequence was that participants' identities were constrained and unsettled and that work had ceased to offer a satisfactory identity in itself' (Warhurst & Black, 2021, p. 12). In contrast, parkrun provided an additional identity dimension, enabling the construction of a more positive and satisfying sense of self. One participant in their study reflected,

> If I go running on my own, I just pootle around, but being among like-minded people helps me push myself and get the best out of myself. And when you do achieve something, everyone bigs you up and you get the recognition that is rare in work. And if you don't achieve, the others make you realise it's worth the effort. I think that they now see me as runner and here among 'this lot' [smiling and pointing to a picture of her group at parkrun] I am pleased that I am no longer just 'Dianne the doctor.'
>
> (p. 11)

This testimony not only illustrates how the parkrun community enables and sustains an alternative, desired, identity but also reveals some of the deficiencies in professional and managerial work and how workers wish to be more than their occupation. As such 'parkrun provided a resource for coping by enabling the construction of a coherent and secure sense-of-self to replace the fragmented and often threatened identities built around work' (p. 12). It is noted how the parkrun community provided distinct discursive resources that were separate from work and that enabled and sustained new identity narratives; in this community individuals were first and foremost runners and not managers or professionals. As this respondent remarked,

> Through running I have realised I am good at something. I am finding myself. I like people to know that I do parkrun and to be seen as a runner. It makes me feel better about myself, makes me feel different. It has improved my self confidence as a result. It is almost like being an actor, I am becoming a different type of person; it's given me a new identity, here [pointing to his well-worn running shoes] I'm not Dave the teacher but Dave the runner.
>
> (p. 9)

Conversely, it is acknowledged how parkrun could readily constrain and regulate runners' identities with an emphasis on self-surveillance and where performance comparisons are normalised.

> While certain participants complained about routinisation of their work, there is some irony in their running and valuing parkrun given the totally predictable nature of the weekly event. Identities built around parkrun might thus be just as instrumentalised and as performance and achievement orientated as identities built upon managerial and professional occupations given the constraining ways that these occupations are now typically defined under neo-liberalism.
>
> (p. 13)

In concluding Warhurst and Black (2021) adopt a nuanced stance, stressing that identities are multiple, interleaved, and potentially conflicted. Consequently, it is likely that participants within their study might identify both as a professional or manager *and* as a parkrunner.

★

There is a growing body of evidence which suggests that social identities may have profound implications for physical activity participation. This was the premise behind the study by Stevens et al. (2019) which drew upon a sample of 289 parkrunners in the south of England, all of whom had completed at least one parkrun in the 6 months prior to completing the study. The authors hypothesised that the stronger the identification with parkrun, the more motivated the individual will be to engage in behaviours normative of the group; in this case, running. Their study examined associations between group identification, participation, an affective exercise outcome, a key group construct, and an indicator of overall health in parkrun. Results revealed an array of exercise-specific benefits associated with developing a strong social identity in the parkrun setting. These included observing a significant relationship between group identification and participation. The authors contended that, in this case where regular participation is a group norm, individuals' desire to align their behaviour with this norm may have positive implications. The findings also suggested that the strength of individuals' identity as a parkrunner is associated with their satisfaction with their parkrun experiences. It is important to note, however, that whilst previous research has demonstrated that individuals' overall exercise participation and life satisfaction are positively associated (Grant et al., 2009), the findings of this study indicated that parkrun participation alone (at most a once-per-week activity) is not associated with greater life satisfaction. In seeking to explain the non-significant relationship between parkrun identification and life satisfaction, Stevens et al. (2019) cite the work of Sato et al. (2015), who suggest that for running to boost life satisfaction, an increase in running volume is necessary.

In a later study, Davis et al. (2021) examined the influence of social perceptions and behaviour on enjoyment, energy, fatigue, effort, and performance among a sample of adult parkrunners in southern England. The authors highlight that preliminary evidence suggests exercising with others as opposed to exercising alone has a number of benefits, including greater exercise adherence, greater pain thresholds, and improvements in performance. The aim of their study was to build on these findings to develop and test the hypothesis that social reward and support in exercise are associated with positive exercise experiences and enhanced performance. Participants were recruited from six parkrun sites, situated in close proximity to Oxford. Surveys were administered online every Saturday morning for the duration of the study, requesting that participants completed the survey as soon as possible after their run. In total, 188 parkrunners consented to take part; 144 participants completed the survey at least once with a total of 734 usable surveys. Survey responses confirmed previous findings of high levels of sociality at parkrun with running with others being the predominant motivation for attending. Perceived support from others and being a part of the parkrun community was reported as high, as were subjective enjoyment, energy, effort, and fatigue. In short 'the descriptive picture is of a positive and facilitative social context for invigorating and challenging self-paced exercise' (p. 11). Social predictors meanwhile had positive effects on subjective enjoyment, energy, and performance. Overall, the results suggest potential beneficial effects of social reward and perceived social support on enjoyment and energy with potential regulatory effects on performance. These lead the authors to advise

> that there should be greater research attention on how positive and rewarding social behaviours and experiences – particularly subjective enjoyment and energy, and perceptions of community social support and belonging – influence exercise-related behaviour, psychology, and physiology, and promote health through collective physical activity.
>
> (p. 1)

★

There is an emerging body of literature investigating how motivation affects physical activity participation and what influences individuals' initiation and maintenance of active behaviour. That said, existing studies have concentrated on analysing the motivations of seasoned runners, for example, long-distance runners; in contrast, there is little research on the initial impetus to take up running, for example, what motivates an inactive individual to start attending parkrun. This was the focus of a study by Malchrowicz-Mosko et al. (2020) published in *Frontiers in Public Health*, which aimed to investigate the motivations of beginner runners to take part in parkrun in Poznan, Poland. Understanding the reasons why people decide to engage in physical activity is obviously important from the perspective of health promotion and the potential of mass participation events to encourage physically active leisure (Funk et al., 2011). Also incorporated within their study was City Trail, a mass participation initiative that was started in Poland in 2010 as a response to a shortage of 5 km runs, in contrast to the rising number of marathons and half marathons. Not dissimilar to parkrun, City Trail is predicated on the assumption that running is for everyone, including novice runners and families with children. Runs are regularly organised in the autumn and winter in major Polish cities, attracting up to 20,000 participants annually.

For the purposes of the study a beginner runner was defined as an individual with no prior running training and not being involved in regular sporting activities. Sociodemographic variables were also considered, including age, gender, and educational level. A total of 165 inexperienced runners, taken from across parkrun and City Trail, were surveyed, completing a MOMS (Motivations of Marathoner Scale) questionnaire. The sample consisted of 82 men and 83 women. Only individuals who had not previously engaged in running and had not led an active lifestyle according to WHO (exercise for at least 150 minutes a week) prior to participating in parkrun and City Trail were asked to participate. The sample allowed the researchers to study individuals who took up physical activity and running thanks to initiatives such as parkrun.

Assessment of the impact that participation in parkrun events had on runners' overall level of physical activity found an increase in activity over 6 months, but this effect was less pronounced after 12 months. The increase was most marked among those individuals with low levels of physical activity, which consequently became close to the recommended weekly level due to their participation in parkrun. According to the study, the highest-rated motivations for beginner runners were related to health orientation and personal goal achievement. In contrast, the lowest-rated motivations were related to recognition and competition. The study reports that almost 75 per cent of respondents made an independent decision to start running in parkrun and City Trail, whereas a statistically significant (higher) difference was found on the affiliation scale among those who had been encouraged to participate by other people. With regard to differences by gender, the results showed that men were more likely to start running due to competition-related motivations, whereas women were more often related to affiliation, psychological coping, life meaning, and self-esteem. As age increased, the level of motivation due to personal goal achievement, competition, and recognition scales decreased. The authors concluded that the study has practical implications for event managers and practitioners working in public health, suggesting that promoting safe running among people who have no experience with this sport is as important as encouraging them to run.

In a separate empirical study, researchers sought to determine the reasons for practising different running distances, which incorporated the Pozman parkrun in its analysis. Additionally, the analysis considered sociodemographic variables including gender, age, and marital status. The study by Rozmiarek et al. (2021) was conducted during the 2020 Karkonosze Winter Ultramarathon, 20th PKO Poznan Marathon, and the two aforementioned 5 km runs, Poznan parkrun and City Trail. A total of 267 ultramarathoners, 493 marathon runners, and 165 parkrun and City Trail participants took part in the cross-sectional study. Data were collected using an online interview questionnaire, which employed the division of motives used by the MOMS cited earlier. Focusing on the 5 km distance, the authors cited motivation studies by Bell (2013) and Bell and Stephenson (2014) in relation to the Theory of Reasoned Action, looking at attitude motivation during the race according to skill levels. Past results from Pennsylvania runners indicated that health, social affiliation, and altruism influenced the attitudes of low- and medium-ability runners. It is observed that the results of their study showed how motivation scores related to health orientation and affiliation are higher in 5 km and marathon runners than in ultramarathoners. Drawing on existing studies, it is noted that younger athletes were more motivated by personal achievement, whilst 'older runners were motivated by the meaning of life and a sense of belonging with other runners, but above all, by general health orientation and concern about weight' (p. 8). Additionally, among 5 km and marathon runners, weight concern decreased in the 36 to 50 age range and subsequently increased in those over 51 years of age. The authors advised that understanding the differences in motivation noted between the groups of runners identified can be useful for practitioners, for example, coaches, sports psychologists, and health professionals, when promoting participation.

Chivunze et al. (2021) also sought to identity the motives for participation in parkrun, in this case seeking to ascertain the physical activity-related behavioural changes among registered parkrunners in the Western Cape Province of South Africa. Participants ($n = 1,787$) completed either an online questionnaire or face-to-face survey consisting of demographic history, parkrun participation history, motivations for participation, and physical activity-related behaviour changes associated with parkrun participation. To be eligible in either format, participants had to be over 18 years of age, registered with one of 37 parkrun sites located in the Western Cape, and completed a minimum of two parkrun events in the preceding 6 months. The majority of participants surveyed were female (53.3 per cent) and aged 50 years or over, which as the authors note is comparable with parkrun participation globally. Participants reported having a higher education qualification similar to previous studies (Stevinson & Hickson, 2018) with only 3 per cent of respondents reported to be unemployed, significantly less than the national unemployment rate at the time of the study. As with the studies outlined earlier in the chapter, multiple motives were identified for initiating participation in parkrun. These involved the perceived health and fitness-related benefits, including positive changes in weight, increases in cardiorespiratory fitness, and improvements in mental wellbeing. An additional benefit highlighted by the authors was the potential to earn Discovery Health Vitality points. Discovery Health is South Africa's largest private medical aid covering healthcare costs, which rewards its members with points when engaged in health/fitness-related activities. 'Almost half of the participants in this study reported the ability to earn these points as a key motivation for participation' (p. 6). As with the study by Rozmiarek et al. (2021), the provision of a safe environment for physical activity by parkrun was identified as a motive for participation, particularly among women respondents. Additionally, the social connectedness from an organised, weekly mass participation event was cited with over half the sample reporting socialisation to be influential to their participation. This supports previous findings (e.g. Stevinson et al., 2015). The large majority of participants (83.4 per cent) were physically active (regular or occasional exercisers) prior to joining parkrun with only a small percentage classifying themselves as inactive. Almost half of all respondents self-reported increased physical activity levels since beginning parkrun with close to three quarters of non-exercisers integrating regular exercise into their daily life. In summary, Chivunze et al. (2021) noted that 'parkrun provides a protected and engaging environment that provides opportunity for increased physical activity and potentially reducing the burden on the healthcare system' (p. 1).

The importance of having a safe environment when exercising was a theme identified in the findings of a study published in the journal *Critical Public Health*. Barnfield (2016) examined recreational running in Sofia, Bulgaria, a country traditionally with low levels of physical activity participation. The study incorporated two recreational running groups, one of which was Sofia parkrun, which takes place in South Park (Yuzhen Park) in Sofia. A range of methods were employed, including participant observation, with the author drawing on their own experiences of running as a source of insight into runners' practices. Additionally, an online survey was sent to members of the running groups (153 responses) with participants varying in levels of experience and expertise, which was followed by semi-structured interviews with 14 runners. The interviews questioned, among other things, runners' use of urban space, how they constructed their running routines, the meanings they attached to their running practices, and the technologies they used to participate. Barnfield (2016) concluded that recreation running groups, such as parkrun, helped to challenge the constraints of the urban space of Sofia by providing settings where a variety of bodies and objects can be brought together to open up new opportunities for organisation and participation. It was noted that recreational runners in Sofia are faced with many challenges, which include the quality and provision of facilities, surfaces and routes, air pollution, and volume of traffic. Barnfield (2016) contended that developing an openness towards bodily movement was vital, advocating support for running infrastructure and better maintenance of green spaces to help nurture the wider spread of participation.

★

In conclusion, this chapter has set out to explore the transformative potential of parkrun, presenting published empirical research which has reported how parkrun may provide individuals with the opportunity to become 'runners' by cultivating the conditions for them to develop a running habitus (Bowness et al., 2021). In turn, I have drawn upon recent scholarship which has sought to understand how parkrun can alter physical activity behaviours and how parkrun might work in encouraging individuals to engage in opportunities that exist beyond parkrun, for example, through the use of community running groups or registering for organised running events. More broadly, our attention has extended to consider the serious leisure perspective in explaining how individuals come to acquire their running identity. In this way parkrunners become part of a social world that allows for both individual engagement and a shared, communal experience. Latterly, we have contemplated how group identification may promote greater exercise participation so that participants who identified more strongly as a member of the parkrun community may lead them to engaging more regularly. This leads us finally to consider the motivations of parkrunners, in particular the motivations of novice runners to take part; the resulting literature adds to what we already know about parkrun and has implications for our understanding of how mass participation events may increase positive attitudes towards physical activity.

Note

1 For example, it has been asserted that running shares some similarities with work and as such has depicted the practice less favourably (see Bale, 2004).

References

Allen-Collinson, J., & Hockey, J. (2007). 'Working Out' identity: Distance runners and the management of disrupted identity. *Leisure Studies*, 26:4, 381–398.

Altheide, D.L., & Pfuhl, E.H. (1980). Self-accomplishment through running. *Symbolic Interaction*, 3, 127–142.

Barnfield, A. (2016). Public health, physical exercise and non-representational theory – A mixed method study of recreational running in Sofia, Bulgaria. *Critical Public Health*, 26:3, 281–293.

Baxter, N. (2021). *Running, Identity and Meaning: The Pursuit of Distinction Through Sport*. Bingley: Emerald Publishing.

Bell, N.M. (2013). *Motivation to Run: Using Fishbein & Ajzen's Theory of Reasoned Action to Predict Participation in 5K Races*. Indiana, PA: ProQuest Dissertations Publishing.

Bell, N.M., & Stephenson, A.L. (2014). Variation in motivations by running ability: Using the theory of reasoned action to predict attitudes about running 5K races. *Journal of Policy Research in Tourism, Leisure and Events*, 3, 231–247. https://doi.org/10.1080/19407963. 2014.933227.

Borgers, J., Vos, S., & Scheerder, J. (2015). Belgium (Flanders). Trends and governance in running. In Scheerder, J., Breedveld, K., & Borgers, J. (Eds.), *Running Across Europe: The Rise and Size of One of the Largest Sport Markets* (pp. 28–58). Basingstoke: Palgrave.

Bowness, J., McKendrick, J., & Tulle, E. (2021). From non-runner to parkrunner: Subjective athletic identity and experience of parkrun. *International Review for the Sociology of Sport*, 56:5, 695–718.

Chivunze, E., Burgess, T.L., Carson, F., & Buchholtz, K. (2021). Motivation and behaviour change in parkrun participants in the Western Cape Province, South Africa. *International Journal of Environmental Research and Public Health*, 18, 8102. https://doi.org/10.3390/ ijerph18158102.

Cleland, V., Nash, M., Sharman, M.J., & Claflin, S. (2019). Exploring the health-promoting potential of the parkrun phenomenon: What factors are associated with higher levels of participation? *American Journal of Health Promotion*, 33:1, 13–23.

Davis, A.J, MacCarron, P., & Cohen, E. (2021). Social reward and support effects on exercise experiences and performance: Evidence from parkrun. *PLoS ONE*, 16:9, e0256546.

Dilley, R.E., & Scraton, S.J. (2010). Women, climbing and serious leisure. *Leisure Studies*, 29:2, 125–141.

Elkington, S., & Stebbins, R.A. (2014). *The Serious Leisure Perspective: An Introduction*. London: Routledge.

Evans, B. (2020). Why we run: An exploration of who and what motivates us to run. *Strava*. Retrieved from https://whywerun.strava.com/assets/whitepaper/Whitepaper_Strava_WhyWeRun_012320.pdf

Fitzpatrick, K., & Tinning, R. (Eds.). (2014). *Health Education: Critical Perspectives*. London: Routledge.

Fullagar, S., Petris, S., Sargent, J., Allen, S., Akhtar, M., & Ozakinci, G. (2020). Action research with parkrun UK volunteer organisers to develop inclusive strategies. *Health Promotion International*, 35, 1199–1209.

Funk, D., Jordan, J., Ridinger, L., & Kaplanidou, K. (2011). Capacity of mass participant sport events for the development of activity commitment and future exercise intention. *Leisure Sciences*, 33:3, 250–268.

Grant, N., Wardle, J., & Steptoe, A. (2009). The relationship between life satisfaction and health behaviour: A cross-cultural analysis of young adults. *International Journal of Behavioural Medicine*, 16:3, 259–268.

Hindley, D. (2020). 'More than just a run in the park': An exploration of parkrun as a shared leisure space. *Leisure Sciences*, 42:1, 85–105.

Hitchings, R., & Latham, A. (2017). How 'social' is recreational running? Findings from a qualitative study in London and implications for public health promotion. *Health & Place*, 46, 337–343.

Jones, E. (2021). *How Parkrun Changed Our Lives*. Hebden Bridge: Gritstone Publishing.

Latham, A. (2015). The history of a habit: Jogging as a palliative to sedentariness in 1960s America. *Cultural Geographies*, 22(1): 103–126.

Lee, I.S., Brown, G., King, K., & Shipway, R. (2016). Social identity in serious sport event space. *Event Management*, 20, 491–499.

Malchrowicz-Mosko, E., Leon-Guereno, P., Tapia-Serrano, M.A., Sanchez-Miguel, P.A., & Waskiewicz, Z. (2020). What encourages physically inactive people to start running? An analysis of motivations to participate in parkrun and City Trail in Poland. *Frontiers in Public Health*, 8.

McKendrick, J.H., Bowness, J., & Tulle, E. (2020). In search of parkrun tourism: Destabilising contradictions or progressive conceptual tensions? *International Journal of Culture, Tourism and Hospitality Research*, 14:3, 335–347.

Mols, F., Haslam, S.A., Jetten, J., & Steffens, N.K. (2015). Why a nudge is not enough: A social identity critique of governance by stealth. *European Journal of Political Research*, 54:1, 81–98. https://doi.org/10.1111/1475-6765.12073.

Nash, J.E. (1979). Weekend racing as an eventful experience: Understanding the accomplishment of well-being. *Urban Life*, 8:2, 199–217.

Perrier, M.-J., & Bridel, W. (2016). An interdisciplinary conversation about running between two academics who run. In Bridel, W., Markula, P., & Denison, J. (Eds.), *Endurance Running: A Socio-cultural Explanation* (pp. 196–211). Abingdon: Routledge.

Poulson, S.C. (2016). *Why Would Anyone Do That?: Lifestyle Sport in the Twenty-First Century*. New Brunswick, NJ: Rutgers University Press.

Qvistrom, M. (2017). Competing geographies of recreational running: The case of the "jogging wave" in Sweden in the late 1970s. *Health & Place*, 46, 351–357.

Rozmiarek, M., Malchrowicz-Mosko, E., Leon-Guereno, P., Tapia-Serrano, M.A., & Kwiatkowski, G. (2021). Motivational differences between 5K runners, marathoners and ultramarathoners in Poland. *Sustainability*, 13:6980. https://doi.org/10.3390/su13126980.

Sato, M., Jordan, J.S., & Funk, D.C. (2015). Distance running events and life satisfaction: A longitudinal study. *Journal of Sport Management*, 29:4, 347–361.

Sharman, M.J., Nash, M., & Cleland, V. (2018). Health and broader community benefit of parkrun – An exploratory qualitative study. *Health Promotion Journal of Australia*, 30, 163–171.

Shilling, C. 2003. *The Body and Social Theory* (2nd ed.). London: Sage.

Shipway, R. (2008). Road trip: Understanding the social world of the distance runner as sport tourist. In *Proceedings of CAUTHE 2008 Annual Conference: Tourism and Hospitality Research, Bowness et al. 717 Training and Practice: 'Where the "Bloody Hell" Are We?', Griffith University, Gold Coast, Queensland, Australia, 11–14 February*.

Shipway, R., Holloway, I., & Jones, I. (2013). Organisations, practices, actors, and events: Exploring inside the distance running social world. *International Review for the Sociology of Sport*, 48:3, 259–276.

Shipway, R., & Jones, I. (2007). Running away from home: Understanding visitor experiences in sport tourism. *International Journal of Tourism Research*, 9:5, 373–383.

Shipway, R., & Jones, I. (2008). The great suburban Everest: An 'insiders' perspective on experiences at the 2007 Flora London Marathon. *Journal of Sport & Tourism*, 13:1, 61–77.

Smith, S.L. (1998). Athletes, runners, and joggers: Participant-group dynamics in a sport of "Individuals". *Sociology of Sport Journal*, 15:2, 174–192.

Stebbins, R.A. (1992). *Amateurs, Professionals, and Serious Leisure*. Montreal, QC and Kingston, ON: McGill-Queen's University Press.

Stebbins, R.A. (2012). *The Idea of Leisure: First Principles*. New Brunswick, NJ: Transaction.

Stebbins, R.A. (2014). *Careers in Serious Leisure: From Dabbler to Devotee in Search of Fulfilment*. Basingstoke: Palgrave.

Stevens, M., Rees, T., & Polman, R. (2019). Social identification, exercise participation, and positive exercise experiences: Evidence from parkrun. *Journal of Sports Sciences*, 37:2, 221–228.

Stevinson, C., & Hickson, M. (2014). Exploring the public health potential of a mass community participation event. *Journal of Public Health*, 36:2, 268–274.

Stevinson, C., & Hickson, M. (2018). Changes in physical activity, weight and wellbeing outcomes among attendees of a weekly mass participation event: A prospective 12-month study. *Journal of Public Health*, 41:4, 807–814.

Stevinson, C., Wiltshire, G., & Hickson, M. (2015). Facilitating participation in health-enhancing physical activity: A qualitative study of parkrun. *International Journal of Behavioural Medicine*, 22, 170–177.

Tulle, E. (2007). Running to run: Embodiment, structure and agency amongst veteran elite runners. *Sociology*, 41:2, 329–346.

Unruh, D. (1980). The nature of social worlds. *Pacific Sociological Review*, 23, 271–296.

Warhurst, R., & Black, K. (2021). Lost and found: parkrun, work and identity. *Qualitative Research in Sport, Exercise and Health*. https://doi.org/10.1080/2159676X.2021.1924244.

Weiss, O. (2001). Identity reinforcement in sport. Revisiting the symbolic interactionist legacy. *International Review for the Sociology of Sport*, 36:4, 393–405.

Wilson, A. (2019). Parkrun tourism: 10 of the best routes in the UK and worldwide. *The Guardian*. Retrieved from www.theguardian.com/travel/2019/feb/07/10-most-scenic-parkruns-in-uk-worldwide-running-routes

Wilson, K. (1995). Olympians or lemmings? The postmodernist fun run. *Leisure Studies*, 14:3, 174–185.

Chapter 7

Green Exercise

The coronavirus pandemic and subsequent restrictions have unarguably turned our ways of living upside down. Our new anxiety-filled world of uncertainty has, during periods of lockdown, diminished opportunities to see loved ones and constrained opportunities for recreation and restoration. For many, parks have taken on a heightened significance, becoming one of few accessible public spaces for exercise, relaxation, and where social interaction with others was deemed permissible. At the time politicians and scientists advocated these municipal green spaces as central to maintaining individuals' physical and mental well-being, 'being outside in the park is a very good thing to do,' endorsed Chief Medical Officer Chris Whitty in a statement that is often recycled.[1] In the UK, park visits increased dramatically as many used their local park for the first time during the first national lockdown and as restrictions were eased parks became busier than they ever had previously.[2] As Matthew Bradbury, Chair of the Parks Alliance, observed, 'the pandemic changed the relationship between people and their local parks for ever' afore underlining the numerous and established benefits such accessible green spaces provide for health and wellbeing.[3]

Such proclamations are nothing new but whose antecedents can be traced back to the municipal park movement of the Victorian era when it was envisaged that parks would provide health benefits, help ameliorate social unrest and crime, as well as providing 'green lungs' for congested and polluted towns and cities (Maller et al., 2009). At the time when parks were 'invented' in response to increasingly high-density, industrialised conditions, the bulk of the population were unlikely to have access to a garden or even a yard. Historian Travis Elborough (2016) evocatively recites 'ecologically speaking, parks were widely deployed as tools to tame supposed wildness among the population, ease alienation and see off social discord' (p. 4). As Dr Hilary Taylor (1994) contends, the public park was a metaphor for a notion of the civilised society, 'cementing a society which was viewed as threateningly unstable in its diversity and growth.' Municipal parks were places, which, on a utilitarian level, can be understood as a rational response to the rapidly expanding urban population, associated with notions of public health, and envisaged as a way to improve the wellbeing of Victorian city dwellers.

DOI: 10.4324/9781003121961-7

Fast-forward and to the present-day urbanite, parks are perceived as part of the fabric of the city, not separate from it (Burgess et al., 1988). Layton and Latham (2021) make a compelling case for framing parks as key pieces of 'social infra-structure' as a way of thinking about the social lives of parks and the potential of such public spaces in facilitating a diverse range of social connections. Public parks inhabit a unique temporal zone, a sanctuary where one is able to feel a sense of 'being away' from the bustle of workaday life and often imbued with affectionate childhood recollections of exploration and discovery (Elborough, 2016). But our cosy familiarity with public parks should neither overshadow nor distract us from their increasing vulnerability through years of underfunding and neglect. With local authorities under intensifying financial pressure, they are likely to prioritise statutory obligations, leaving discretionary services, including parks, under threat. According to the *State of UK Public Parks* 2016 report, 92 per cent of council parks departments have experienced tightening budgets. In 2019, Bristol City Council announced that spending on parks would be with-drawn, relying solely on revenue generated. The parks budget for Newcastle City Council has been reduced by 90 per cent over 7 years. Rather than treasured community assets, parks have been reduced to a Cinderella service, leading to inattention and disrepair.

This pattern of declining provision of publicly accessible parks and green spaces needs to be situated in the broader context of urbanisation where the majority of us live isolated indoor lives, separated from the natural world. According to the charity Fields in Trust, over 2.69 million people don't live within easy walking distance of a green space.[4] As Lucy Jones (2020) laments in her book *Losing Eden*, 'within the winnowing landscape and downward trends, there is deep inequality in access and connection' (p. 124). Research high-lights children from low-income families and black, Asian, and minority ethnic households are markedly less likely to regularly visit natural settings than white children and those from higher income households (Natural England, 2019). These disparities became exacerbated during the coronavirus pandemic with people living in deprived wards and those from BAME backgrounds occupying the most densely populated neighbourhoods and having less access to private gardens and municipal parks. Ethnographic researcher Beth Collier (2019) sug-gests this chain of disconnect for people of colour is generational with deep-rooted cultural attitudes and racialised narratives contributing to a process of disenfranchisement.

Since entering fatherhood, I am well aware (pre-pandemic) of the incontro-vertible fact that my infant daughter, Rowan, and her generation will spend an increasing amount of time confined indoors. This is most starkly illustrated in a 2016 survey which found that three quarters of UK children (aged 5 to 12) spend less time outdoors than prison inmates[5] whereas it has been reported that only 10 per cent of today's generation of youth has regular access to nature, compared to 40 per cent of adults who did so when they were young (Natural England, 2009). Concerns about children's disconnection from nature have been brought to the fore by author Richard Louv, whose book *Last Child in the Woods* introduced the term 'nature-deficit disorder' to describe how the cosseted young no longer spend time alone, exploring nature. Alienation from the natural world, Louv (2005) suggests, leads to diminished use of the senses, difficulties with paying attention, and higher rates of physical and emotional illnesses. Like many parents, I'm keen to cultivate for my daughter the same wide-eyed fascination for nature and the outdoors that I experienced during my formative years, albeit in a metropolitan city where we live rather than a rural Leicestershire village where I was brought up. Parks and play areas have become an established fixture at weekends, sometimes incorporating parkrun, although it is away from these manicured and managed environments that perceptibly Rowan is most at ease and her most animated. She is happiest exploring wilder environs or woodland, clambering up trees, searching for ladybirds, and letting her imagination roam free.

We know, instinctively, that being exposed to nature makes us feel better. This observation has spawned a number of theoretical accounts for why spending time in natural environments can improve our moods, many of which use an evolutionary framework (Schertz et al., 2021). As biologist Edward O. Wilson proposes in his book, *Biophilia* (1984), through our evolution as human beings rooted in ecology, we have a primal emotional connection with other living organisms. Innately, we are drawn to be in and around nature. This idea is central to the Biophilia Hypothesis and helps to account for why there is a booming millennial economy in houseplants, the popularity of majestic natural landscapes as laptop screensavers, as well as how we regularly turn to aspects of the natural world on a linguistic and mental level (see Jones, 2020; Williams, 2017). However, this theory does not specify how nature impacts emotional functioning (Kellert & Wilson, 1995).

As stated, there is a mounting body of robust and wide-ranging scientific evidence that exposure to, or contact with, natural environments (such as parks, playing fields, and beaches) is associated with health and wellbeing benefits. Research studies and systematic reviews have shown that contact (either presence or visual) with nature – trees, grass, indoor plants, or even a view from a window – has therapeutic potential for mental health, proven to elevate mood, vitality, and feelings of restoration, reducing blood pressure and stress levels (e.g. Kaplan, 2001; Wells, 2000). Additionally, there is growing peer-reviewed evidence that exercise in natural spaces has greater psychological benefits than the equivalent physical activity indoors or in-built environments (Pretty et al., 2005; Thompson Coon et al., 2011). Moreover, access to local green spaces increases the probability that individuals will achieve the recommended physical activity guidelines by over four times (Flowers et al., 2016). Consequently, green space has a multilayered potential – what Lucy Jones describes 'a club sandwich' – to influence a range of positive health outcomes. In contrast, relatively little is known with regard to how much time in nature, and how often, is needed to generate these apparent benefits. What form(s) exposure or experience of nature is required? Is the type or quality of green space important when considering optimal psychological benefits? In other words, how might the health benefits of parkrun compare between different locations which vary in their environmental scenery such as the presence of water features? Evidence is also sparse when it comes to being able to demonstrate to what extent the short-term physiological and psychological changes we experience in natural environments translate into longer-term benefits.

Past studies have shown that looking at the natural world – even if it is just a picture – can ameliorate stress levels and provide wellbeing benefits. A seminal, frequently cited 1984 study by physician Roger Ulrich (1984) discovered how post-operative hospital patients that were assigned a room with a natural view out of a window (in this case looking out onto deciduous trees) in contrast to those that looked out onto a brick wall had a demonstrative restorative effect. The researchers reported that these recovering patients had shorter post-surgical stays, had fewer negative evaluative comments in nurses' notes, and took fewer moderate and strong analgesic dosages. This early study provides a partial confirmation of the Biophilia Hypothesis with implications for the practice of medicine and the design of healthcare facilities.

In the intervening period, studies have sought to expand on Ulrich's work, exploring the association between the natural environment and human health (and conversely, whether our modern-day estrangement from nature is making people less physically active and more mentally stressed). In 2019, research published by White et al. in the journal *Scientific Reports* suggested that a 2-hour 'dose' of nature a week has significant health and wellbeing benefits. Participants ($n = 19,806$) were drawn from the Monitor of Engagement with the Natural Environment Survey, which was weighted to be nationally representative. Analyses controlled for residential green space and other neighbourhood and individual factors, whilst also explicitly excluding time spent in one's own garden. Compared to those who reported no nature contact in the previous week, the likelihood of reporting good health or high wellbeing became significantly greater with contact of 2 hours or more. Interestingly, the pattern was consistent across key groups including older adults and those with long-term health illnesses and disabilities. The researchers were also intrigued to discover that it did not matter how the 120-minute threshold was achieved – for example, whether taken in one go or a series of shorter visits – whilst exposure 'quality' in terms of wildlife richness suggests that health and wellbeing outcomes may be more pronounced in more biodiverse settings.

Liisa Tyrainen and colleagues at the National Resources Institute of Finland studied different environments in Helsinki that are accessible to city dwellers, comparing a built-up area, an urban park, and managed woodland. The team of researchers was interested in the influence of the settings on participants' feelings of restoration, vitality, mood, creativity, and salivary cortisol concentration (commonly used as a biomarker of psychological stress). As part of the experiment, which was published in the *Journal of Environmental Psychology*, after-work volunteers (n = 82 office employees) spent time in each of the three sites, sitting for 15 minutes before walking leisurely for 30 minutes. The results showed that the park and urban woodland had almost the same restorative influence with increased feelings of vitality and positive mood. Fascinatingly, the findings suggest that even short-term visits to nature areas have positive effects on perceived stress relief compared to built-up environment.

An early experimental study by Bodin and Hartig (2003) similarly sought to explore the psychological benefits of different types of outdoor environment that are readily accessible to city dwellers, investigating the relative effects of park and urban environments on a small group of runners (n = 12). Underpinning the study rationale, it is noted, '[P]arks are meant to provide a setting for exercise, among other activities. Urbanites without ready access to parks may have few other places to run aside from streets and sidewalks' (p. 142). The participants, described as 'regular runners' with the majority recruited from a local running club, provided self-reports of emotions and behavioural measures of attention before and after each of two 1-hour runs in each of the two environments. It was found that the runners preferred the park route, which was almost entirely situated within a large nature reserve. This was perceived to be a more restorative environment than the urban route, which incorporated sidewalks and city streets with varying volumes of traffic. Interestingly, the authors reported that whilst running did produce beneficial emotional changes as expected, 'our results do not indicate that greater emotional (or attentional) benefits came from running in the park versus the urban environment' (p. 151). A number of methodological issues were highlighted in interpreting the results, including the suggestion that experienced runners, such as those who took part in the study, may focus on physiological states such as heart rate and perceived exertion more than the environment at a given level of exertion.

Just as studies have consistently linked urban city living with poorer mental health, how close we live to nature has been shown to make a demonstrable difference to physical and mental health. In 2006, a pioneering study by Jolanda Maas and colleagues based at the Netherlands Institute for Health Services Research in Utrecht found that those with a high percentage of green space nearby (calculated as between 1 and 3 km) reported better general health, including mental health and fewer health complaints. Critically, the study which involved more than 250,000 residents in the Netherlands controlled for socio-economic and demographic variables. These findings have been replicated with different populations, health measures, and green space indicators in studies in the Netherlands and other countries such as England.

An exploratory study conducted by Catharine Ward Thompson and colleagues (2012) in the city of Dundee on the east coast of Scotland found a positive relationship between living in greener environments and health, measured by salivary cortisol. Self-reported measures of stress and general wellbeing were also captured, suggesting that the percentage of green space near home was, alongside physical activity, a significant predictor of their 'cortisol slope.' The authors concluded that the need for adequate levels of nearby greens pace is an important consideration for landscape and urban planners when designing new residential developments and renovating existing urban infrastructure, particularly in deprived communities.

In an observational population study published in *The Lancet* (2008) authors Mitchell and Popham obtained individual mortality records ($n = 366,348$) to establish whether the association between income deprivation and mortality varied by exposure to green space. It was shown that populations that are exposed to the greenest environments also enjoy lower levels of income-related health inequality. Conversely, populations exposed to fewer green environments could be less protected from health inequality related to income deprivation. Mitchell and Popham (2008) coined the term 'equigenesis' for this process; if an environment is equigenic, it has the potential to level up or level down. The former supports the health of the less advantaged as much as, or perhaps more than, the more advantaged, whereas the latter presumably limits the health of the more advantaged to a greater extent than the less advantaged. The implications of the study are clear: physical environments that promote good health might be crucial to reduce socio-economic health inequalities. Crucially, of course, many people don't necessarily frequent woodland or publicly accessible green space, even if it is proximity to where they live.

A systematic review and meta-analysis of the impact of exposure green space on health outcomes was published by colleagues at the University of East Anglia (Twohig-Bennett & Jones, 2018). The research team gathered evidence from 103 observational and 40 interventional studies investigating over 100 health outcomes and with a combined population size of over 290 million. The evaluation provided evidence that exposure to 'greenspace' (defined as 'open, undeveloped land with natural vegetation' as well as including urban parks, and street trees and greenery) is associated with wide-ranging health benefits. The authors reported that spending time in, or living close to, natural green spaces is found to reduce the risk of type II diabetes, cardiovascular disease, premature death, and preterm birth and increases sleep duration. People living near nature also had reduced diastolic blood pressure, heart rate, and stress.

Whilst the corpus of empirical research is persuasive, nevertheless, there remain several noteworthy caveats. Crucially, we understand relatively little about what causal mechanisms may explain the positive nature-health nexus. Graham Rook, Emeritus Professor of Medical Microbiology at UCL, emphasises that many psychosocial studies lack specificities. Put simply, one cannot compare the experience of a scalloped park with that of a bustling city street. Similarly, an urbanite may be able to find restoration in a quiet cafe, cinema, or art gallery, just as for some the prospect of spending time trudging along a country lane isn't an attractive proposition. Sceptics have also intimated that one explanation might be that time spent in nature is a proxy for physical activity, socialisation, and relaxation, and therefore it is this which is driving the relationship, not contact with nature per se. Moreover, it is important to acknowledge that contact with nature is more than just a complex multisensory experience, which needs to consider to varying degrees personal histories, meanings, and a sense of place.

★

We know then that both exercise and nature are independently facilitative of positive health and wellbeing. There is also now growing interest in the idea that the combination may have an even more compelling effect. This is manifest in the emerging green-prescriptions movement with scores of green gyms, green-therapy groups, care farms, and GPs connecting patients with local parks to improve their mental, physical, and social health. The idea has been validated with numerous reports and studies suggesting that physical activity in the presence of nature – a practice known as 'green exercise' – can provide additional health benefits in comparison to physical activity in built-up urban environments or indoors.[6] Alongside this realisation is the premise that green space can both facilitate and have a supportive role for partaking in physical activities such as walking, cycling, and running. The benefits are manifold: exercise outdoors makes people happier, less fatigued, more relaxed, and is more likely to increase an individual's frequency of exercise compared to indoor exercise.

Mike Rogerson and colleagues at the Green Exercise Research Team at the University of Essex conducted a study (2016b) comparing psychological and social outcomes of exercise in green outdoors versus built settings indoors. Participants completed two conditions of 15 minutes of cycling on an exercise bike located outside in a natural environment and inside in a laboratory setting. Following each session, respondents provided self-reports of their enjoyment of the exercise, perceived exertion, and intention for future exercise in the same environment. The findings showed that exercise in an outdoors environment may promote directed attention and social interactions, which may positively influence future exercise intentions.

The suggestion that exercise may feel easier when performed in natural environments has attracted interest from a number of scientists. Brian Focht (2009), for example, studied the effect of brief walks on affective responses, enjoyment, and adherence to exercise. Participants were asked to walk for 10 minutes on a laboratory treadmill and 10 minutes in an outdoor environment at a self-selected intensity. Results revealed that although both walks resulted in improvements in affective responses, participants reported greater pleasant affective states, enjoyment, and intention for future participation with outdoor walking. Results of correlation analyses also revealed that affective responses were only consistently related to enjoyment in the outdoor environment. Similarly, a study by Dasilva et al. (2011) published in the journal *Medicine and Science in Sports and Exercise* found that when asked to reproduce a given level of perceived effort indoors and outdoors, individuals tend to walk faster at a greater physiological effort, suggesting they perceive exercise to be less demanding when performed in a natural setting.

One explanation developed by psychologists Rachel and Stephen Kaplan is that natural environments provide positive distractions from workaday stresses and invoke feelings of interest and calm. The 'attention restoration theory' defines two types of attention: directed and involuntary attention. The former requires mental effort and concentration, often resulting in mental fatigue, irritability, and difficulties focusing on a task; whereas the latter – which natural environments promote – is a kind of 'fascination,' an antidote, enabling recovery and restoration. It takes no effort, for instance, to watch leaves moving in the breeze, a river flowing or to gaze at the birds outside your window. Moreover, the suggestion is that natural objects such as trees, leaves, and vegetation have a unique capacity for mental refreshment. Thus, Kaplan and Kaplan propose that spending time in natural settings and contact with green landscapes can have a positive impact on attention restoration and that this may be enhanced through interactions that help us tune in to the external environment.

According to a study published in the *British Journal of Sports Medicine*, walking through green spaces may affect the brain in a similar way to meditation with evidence of reductions in arousal, frustration, and directed attention. Researchers from Heriot-Watt University used mobile electroencephalography (EEG) as a method to record and analyse the emotional experience of participants ($n = 12$) who were asked to walk around Edinburgh. The route took the student volunteers through three types of urban environment: an old shopping district, a city park, and a bustling commercial area. The study reported the systematic differences in EEG recordings between the three urban areas were in line with attention restoration theory, which has implications for promoting urban green space as a mood-enhancing environment for walking or for other forms of physical or reflective activity (Aspinall et al., 2013).

A recent study published in 2018 conducted by researchers at Indiana and Illinois State Universities joins the attempt to unravel which factors are most crucial to nature's restorative benefits. The study compared three differing 'levels of nature' – a wilderness setting, a municipal city park, and a third site representing a built environment (an indoor exercise club) to ascertain how they affect levels of stress, as measured by a psychological test and using biophysical markers (cortisol and amylase). Findings suggest that visiting natural environments can be beneficial in reducing both physical and psychological stress levels with visitors to a natural environment reporting significantly lower levels of stress than their counterparts visiting a more urbanised outdoor setting or indoor exercise facility (Ewert & Chang, 2018).

A systematic review of literature conducted by Gladwell et al. (2013) noted the range of physiological, psychological, biochemical, and social 'evidence' that exists to demonstrate how exercising in outdoor natural environments can bring a significant range of health benefits to the general population. It is emphasised that such advantages include improving motivation for exercise and greater adherence of regimes that increase physical activity, as well as citing research that suggests that exercising in rural rather than urban settings appears to have greater benefits in relation to some health outcomes. The authors summarise that exercise within green spaces may provide the best all-round health benefits by increasing physical activity levels with lower levels of perceived exertion, altering psychological functioning including stress reduction, restoring mental fatigue, and improving mood and self-esteem.

This is something habitual parkrunners have instinctively known for some time, although empirical research that specifically focuses on parkrun to examine the relationship between nature and health remains underdeveloped. 'Relatively little research has been reported about the experience of parkrun as an opportunity to engage in physical activity in natural settings,' observe Wiltshire and Merchant (2021, p. 214). Furthermore, limited attention has been paid to what participants themselves believe different environments do to their experience and to what extent this may shape their continued participation (Hitchings & Latham, 2017). In a similar vein, Barnfield (2016) has argued that public health promoters may profit from acknowledging how the environment is much more than an 'inert backdrop' (p. 282) for exercise. That parkrun settings manifestly vary, taking in highly managed metropolitan parks as well as woodland, moorland, and coastline is an obvious enough statement, which makes this seeming blind spot more curious given that natural environments will principally characterise the participant experience. Invariably there are exceptions, although references tend to be relatively brief as opposed to a concentrated focus on the full-sensory experience of green exercise participation. For example, GP Margaret McCartney (2015, p. 1) published a short testimony in the BMJ noting that 'running in a park involves none of the vile mirrors that haunt me in gyms; instead, you are surrounded by trees and grass and encouraged by marshals to keep going.' Moreover, Stevinson et al. (2015, p. 175) described over half of the participants in their interviews mentioned how 'being outdoors in the fresh air among beautiful scenery brought additional pleasure to the experience that increased the desire to return each week.' In contrast, Cleland et al. (2019) study of Tasmanian parkrunners investigated environmental considerations, alongside individual and social factors, associated with driving initial and ongoing parkrun participation. Participants were recruited via electronic communication channels and handing out flyers directly to attendees at three Tasmanian parkrun events (Hobart, Launceston, and Devonport). Data were collected through an online questionnaire ($n = 372$). For environmental-level factors relevant items from a survey developed by Mujahid et al. (2007) were adapted, which included two statements related to safety ('parkrun offers a safe environment to be active' and 'crime/violence is not an issue at parkrun'), two statements related to aesthetics ('parkrun is held in an aesthetically pleasing/attractive location' and 'there is enough shade at parkrun events'), and two items linked to opportunities to be active ('local sports clubs and other facilities in my local area offer many low-cost or free opportunities to be active' and 'without parkrun, there wouldn't be many low-cost or free opportunities to be active').

Interestingly, despite growing evidence of the importance of the physical environment in influencing physical activity (Sallis et al., 2016), the study authors reported no associations between the environmental factors and higher levels of parkrun participation. It was suggested this may be because the physical environment appears to matter less when taking part in strenuous activities such as running because attention is internally focused, citing past experimental studies where during conditions of high workload and prolonged duration, attention was dominated on physiological sensations (Hutchinson & Tenenbaum, 2007). To probe this further, the researchers examined the relationship between average parkrun time and relative parkrun participation but found no association, including when age and BMI were considered. The authors postulate this could be explained by a lack of heterogeneity in the parkrun environments measured (three parkrun sites in one Australian state), advocating additional research, particularly the use of qualitative methodologies, to develop a more detailed appreciation of this finding. Bamberg et al. (2018) and Hitchings and Latham (2017) also advocate for a fuller examination of how exercise and environment interrelate, as well as calling for more qualitative research. In their respective provocations they problematise issues with the positivistic approaches of much green exercise research which tends to downplay how 'natural' environments differ, including how different weather conditions and seasonal environments may shape the diversity in physical experiences. Relatedly, there is a need to pay further attention to the ways in which different material settings play into the exercise experience, including how many of the exercise practices sit uneasily with the notion of sport and the subtleties of how sociality features.

In seeking to contribute to the apparent gap in understanding how the natural context shapes parkrun, Wiltshire and Merchant (2021) offer three explanatory accounts that consider the potential health benefits of green exercise and, in turn, how nature can help maintain people's engagement with physical activity: (a) parkrun provides access to affective 'green space,' (b) parkrun provides an affective and sensory experience, and (c) parkrun fosters affective communities. For the first of these, as previously noted, there now exists an extensive literature that natural environments not only provide a venue for exercise but can also increase exercise intentions and adherence, encourage greater levels of participation by overcoming issues of both boredom and perceived effort, improve enjoyment, promote social interactions, and has the potential to enhance individual wellbeing (Gladwell et al., 2013; Lahart et al., 2019). As Bamberg et al. (2018) witness 'the evidence base supporting the argument for green exercise, when taken as a whole, seems increasingly robust' (p. 270). Indeed, Little (2017) draws our attention to a body of scholarly work investigating exercise and environment, considering the ways in which running practices are shaped by the relationship between nature, environment, and the body. In her own study, involving data gathered from a series of in-depth interviews undertaken with eight women runners (all in their 40s and 50s and who ran regularly) she found from the conversations that all the runners were

influenced by the landscape and preferred running in remoter, rural environments. For some, engagement with nature and the outdoors was perceived to
confer additional health benefits. As one participant noted, 'there's definitely
something you get from running in nature. The smells, the sounds, the sights'
(p. 326). A detailed examination of the coproduction of nature and the running
body is undertaken by Howe and Morris (2009), exploring the different ways
in which nature contributes to, and becomes part of, the numerous practices
employed by the runner. Drawing on participant observation of two groups
of runners over an extended period, Howe and Morris identify three forms
and functions of 'nature' – as a gymnasium, a clinic, and a shrine in the production of the running body – which serve physiological, rehabilitative, and
spiritual purposes respectively. In this way, running in nature can be seen to
offer different challenges and affordances. These arguments resonate with the
work of others (e.g. Allen-Collinson, 2008; Griffin & Pheonix, 2016; Lorimer,
2012; Nettleton, 2015) in exploring how the relationship between running
and environment incorporates a range of sensory, emotional, and embodied
characteristics. Lorimer (2012), for example, depicts the recreational runner as
'a highly accomplished sensualist' (p. 83), discerning of the world according to
the feeling of differently textured terrains – bare rock, sand, soil, concrete. He
opines, '[B]y my reckoning, an appreciation of what is underfoot – as much as
what is overhead – alters runners' moods. In short, the experience of running
is underscored by surfaces' (p. 83). It is certainly true that the 'nature' settings
of parkrun events can vary considerably, being held in different surroundings
and terrains:

> parkruns are held in an amazing variety of locations, from city centres to
> beaches and large nature reserves, and from reclaimed land to World Heri-
> tage Sites. Some runs are held entirely on wide tarmac or concrete paths,
> others on grass, sand, gravel, or bark-covered trail, and many on mixed
> surfaces. Formats vary from single-lap courses to two-, three-, four- and
> even a five-lap course, as well as out-and-back courses and more complex
> layouts.
>
> (Bourne, 2014, p. 276)

The affective outcomes of participation between different parkrun settings
were the focus of a study by Rogerson et al. (2016a) with a view to investigating the possibility of optimum green exercise environments which augment
health benefits. Their study involved 331 attendees at four parkrun event locations: Gorleston Cliffs ($n = 67$); Nowton Park, Bury St Edmunds ($n = 83$);
Chelmsford Central Park ($n = 100$); and Colchester Castle ($n = 81$) with data
collected on four separate dates at each event location. The locations were
selected to enable comparisons between different environments (beach, grass-
lands, riverside, heritage) with two criterion measures: average number of
attendees per week (minimum average of 80) and environmental characteristics

of the 5 km route, in particular, the quantity of water content. At each location participants completed questionnaires pre- and post-run, providing a mixed between-within design. Questionnaires were composite, comprising measures of self-esteem, perceived stress, mood, and nature relatedness. Bespoke questions also included items relating to motivation to attend, membership of a running club, run performance in relation to their expectation, and enjoyment of the run. Collection of data on four dates produced variance measures of the climatic environmental factors (e.g. temperature, cloud cover, rain).

Consistent with previous research, the study findings demonstrate that a single bout of green exercise had improvements in acute psychological wellbeing (self-esteem, stress, and mood), which in the short term may be used by health promotion initiatives. The hypothesis that event locations with greatest presence of water features would facilitate greatest psychological improvements (something that previous research had found, e.g., Barton & Pretty, 2010; Barton et al., 2016; White et al., 2010) was not supported, however. The authors noted, '[E]vent location was not shown to influence the extent of the psychological improvements, despite differences in environmental characteristics' (p. 177). Interpreting the findings, the possibility that participation in parkrun may have been more strenuous than previous studies is mooted with the inference that environmental characteristics might be less influential at greater exercise intensities, as attention is focused more internally (see Hutchinson & Tenenbaum, 2007; LaCaille et al., 2004). This explanation echoes the thoughts of Cleland et al. (2019) and Bodin and Hartig (2003) referred to earlier. The study authors expand further on the finding that outcomes were not different between environments, suggesting that 'large proportions of the psychological benefits of green exercise are universally obtainable, independent of demographic, performance level, climatic, and other environmental characteristics' (p. 178).

As noted earlier, even relatively short encounters with nature have been shown to have positive impacts on psychological functioning (Tyrvainen et al., 2014). For example, White et al. (2019) found that individuals who reported spending at least 120 minutes a week in nature had consistently higher levels of both health and wellbeing than those who reported no exposure. Furthermore, Bratman et al. (2015) suggested that exposure to nature (in their case, a 50-minute nature walk) in comparison to a walk in an urban setting leads to decreases in anxiety, rumination, and negative affect. Their findings extend previous work which supports the idea that nature exposure may provide a 'restorative' affective experience. As such, Wiltshire and Merchant (2021, p. 215) contend, '[S]ituating oneself in one of parkrun's urban parks, beach trails or country estates then, for the duration of the run, would certainly remain significant.' The inference is that not only does participating in parkrun encourage an exposure to nature which otherwise might not have occurred in the weekly routines of many people, but that green exercise may help maintain regular physical activity by virtue of being in nature. Indeed, an individual's emotional response to exercise is a fairly accurate predictor of adherence. Expressed simply, the more someone likes it, the more likely they are to continue. Thus, if the exercise environment created by parkrun can positively influence the emotional response, then it is more likely that participants will return in subsequent weeks.

We turn now to the second theoretical perspective put forward by Wiltshire and Merchant (2021), that one of the reasons why people engage, and continue to engage, is because of the opportunities to experience a range of sensations associated with parkrun, 'in which the body is literally at the whim of the elements' (p. 217). They cite a study by Katrina Brown (2017) as an example, whose mobile video ethnographies involving walkers and mountain bikers 'were often on a quest to feel' (p. 309), highlighting the affective and enlivening capacities of ground textures. As Brown (2017) expresses:

> the texture and shape of the ground emerges as an active, lively, and forcefull agent in the experience of energetically moving one's body. Moreover, it suggests that sensing terrain through bodily touch, or ground-feel, can play a fundamental role in generating a range of valued affects that help secure commitment to regular, outdoor activity.
>
> (p. 312)

In parallel with Lorimer's (2012) writing, which conveys a runner's deep absorption in, and engagement with, the tactile environment, Brown (2017, p. 312) argues that 'surfaces are experienced as more than current narrow conceptions of distance, effort, location or vantage point' and by extension many parkrun settings and terrains 'facilitate a more-than-human 'feeling-with.' Allied to this is the principle, borne out of past studies (Pretty, 2004), that 'the greater the immersion, the more robust the beneficial responses are likely to be, and they are more likely to be longer-lasting' (Rogerson cited in Cregan-Reid, 2016, p. 120).

In relation to parkrun, Wiltshire and Merchant (2021) explain, '[P]articipants . . . are likely to find a common sense of enjoyment in sensing, for example, the warmth of sunshine, the sight of blue skies and the sound of birdsong' (p. 217). In contrast and arguably less palpable is the potential for parkrunners to appreciate and report positively on the challenges associated with, for example, running in inclement conditions, the resistance offered by a steep ascent, and/or exposing the skin to freezing temperatures. In the interviews of Howe and Morris (2009), for example, running 'off-road' on rural footpaths and parkland is valued because 'such spaces, with their typically "softer" and gently undulating surfaces of grass, mud, and wood chips afford impromptu massage of the calf muscles' (p. 319). The attraction for these runners is the alternative to the hard pavements of more urban areas. As Bamberg et al. (2018) assert, these environmental 'affordances' are distinct from, but arguably no less important to, those examined in green exercise research. Indeed, in more urban settings, studies like those of Krenichyn (2004, 2006) and Barnfield (2016) nonetheless demonstrate that many runners reported 'natural' environments such as large urban parks to both stimulate the senses and be calming and restorative.

Women's experiences of undertaking physical activities in Prospect Park, an urban public park located in Brooklyn, New York, are the attention of Kira Krenichyn's work involving semi-structured interviews with 41 women (aged between 18 and 85) who used the park during the summer of 2001 and field notes recorded during observations on 45 different occasions. She found that for some women, the presence of others in the park doing physical activities was a motivator in itself; others commented on the importance of the general presence of other women in the park in fostering feelings of emotional wellbeing and safety. In the 2004 article, Krenichyn applied Gilligan's (1982) 'ethic of care' – the importance of interconnecting relationship networks such as family, friendships, neighbourhood, and community – as a framework for making sense of the women's accounts of their everyday experiences in the park as a public space. Here, Krenichyn (2004) noted the value some women attributed to the park providing opportunities for interacting with others:

> Chance meetings with friends or acquaintances in the park, becoming better acquainted with others whom they saw in the park regularly, or developing a sense of familiarity and friendliness with strangers who nonetheless remained anonymous. Some described very brief, casual encounters, such as a quick smile and a 'hello' when they passed other joggers whom they saw regularly, which were enough to foster a sense of familiarity if not intimacy.
>
> (p. 123)

Closely related to these kinds of interactions is the concept of social support, without which women might otherwise be discouraged, for example, by embarrassment or concerns about safety.

This leads us to the third and final explanatory account that parkrun fosters affective communities, which expands the idea that parkrunners develop a sense of connection and emotional bond 'not merely through engaging in the same activity but by virtue of that activity taking place within a natural landscape' (Wiltshire & Merchant, 2021, p. 218). Of value to the 'affective' sense of connection to other runners is the notion of existential capital, which Nettleton (2013) proposes as a way of capturing the visceral pleasures, corporeal resources, and a novel form of sociality. Existential capital argues Nettleton (2013, p. 207) 'involves not status, monetary reward, or a "healthy" body, but comprises intrinsic values appreciated for their own sake . . . the gains are primarily the embodied residues of the "magic" that forms the basis of sociality of the field.' Whilst her work focuses specifically on fell running, Nettleton offers ways of thinking about the social aspects of parkrun, including how parkrun events seemingly are able to bring together runners from different backgrounds, ages, and abilities in unity rather than differentiate from each other. In this way, what is fostered is camaraderie and a sense of solidarity among those who are part of the parkrun 'family' not merely through taking part in the same activity but by virtue of that activity taking place within a natural landscape. What emerges from Nettleton's writing is the abstract, intrinsic nature of capital, which accrues valued for its own sake and not on the basis of its exchange value.

Notably, the discussion in this chapter has highlighted that many of the potential benefits of parkrun are not solely attributable to nature but rather 'positive experiences are emergent properties of other phenomena occurring in combination with, and in the context of, nature' (Wiltshire & Merchant, 2021, p. 219). Furthermore, our experiences of being in nature through participation in parkrun differ, not only because of the diversity of green exercise environments, and changeable climatic factors, but the different levels of interaction and immersion. In addition, previous studies have pointed to the dilution of environmental characteristics at greater exercise intensities, highlighting the point at which participant attention switches from external awareness to focusing more internally.

★

In this chapter I have considered the growing body of scientific research dubbed 'green exercise' as a way of thinking about parkrun, and the additional physical and psychological benefits that may be accrued by participating in parkrun events, given the outdoor setting is most common in public parks. This body of work provides a robust evidence base illuminating the potential benefits of parkrun on health and wellbeing, as well as exploring the relationship between parkrun, nature, and health in understanding the reasons why people engage, and continue to engage, with parkrun. At the same time, it is important to recognise that many of the benefits are not solely attributable to nature but rather are attribute to a combination of factors occurring with, and in the context of, nature (Wiltshire & Merchant, 2021).

Notes

1 www.theguardian.com/world/live/2020/mar/18/coronavirus-live-news-updates-outbreak-us-states-uk-australia-europe-eu-self-isolation-lockdown-latest-update?page=with:block-5e728afe8f088d7575596052
2 www.ons.gov.uk/economy/environmentalaccounts/articles/howhaslockdownchangedourrelationshipwithnature/2021-04-26
3 www.theparksalliance.org/making-parks-count-the-case-for-parks/
4 www.fieldsintrust.org/News/the-ten-minute-walk-and-why-its-important
5 www.theguardian.com/environment/2016/mar/25/three-quarters-of-uk-children-spend-less-time-outdoors-than-prison-inmates-survey
6 It is not just green space that is of importance: the term 'blue exercise' has been used to refer to physical activity undertaken in and around outdoor 'natural' aquatic environments such as canals, rivers, lakes, and the coast (White et al., 2016).

References

Allen-Collinson, J. (2008). Running the routes together: Co-running and knowledge in action. *Journal of Contemporary Ethnography*, 37:1, 38–61.

Aspinall, P., Mavros, P., Coyne, R., & Roe, J. (2013). The urban brain: Analysing outdoor physical activity with mobile EEG. *British Journal of Sports Medicine*, 49, 272–276. https://doi.org/10.1136/bjsports-2012-091877.

Bamberg, J., Hitchings, R., & Latham, A. (2018). Enriching green exercise research. *Landscape and Urban Planning*, 178, 270–275.

Barnfield, A. (2016). Public health, physical exercise and non-representational theory – A mixed method study of recreational running in Sofia, Bulgaria. *Critical Public Health*, 26:3, 281–293.

Barton, J., Bragg, R., Wood, C., & Pretty, J. (2016). *Green Exercise: Linking Nature, Health and Well-Being*. London: Routledge.

Barton, J., & Pretty, J. (2010). What is the best dose of nature and green exercise for improving mental health? A multi-study analysis. *Environmental Science & Technology*, 44, 3947–3955.

Bodin, M., & Hartig, T. (2003). Does the outdoor environment matter for psychological restoration gained through running? *Psychology of Sport and Exercise*, 4, 141–153.

Bourne, D. (2014). *Parkrun: Much More Than Just a Run in the Park*. Sheffield: Chequered Flag Publishing.

Bratman, G.N., Daily, G.C., Levy, B.J., & Gross, J.J. (2015). The benefits of nature experience: Improved affect and cognition. *Landscape and Urban Planning*, 138, 41–50. https://doi.org/10.1016/j.landurbplan.2015.02.005.

Brown, K.M. (2017). The haptic pleasures of ground-feel: The role of textured terrain in motivating regular exercise. *Health & Place*, 46, 307–314. https://doi.org/10.1016/j.healthplace.2016.08.012.

Burgess, J., Harrison, C.M., & Limb, M. (1988). People, parks, and the urban green: A study of popular meanings and values for open spaces in the city. *Urban Studies*, 25, 455–473.

Cleland, V., Nash, M., Sharman, M.J., & Claflin, S. (2019). Exploring the health-promoting potential of the parkrun phenomenon: What factors are associated with higher levels of participation? *American Journal of Health Promotion*, 33:1, 13–23.

Collier, B. (2019). Black absence in green spaces. *The Ecologist*. Retrieved from https://theecologist.org/2019/oct/10/black-absence-green-spaces

Cregan-Reid, V. (2016). *Footnotes: How Running Makes Us Human*. London: Ebury Press.

Dasilva, S.G., Guidetti, L., Buzzachera, C.F., Elsangedy, H.M., Krinski, K., De Campos, W., Goss, F.L., & Baldari, C. (2011). Psychophysiological responses to self-paced treadmill and overground exercise. *Medicine and Science in Sports and Exercise*, 43:6, 1114–1124. https://doi.org/10.1249/MSS.0b013e318205874c.

Elborough, T. (2016). *A Walk in the Park: The Life and Times of a People's Institution*. London: Jonathan Cape.

Ewert, A., & Chang, Y. (2018). Levels of nature and stress response. *Behavioral Sciences*, 8:49. https://doi.org/10.3390/bs8050049.

Flowers, E.P., Freeman, P., & Gladwell, V.F. (2016). A cross-sectional study examining predictors of visit frequency to local green space and the impact this has on physical activity levels. *BMC Public Health*, 16:420.

Focht, B.C. (2009). Brief walks in outdoor and laboratory environments: Effects on affective responses, enjoyment, and intentions to walk for exercise. *Research Quarterly for Exercise in Sport*, 80:3, 611–620. https://doi.org/10.1080/02701367.2009.10599600.

Gilligan, C. (1982). *In a Different Voice*. Cambridge, MA: Harvard University Press.

Gladwell, V.F., Brown, D.K., Wood, C., Sandercock, G.R., & Barton, J.L. (2013). The great outdoors: How a green exercise environment can benefit all. *Extreme Physiology & Medicine*, 2:3. https://doi.org/10.1186/2046-7648-2-3.

Griffin, M., & Pheonix, C. (2016). Becoming a runner: Big, middle and small stories of physical activity participation in later life. *Sport Education and Society*, 21:1. https://doi.org/10.10 80/13573322.2015.1066770.

Hitchings, R., & Latham, A. (2017). Exercise and environment: New qualitative work to link popular practice and public health. *Health & Place*, 46, 300–306.

Howe, P.D., & Morris, C. (2009). An exploration of the co-production of performance running bodies and natures within 'running taskscapes.' *Journal of Sport & Social Issues*, 33:3, 308–330.

Hutchinson, J.C., & Tenenbaum, G. (2007). Attention focus during physical effort: The mediating role of task intensity. *Psychology of Sport and Exercise*, 8:2, 233–245.

Jones, L. (2020). *Losing Eden: Why Our Minds Need the Wild*. London: Penguin.

Kaplan, R. (2001). The nature of the view from home: Psychological benefits. *Environment and Behaviour*, 33, 507–542.

Kellert, S.R., & Wilson, E.O. (1995). *The Biophilia Hypothesis*. Washington, DC: Island Press.

Krenichyn, K. (2004). Women and physical activity in an urban park: Enrichment and support through an ethic of care. *Journal of Environmental Psychology*, 24:1, 117–130.

Krenichyn, K. (2006). 'The only place to go and be in the city': Women talk about exercise, being outdoors, and the meanings of a large open park. *Health & Place*, 12, 631–643.

LaCaille, R.A., Masters, K.S., & Heath, E.M. (2004). Effects of cognitive strategy and exercise setting on running performance, perceived exertion, affect, and satisfaction. *Psychology of Sport and Exercise*, 5, 461–476.

Lahart, I., Darcy, P.M., Gidlow, C., & Giovanna, C. (2019). Known knowns: A systematic review of the effects of green exercise compared with exercising indoors. In Donnelly, A.A., & Macintyre, T.E. (Eds.), *Physical Activity in Natural Settings: Green and Blue Exercise* (pp. 36–74). London: Routledge.

Layton, J., & Latham, A. (2021). Social infrastructure and public life – Notes on Finsbury Park, London. *Urban Geography*. https://doi.org/10.1080/02723638.2021.1934631.

Little, J. (2017). Running, health and the disciplining of women's bodies: The influence of technology and nature. *Health & Place*, 46, 322–327.

Lorimer, H. (2012). Surfaces and slopes. *Performance Research*, 17, 83–86. https://doi.org/1 0.1080/13528165.2012.671080.

Louv, R. (2005). *Last Child in the Woods: Saving Our Children from Nature-Deficit Disorder*. Chapel Hill, NC: Algonquin Books.

Maas, J., Verheij, R.A., Groenewegen, P.P., de Vries, S., & Spreeuwenberg, P. (2006). Green space, urbanity, and health: How strong is the relation? *Journal of Epidemiology & Community Health*, 60:7, 587–592. https://doi.org/10.1136/jech.2005.043125.

Maller, C., Townsend, M., St Leger, L., Henderson-Watson, C., Pryor, A., Prosser, L., & Moore, M. (2009). Healthy parks, healthy people: The health benefits of contact with nature in a park context. *Parks Stewardship Forum*, 26:2, 51–83.

McCartney, M. (2015). Combination of exercise and social interaction is why I love parkrun. *BMJ*, 350. https://doi.org/10.1136/bmj.h230.

Mitchell, R., & Popham, F. (2008). Effect of exposure to natural environment on health inequalities: An observational population study. *Lancet*, 8, 372:9650, 1655–1660. https://doi.org/10.1016/S0140-6736(08)61689-X.

Mujahid, M.S., Diez Roux, A.V., Morenoff, J.D., & Raghunathan, T. (2007). Assessing the measurement properties of neighbourhood scales: From psychometrics to ecometrics. *American Journal of Epidemiology*, 165:8, 858–867.

Natural England. (2009). *Childhood and Nature: A Survey on Changing Relationships with Nature Across Generations*. Retrieved from http://publications.naturalengland.org.uk/publication/5853658314964992

Natural England. (2019). *Monitor of Engagement with the Natural Environment. Children and Young People Report*. Retrieved from https://assets.publishing.service.gov.uk/government/uploads/system/uploads/attachment_data/file/828838/Monitor_of_Engagement_with_the_Natural_Environment__MENE__Childrens_Report_2018-2019_rev.pdf

Nettleton, S. (2013). Cementing relations within a sporting field: Fell running in the English lake district and the acquisition of existential capital. *Cultural Sociology*, 7:2, 196–210.

Nettleton, S. (2015). Fell runners and walking walls: Towards a sociology of living landscapes and aesthetic atmospheres as an alternative to a Lakeland picturesque. *The British Journal of Sociology*, 66:4, 759–778.

Pretty, J. (2004). How nature contributes to mental and physical health. *Spirituality and Health International*, 5:2, 68–78.

Pretty, J., Peacock, J., Sellens, M., & Griffin, M. (2005). The mental and physical health outcomes of green exercise. *International Journal of Environmental Health Research*, 15, 319–337.

Rogerson, M., Brown, D.K., Sandercock, G., Wooller, J.J., & Barton, J. (2016a). A comparison of four typical green exercise environments and prediction of psychological health outcomes. *Perspectives in Public Health*, 136:3, 171–180.

Rogerson, M., Gladwell, V.F., Gallagher, D.J., & Barton, J.L. (2016b). Influences of green outdoors versus indoors environmental settings on psychological and social outcomes of controlled exercise. *International Journal of Environmental Research and Public Health*, 13:363. https://doi.org/10.3390/ijerph13040363.

Sallis, J.F., Cerin, E., Conway, T.L., Adams, M.A., Frank, L.D., Pratt, M., Salvo, D., Schipperijn, J., Smith, G., Cain, K.L., Davey, R., Kerr, J., Lai, P.C., Mitáš, J., Reis, R., Sarmiento, O.L., Schofield, G., Troelsen, J., Van Dyck, D., De Bourdeaudhuij, I., & Owen, N. (2016). Physical activity in relation to urban environments in 14 cities worldwide: A cross-sectional study. *Lancet*, 387:10034, 2207–2217. https://doi.org/10.1016/S0140-6736(15)01284-2.

Schertz, K.E., Meidenbauer, K.L., & Berman, M.G. (2021). Understanding the affective benefits of interacting with nature. In Brymer, E., Rogerson, M., & Barton, J. (Eds.), *Nature and Health: Physical Activity in Nature* (pp. 8–22). London: Routledge.

Stevinson, C., Wiltshire, G., & Hickson, M. (2015). Facilitating participation in health-enhancing physical activity: A qualitative study of parkrun. *International Journal of Behavioural Medicine*, 22, 170–177.

Taylor, H.A. (1994). *Age and Order: The Public Park as a Metaphor for a Civilised Society*. Working Paper No 10, Comedia/Demos.

Thompson Coon, J., Boddy, K., Stein, K., Whear, R., Barton, J., & Depledge, M.H. (2011). Does participating in physical activity in outdoor natural environments have a greater effect on physical and mental wellbeing than physical activity indoors? A systematic review. *Environmental Science and Technology*, 45:5, 1761–1772.

Twohig-Bennett, C., & Jones, A. (2018). The health benefits of the great outdoors: A systematic review and meta-analysis of greenspace exposure and health outcomes. *Environmental Research*, 166, 628–637.

Tyrvainen, L., Ojala, A., Korpela, K., Lanki, T., Tsunetsugu, Y., & Kagawa, T. (2014). The influence of urban green environments on stress relief measures: A field experiment. *Journal of Environmental Psychology*, 38, 1–9.

Ulrich, R.S. (1984). View through a window may influence recovery from surgery. *Science*, 224:4647, 420–421.

Ward Thompson, C., Roe, J., Aspinall, P., Mitchell, R., Clow, A., & Miller, D. (2012). More green space is linked to less stress in deprived communities: Evidence from salivary cortisol patterns. *Landscape and Urban Planning*, 105:3, 221–229. https://doi.org/10.1016/j.landurbplan.2011.12.015.

Wells, N. (2000). At home with nature: Effects of 'greenness' on children's cognitive functioning. *Environment and Behaviour*, 32, 775–795.

White, M.P., Alcock, I., Grellier, J., Wheeler, B.W., Hartig, T., Warber, S.L., Bone, A., Depledge, M.H., & Fleming, L.E. (2019). Spending at least 120 minutes a week in nature is associated with good health and wellbeing. *Scientific Reports*, 9:7730. https://doi.org/10.1038/s41598-019-44097-3.

White, M.P., Bell, S., Elliott, L.R., Jenkin, R., Wheeler, B.W., & Depledge, M.H. (2016). The health benefits of blue exercise in the UK. In Barton, J., Bragg, R., Wood, C., & Pretty, J. (Eds.), *Green Exercise: Linking Nature, Health and Well-Being* (pp. 69–78). London: Routledge.

White, M.P., Smith, A., Humphryes, K., Pahl, S., Snelling, D., & Depledge, M. (2010). Blue space: The importance of water for preference, affect, and restorativeness ratings of natural and built scenes. *Journal of Environmental Psychology*, 30, 482–493.

Williams, F. (2017). *The Nature Fix: Why Nature Makes Us Happier, Healthier, and More Creative*. New York: Norton.

Wilson, E.O. (1984). *Biophilia*. Cambridge, MA: Harvard University Press.

Wiltshire, G., & Merchant, S. (2021). What can we learn about nature, physical activity, and health from parkrun? In Brymer, E., Rogerson, M., & Barton, J. (Eds.), *Nature and Health: Physical Activity in Nature* (pp. 208–222). London: Routledge.

Chapter 8

Conclusion

The Future of parkrun

In this chapter, I bring together previous discussions with the aim of identifying the key findings of the book. This will include highlighting some of the lessons learnt, as well as discussing current and future challenges. I specifically focus on parkrun as a community-based physical activity opportunity in its capacity to incrementally promote positive changes to physical activity over time, as well as its potential to encourage positive attitudes towards future exercise among the least active, inexperienced, and novice runners. I argue that as a multi-component intervention, parkrun can illuminate new ways of understanding the potential of mass participation events in catering for the non-elite, as well as encouraging participation among those traditionally hard to engage in physical activity.

Throughout the book I have focused on underlining the distinctive features and characteristics of the initiative through a review of the scholarly research on parkrun that has emerged over the last 7 years. Each of the chapters spotlights a specific aspect, outlining relevant findings from the published literature on parkrun, alongside documenting parkrun's evolution into a global movement striving for healthier and happier communities. One of the overarching themes that emerges is the prevailing narrative that is central to parkrun, that of social inclusion. The overarching ethos of parkrun being open to all – reflected within discourse around 'mass' participation (see Bauman et al., 2009) – is both championed by its administration and endorsed by participants. The simplicity of parkrun's free, one-off registration gives sense to this ambition, alongside other elements designed to mitigate long-standing barriers to physical activity. An example is the prominence given to presenting parkrun as 'not a race,' distancing itself from more traditional (and potentially problematic) conceptualisations of sport. Hillman et al. (2021) contend that in this context the dominant conceptual lens of 'sport' is limiting, as it privileges interpersonal competition. The term 'active leisure events' is proposed as a more accommodating alternative, encouraging broader thinking about why people participate, acknowledging motives spanning non-competitive, personal challenge, as well as highly competitive participants. With no time limit, and without any overt pressure to be competitive, parkrun can be seen to stretch the conceptual boundaries that sport has imposed. Relatedly, applying active leisure as an inclusive foundational

DOI: 10.4324/9781003121961-8

concept encourages us to consider the malleability of parkrun and, in so doing, diluting hegemonic connotations of running, competitiveness, or athleticism (which I explored in Chapter 5). It is the flexibility and informality of parkrun, the pliability of parkrun to its participants in terms of motivation and meaning, and its egalitarian principles in ascribing equal value to all that distinguish park-run events from most participant events catering for the masses.

One of the striking features of parkrun is the ways in which it seeks to diverge from convention. What started as a timed running event for runners has unde-niably morphed into something broader and much more ambitious, whilst still managing to retain its original appeal. It is worth emphasising that during the formative years, the response to parkun by running clubs has been mixed. As I explored in Chapter 6, there is some evidence that parkrun has proved benefi-cial to the membership of running clubs, as well as entries to organised running events. This is also reflected in the synergistic relationship which exists between some parkruns and running clubs (Bourne, 2014). However, there have been some running club runners who were initially hesitant and a disapproving vocal minority who believed parkrun to be detrimental to the sport of athletics.

Another powerful feature identified in the book is the sense of a community fostered at parkrun events and related social structures through which partici-pants may engage against a backdrop of casual social interaction, solidarity, and enjoyment. As I have written previously, part of parkrun's appeal is in 'moving away from serious competition and towards sociality, camaraderie, and experi-ence' (Hindley, 2020, p. 86) with events providing a liminal space where mem-bers of social worlds coalesce. Nonetheless, as has been discussed, the claim that parkrun is welcoming and accessible to anyone shouldn't merely be assumed as self-evident or irrefutable. In Chapter 2, for example, I highlighted the anxieties of first-timers whose preconceptions may limit attendance, as well as the reliance on social capital to encourage participation which may as a result dispropor-tionately engage individuals from middle- to high-income groups. Relatedly, evidence suggests that whilst access to parkrun is generally good and is similar across socio-economic groups, participation is markedly higher in less-deprived areas.

Understanding parkrun as an opportunity for physical activity is another defining characteristic discussed in the book, with participants encouraged to complete the 5 km course at a pace suitable to their ability, which may include walking. In the case of parkrun, the degree of physicality may vary considerably, shaped by a combination of variables such as terrain and weather conditions, as well as participants' personal agendas for participation. As Hillman et al. (2021) explain, 'parkrun is framed first and foremost as an accessible opportunity for practicing healthy behaviours, whilst concurrently offering a space for those who seek a competitive outlet' (p. 5). Event physicality is noteworthy, not least because it is inherently a physical challenge which, as the emerging research has reported, is deemed to be associated with enhancing personal health and wellbeing. This was the focus of Chapter 4, outlining the evidence which is growing of the health and wellbeing benefits of taking part in parkrun. For those participants who elect to walk the 5 km course, encouragingly there is now an emerging body of evidence that indicates that walking in nature, especially in regular doses, can improve the way we feel (O'Mara, 2019). Further, as discussed, the benefits can extend beyond encouraging more people to be physically active for health reasons. Potential social impacts include fostering engagement with others and cultivating a sense of group belonging, thus providing a buffer against social isolation, loneliness, and poor mental health (Holmes et al., 2020). However, when considering the impacts generated by parkrun events it is important to be reflective of the respective methodological considerations. For example, a number of studies employ self-reporting measures which may have been biased by measurement errors and reporting biases. Additionally, event frequency may be seen as a limitation given that parkrun takes place only once a week (McIntosh, 2021).

I have argued the attractiveness of parkrun may, in part, be attributed to its relatively simple, standardised, and scalable operational model. This is echoed by Grunseit et al. (2020) in their scoping review who observe '[parkrun] stands out among other physical activity interventions in terms of its scalability, sustainability, accessibility, and potential to disrupt the socio-economic gradient of health behaviours' (p. 1). On the one hand, parkrun's remarkable growth appears to have been largely organic, established by enthusiastic volunteers in their local community. An unintended consequence of this is there may be a risk that, as with other public health interventions, parkrun events may not be as accessible or as well attended by people living in deprived areas as in less-deprived areas (Smith et al., 2021). What began as a 5 km time trial in Bushy Park is now a global movement with events (in excess of 2,200) across 22 countries. On the other, in recent years parkrun's commitment to create accessible and welcoming events has subtly shifted to engage with socio-economically deprived communities and areas of higher ethnic density. As discussed earlier in the book, this aspiration brings with it sizeable challenges, and establishing parkruns in deprived areas, whilst necessary, is not sufficient on its own for equity of participation (Haake et al., 2021). Other challenges include the immediate issues with managing the growing numbers of parkrunners (and consequently the need to recruit more volunteers), which was explored in Chapter 3. Further, published studies have noted possible tensions with the growth in popularity and participant numbers contributing to a diminished sense of belonging (Bowness et al., 2020). There remain questions about how to engage with culturally diverse communities (Fullagar et al., 2020) as well as considering the effects of austerity policies in the UK with local authorities experiencing savage cuts from central government. As a consequence, councils have looked to novel – and controversial – ways of replacing lost funding, including the introduction of charges for parking, as well as outsourcing the management of parks (Layton & Latham, 2021). One illustration is the threat of parkrun being negatively impacted by other events that have paid for park use which result in the cancellation of parkrun events.

A further consideration aligned to the future sustainability of parkrun is the environmental impact. As documented, encouragingly, the mean geodesic distance to the nearest parkrun event has decreased from 34.1 km in 2010 to 4.6 km in 2019 (Smith et al., 2021). Conversely, access to local parks has also been identified as a constraint for sites that are not easily reached by foot or public transport (Fullagar et al., 2020) making access challenging without using a car. This is certainly true of parkrun events that I have attended, which, combined with an upsurge in participant numbers, has resulted in pressures on car parking and associated issues with car parking charges. Whilst parkrun is a free event, the transport and/or parking costs and car use is an issue of equity, as well as contributing to parkrun's carbon footprint. It is commendable that parkrun encourages participants, wherever possible, to walk, jog, cycle, or use public transport when attending, emphasising on parkrun event webpages that 'if you do have to drive, consider car-sharing to reduce our impact on both the environment and other park users.' Given parkrun's expansion and projected future growth, consideration of its transport footprint, particularly for sites where car usage is likely, represents a significant conundrum.

Arguably the greatest challenge in parkrun's 17-year history has been the impact of the COVID-19 pandemic with lockdown restrictions resulting in the abrupt cancellation of parkrun events in March 2020. It has been widely acknowledged that the suspension of parkruns during the coronavirus pandemic has had significant impacts on physical and mental health. Writing in support of the resumption of parkrun events across the UK, Tom Williams argued:

> We're often asked why parkrun is so successful, and our answer is that we believe all human beings have an innate need to be active, social, and outdoors. We believe that these are fundamental building blocks of health and happiness, and that without any one of them, regardless of steps counted or calories burned, our health deteriorates. It is critical then, that as we look toward the future of sport and physical activity, we hold on to the human interaction that makes people healthier and happier, and that we continue to remove barriers to participation.[1]

The impact of the coronavirus pandemic on the wellbeing of parkrun participants in the UK was the focus of a study by Quirk et al. (2021) which surveyed a sample of parkrunners pre-COVID 19, early in 2019, and during the pandemic in September 2020. The authors reported that the overall wellbeing of a cohort of 450 parkrun participants declined during the pandemic. Physical activity dropped by 6 per cent, whereas happiness and life satisfaction fell by 12 per cent. The data showed that the most notable negative impact among the sample was on people's connections with others. 'Our open-text responses captured how people missed the socialisation and community parkrun provides, perhaps more so that the physical activity itself' (Quirk et al., 2021, p. 9). This is supported by findings in this book that emphasise both the sense of community and social connectedness as being an appeal and positive outcome of parkrun participation.

After a total of 497 days parkrun events finally resumed on 26 June 2021 in England. The recommencement came after a series of false dawns and overcoming a combination of obstacles – what Nick Pearson has described as 'ugly conversations' and a 'significant existential threat.' Whilst the government had advised that parkrun be given the green light, the decision to grant permission for each event had been devolved to local levels, resulting in parkrun becoming a 'political football,' caught up in a web of administration and bureaucracy. Eventually the decision came after more than 500 of the 589 local councils and landowners across England gave permission for the restart (Ingle, 2021). The number is significant; parkrun had been transparent in explaining that, unlike junior parkrun which returned in phases, the 5 km events needed all to come back at the same time (with 'all' defined as being over 90 per cent).[2] This was due to the relatively large attendances, and significant opportunities for tourism, meaning that if only a subset of parkrun events reopened, they would likely be overwhelmed with no mechanism to control or limit numbers attending. Nevertheless, if there is one positive to emerge from this, it is the resilience of parkrun's financial model, which successfully withstood the financial shock of COVID-19 with significantly reduced revenues with the suspension of all parkrun events.

I am mindful that some of the analysis presented in this book may be perceived by some parkrun evangelists as unduly critical, an affront to a community, and a practice that is widely celebrated, and is seen as analogous to a 'new religion' in terms of devotion and providing a sense of belonging, and for whom parkrun has personally proved transformative. As Wiltshire and Merchant (2021) contend, it is possible to view parkrun as a 'tonic' in that this mass participation initiative presents creative solutions to a variety of societal ills, including inequities in physical activity participation, a rise in sedentary lifestyles disconnected from the natural world, a reduction in a sense of community, and epidemic levels of loneliness. The purpose of the book has been to probe and ask questions, as opposed to deliberately setting out to expose or undermine; arguably this would be duplicitous given my own personal attachment as a parkrunner for a number of years. It is only by asking questions that we can begin to understand how participating in free, weekly, timed 5 km event in a local park comes to make sense as a meaningful and pleasurable leisure practice with positive health and wellbeing outcomes.

Invariably there are questions in a book of this length that remain unanswered and several under-researched aspects which still exist. To paraphrase the author Alex Hutchinson (2019), debatably the most crucial research question is how parkrun generates such levels of commitment and devotion. In some ways this feels counterintuitive, given a key feature of the parkrun is flexibility and informality; put simply, there is neither expectation to attend weekly nor any overt pressure to volunteer. Originally, I had planned for the book to contain a chapter specifically devoted to parkrun's global expansion, which, with hindsight, proved too ambitious. There remains a notable gap in the fledgling literature on parkrun which seeks to improve our understanding of cultural relevance and specificity of the parkrun model (Grunseit et al. 2020). Indeed, the majority of studies to date have been conducted in the UK with only a handful of studies conducted in other countries (most notably Australia). Further, as Wiltshire and Merchant (2021) have identified and the subject of discussion in the penultimate chapter on green exercise, there remains a gap in understanding how the natural context shapes parkrun and a need to unpack, theorise, and better understand this relationship.

Notes

1 www.sportengland.org/blogs/why-its-vital-we-get-parkrun-and-running-soon-possible
2 https://blog.parkrun.com/uk/2021/02/26/restarting-parkrun-in-england/#:~:text= junior%20parkrun%20events%20across%20England%20will%20be%20able,England%20 will%20return%20on%20Saturday%205%20June%202021

References

Bauman, A., Murphy, N., & Lane, A. (2009). The role of community programmes and mass events in promoting physical activity to patients. *British Journal of Sports Medicine*, 43:1, 44.

Bourne, D. (2014). *Parkrun: Much More than Just a Run in the Park*. Sheffield: Chequered Flag Publishing.

Bowness, J., Tulle, E., & McKendrick, J. (2020). Understanding the parkrun community; sacred Saturdays and organic solidarity of parkrunners. *European Journal for Sport and Society*, 18:1, 44–63. https://doi.org/10.1080/16138171.2020.1792113.

Fullagar, S., Petris, S., Sargent, J., Allen, S., Akhtar, M., & Ozakinci, G. (2020). Action research with parkrun UK volunteer organisers to develop inclusive strategies. *Health Promotion International*, 35, 1199–1209.

Grunseit, A.C., Richards, J., Reece, L., Bauman, A., & Merom, D. (2020). Evidence on the reach and impact of the social physical activity phenomenon parkrun: A scoping review. *Preventative Medicine Reports*, 20, 1–8. https://doi.org/10.1016/j.pmedr.2020.101231.

Haake, S., Heller, B., Schneider, P., Smith, R., & Green, G. (2021). The influence of neighbourhood equity on parkrunners in a British city. *Health Promotion International*, 1–8. https://doi.org/10.1093/heapro/daab138.

Hillman, P., Lamont, M., Scherrer, P., & Kennelly, M. (2021). Reframing mass participation events as active leisure: Implications for tourism and leisure research. *Tourism Management Perspectives*, 39, 1–13.

Hindley, D. (2020). 'More than just a run in the park': An exploration of parkrun as a shared leisure space. *Leisure Sciences*, 42:1, 85–105.

Holmes, E.A., O'Connor, R.C., Perry, V.H., Tracey, I., Wessely, S., Arseneault, L., Ballard, C., Christensen, N., Silver, R.C., & Everall, I. (2020). Multidisciplinary research priorities for the COVID-19 pandemic: A call for action for mental health science. *The Lancet Psychiatry*, 7:6, 547–560.

Hutchinson, A. (2019). Parkrun's community feel inspires devotion. *The Globe and Mail*. Retrieved from www.theglobeandmail.com/life/health-and-fitness/article-parkruns-community-feel-inspires-devotion/

Ingle, S. (2021). Parkrun events to return in England at end of June after late approvals. *The Guardian*. Retrieved from www.theguardian.com/sport/2021/jun/11/parkrun-events-to-return-in-england-at-end-of-june-after-late-approvals-athletics

Layton, J., & Latham, A. (2021). Social infrastructure and public life – Notes on Finsbury Park, London. *Urban Geography*. https://doi.org/10.1080/02723638.2021.1934631.

McIntosh, T. (2021). parkrun: A panacea for health and wellbeing? *Journal of Research in Nursing*, 26:5, 472–477.

O'Mara, S. (2019). *In Praise of Walking: The New Science of How We Walk and Why It's Good for Us*. London: Vintage.

Quirk, H., Haake, S., Goyder, E., Bullas, A., Graney, M., & Wellington, C. (2021). Impact of the COVID-19 pandemic on the wellbeing of parkrun participants in the United Kingdom. *Research Square*. https://doi.org/10.21203/rs.3.rs-690431/v1.

Smith, R.A., Schneider, P.P., Cosulich, R., Quirk, H., Bullas, A.M., Haake, S.J., & Goyder, E. (2021). Socioeconomic inequalities in distance to and participation in a community-based running and walking activity: A longitudinal ecological study of parkrun 2010 to 2019. *Health and Place*, 71. https://doi.org/10.1016/j.healthplace.2021.102626.

Wiltshire, G., & Merchant, S. (2021). What can we learn about nature, physical activity, and health from parkrun? In Brymer, E., Rogerson, M., & Barton, J. (Eds.), *Nature and Health: Physical Activity in Nature* (pp. 208–222). London: Routledge.

Index

Abel, J. 7, 53
accessibility 10, 15, 16, 52, 61, 62, 98, 129, 130; and deprivation 35–36; geographic 35–37; Oldenburg's conceptualisation of 56; research 26–34
accomplishment, sense of 63
active leisure events 129–130
Active Lives (Sport England) 5–6
Adidas 9
Alberti, F.B. 13
American Journal of Health Promotion 32–33, 65
Amin, A. 53
Andrews, G. 86
apprehension 31–32
asthma 60
attachment, feeling of 22–23
attendance 5, 8
attention restoration theory 117
Australia 28–30, 64–65, 67

Baber, M. 8
Bale, J. 12, 84
Bamberg, J. 119, 122
Barnfield, A. 55, 106, 122
Bauman, A. 12
Baxter, N. 93
behavioural science 8
behaviour changes 62
behaviour change theory 71
Bell, N.M. 104
belonging, sense of 2, 8, 21, 22–23, 24, 52, 54, 131
benefits 5, 8, 14, 15, 16, 22, 27, 29, 54–55, 94, 102; volunteering 49–51, 57; *see also* health and wellbeing impacts
Bingham, J. 80
Biophilia Hypothesis, the 112, 113

Bishop, J. 43
Black, K. 14, 96, 100–102
blue exercise 124n6
BMC Sports Science, Medicine and Rehabilitation 69–71
Bodin, M. 114
Borgers, J. 97
Bourne, D. 120
Bowness, J. 10, 22–23, 25, 98, 99, 100
Bradbury, M. 110
Brissett, D. 56
Bristol City Council 111
British Journal of General Practice 72, 74–75
British Journal of Sports Medicine 117
Brown, K. 122
Buckingham, A. 84
Bushy Park, London 2–3

camaraderie 30
carbon footprint 132
Carter, D. 25
Castle parkrun 37–38
celebrations 22
Chakrabortty, A. 21–39, 79
challenge 8
charitable fundraising 12
Chavis, D. 24
children 9
China, 26
Chivunze, E. 105–108
Clarke, L. 7, 53
Cleland, V. 32, 65, 98, 118
clothing line 10
collective bodywork 68
collective identity 24, 26
Colwick parkrun 31–32, 51–56, 59n6, 98
communal experience 16
communication barriers 70–71

community 13; accessibility research 26–34; definition 24; ecological analysis 35–38; elements of 24; ethos 26; idea of 24–26; and inclusivity 21–39; sense of 25, 29, 52, 54, 130, 133; social networks 30–31
community-based intervention 61
community-building 21–39
community membership 96–97
community wellbeing 2
competition 80, 84
comradeship 25
confidence 66
council politics 29
course 4–5
COVID-19 pandemic 14, 51, 110, 132–133
Craig, G. 86
Cregan-Reid, V. 81
Critical Public Health 106
Crossfit 32
Crouch, T. 10
cultural capital 31
cut-off times 79, 85

Dasilva, S.G. 116
Das, P. 7
Davis, A.J, 102–103
deaths, inactivity 6
definition 1
deign 8
democratic values 4
demographics, participants 5
depression 60
deprivation, and accessibility, 35–36
diabetes 60, 61
disability 69–71
disciplined leisure 81
Discovery Health Vitality points 105
distance 4–5
distinctive features 59
Dundee 114–115, 115
Dunn, E.W. 54
Durham University 47–48
Durkheim, E. 22

East Anglia, University of 115
ecological analysis 35–38
economic theory 8
Edinburgh 117
Edwards, A. 79
Eichberg, H. 83
Elborough, T. 110
embodied subjectivities 68–69

emotional connection 24
emotional support 54
encouragement 30
environmental context 28, 106
environmental impact 132
equality 63
equigenesis 115
ethnic density 36, 37
ethnic minorities 27
ethos 7, 81, 97
European Journal for Sport and Society 22
Evans, B. 97
event research 2
evolution 6
exercise 3; definition 6
ExercisePLUS 8
existential capital 123–124
Exodus Travel 95–96

fees 10
Fields in Trust 111
finishing times 16, 32–33, 79, 85, 88
first finisher 82
fitness 59, 60–61, 71
Fitzpatrick, K. 93–94
Fleming, J. 72–75
Fletcher, T. 2
flexibility 9–10, 61, 130
Focht, B. 116
free at the point of use model 10, 26–27
freedom 5, 27, 61
friction 13
Frontiers in Public Health 103–104
Fullagar, S. 27, 33–34, 82, 97
funding 9, 10, 11, 35

Gard, M. 7
gender 47–48
general practice 71–75
geographical access 35–37
Gilligan, C. 123
Gladwell, V.F. 117–118
Global Action Plan on Physical Activity 2018–2030 (WHO) 23
goals 68–69
Graham, P. 9
Grant, A, 50
Great North Run 80–81
green exercise 16; health and wellbeing impacts 116–124
green-prescriptions movement 116
Greenwood, S. 2
group identification, and participation 102

group-related performance 43
growth 8–14, 34–35, 69, 130, 131
Grunseit, A.C. 64–65, 67, 131

Haake, S. 37–38, 65–66, 69–71
Hallam parkrun 37–38
Hallett, R. 43–45, 45–46, 83–84
Hanstad, D.V. 48
happiness 66
Hartig, T. 114
Health and Place 36–37
Health and Social Care in the Community
    72–74
health and wellbeing impacts 59–76,
    100, 105–108, 131; behaviour changes
    62; LTCs 69–71, 72; medical interest
    71–75; mental health 59, 62–64; nature
    112–116; negative 66–67; of physical
    activity 59–69; potential 59; PROVE
    project 69–71; psychological 59–60,
    61; research 60–69; role of technology
    71; sociological interpretation 68–69;
    volunteers and volunteering 63;
    women 66
Health and Wellbeing Survey 4
healthiness 92
healthism 5–8, 93–94
health practice 59, 68–69
heart disease 60
Henderson, J. 80
Her Majesty's Prison and Probation
    Service 11
Hickson, M. 5, 27, 33, 60–62, 98, 98–99
Hillman, P. 130
Hindley, D. 31–32, 51–56
Hitchings, R. 53, 55, 81, 84, 92–93, 95,
    119
Hoggett, P. 43
Honore, C. 86
Horton, R. 7
Howe, P.D. 120, 122
human condition, the 6
Hustinx, L. 48–49
Hutchinson, A. 133
hybrid organisation 12

identification 94
identity 16, 25, 92, 94–95, 97–102;
    collective 24, 26; non-runners 99–100;
    runner 97–98; social 96–97, 102–103
inactivity 5–6, 6–7, 60; deaths 6
inclusivity 3, 5, 52, 61, 62; apprehension
    31–32; Colwick parkrun case study 54–55;

and community 21–39; ecological
    analysis 35–38; ethos 26, 81; free at the
    point of use model 26–27; paid-entry
    events 32–33; research 26–34
Index of Multiple Deprivation 35
influence 24
informality 3, 8, 12, 130
injuries 66
International Journal of Behavioural Medicine
    61–62
*International Journal of Culture, Tourism and
    Hospitality Research* 95–96
*International Review for the Sociology of
    Sport* 99

Joggers and jogging 80, 84, 92
joined-up relationships 34
Jones, E. 21
Jones, L. 111
Journal of Environmental Psychology
    113–114
Journal of Public Health 60–61
junior parkrun 9, 82

Kaplan, R. 117
Kaplan, S. 117
key findings 129–134
Kingston University 43–45
Kohl, H. 59–69
Krenichyn, K. 122, 123

Lammertyn, F. 49
Lancet The 7, 115
Latham, A. 53, 55, 81, 84, 92, 92–93, 95,
    111, 119
Layton, J. 111
Leeds Beckett University 47–48
Lee, I.S. 94
leisure space 52
levellers 55
Lieberman, D. 6
life satisfaction 102
lifestyle behaviours 59
light sociality 53
Linton, L. 66
Little, J. 119
local organisation 29
London, Bushy Park 2–3
London Marathon 81
long-term conditions 60, 69–71, 72
Lorimer, H. 120, 122
Louv, R. 112
Lower Layer Super Output Areas 35, 36

Maas, J. 114
McCartney, M. 118
McIntosh, T. 60, 72, 76
McKendrick, J.H. 95–96
Mcmillan, D.W. 24
maiden event 2–3
Mair, H. 55
Malchrowicz-Mosko, E. 103–104
Managing Sport and Leisure 46–47
marathon runners 104–105
mass participation events 12, 15, 80–81,
    129
Masters, N. 84
media coverage 10, 27
medical interest 71–75
Medicine and Science in Sports and Exercise
    116
Mensah, B. 75
mental health 14, 59, 62–64, 112–114
merchandise 10
Merchant, S. 26–27, 118, 119, 121–122,
    133, 134
micro-economies 42
Montanari, M. 86
moral responsibility 24
Morris, C. 120, 122
Morris, P. 25–26, 62–64
motivation 4, 8, 12, 28, 55, 61–62, 66, 74,
    92, 92–93, 117–118; and participation
    103–106; volunteers 43–45, 46–47,
    48–49, 56
Mowday, R.T 47
Muniz, A.M. 24
Murphy, N.M. 12

Nash, J.E. 93
National Council for Voluntary
    Organisations 50–51
nature 110–124; and the body 119–120;
    disconnection from 111–112, 113;
    functions 120; health and wellbeing
    impacts 112–116, 116–124;
    psychological benefits 113–114;
    restorative benefits 117
nature-deficit disorder 112
nature relatedness 88
Netherlands, the 114
Nettleton, S. 123–124
networks 2
Newcastle Business School 100–102
Newcastle City Council 111
new exercisers 60–61
non-runners 92, 99–100

non-volunteering behaviour 45–46
Nudge Unit, The 8
Nuzzo, J.L. 32–33

obesity 61
Occupational Therapy News 9
O'Guinn, T.C. 24
Oldenburg, R. 51, 55–56
operativism 42
organisation 1
organisational identity 16
origins 2–3
Osbaldiston, N. 86
Outreach Ambassadors 69–71

pacers 83
paid-entry events 32–33
paradoxes 14–15
Parkins, W. 86
parkrun practice initiative 71–75
parkrun tourism 95–96
parks and green spaces 110–113, 118, 132
participant observation 52
participants 92–107; demographics 5,
    27, 32–33, 33; diversity 21–39, 27,
    34, 98–99; ecological analysis 35–38;
    gender breakdown 33; goals 68–69;
    new exercisers 60–61; non-runners 92,
    99–100; non-traditional 32–33; numbers
    37, 131, 132; occupations 100–102;
    sociodemographic profile 61
participation 4, 8–9, 67, 129–130;
    apprehension 31–32; environmental
    factors 119–123; and ethnic density
    36, 37; and group identification 102;
    and motivation 103–106; and physical
    activity 104; rates 37, 131, 132;
    volunteering opportunities 47–56
partnership working 8
Pearson, N. 1, 34–35, 85, 133
Pedersen, H. 26
Pedlar, C.R. 85
performance 82–83
Personal Best 83
personal support 8
philosophy 3
physical activity 8; benefits 5, 8, 15, 29,
    102; deficit narrative 6; health and
    wellbeing impacts 59–69; healthism
    5–8; negative connotations 7; and
    participation 104; prescribed 59;
    promotion 7, 8; recommended levels 6
physical activity opportunities, provision 5

physicality 130–131
Poland 103–104
Popan, C. 87
popularity 10, 12–13
portrayal 1–2
presentation 1
Preventive Medicine Report 67
Price, Jennie 12
prison environments 11
proportionate universalism 11
PROVE project 69–71
psychological benefits 59–69, 61; nature 113–114
public health 1, 7, 12, 15, 27, 30, 31, 36, 42, 60, 62, 65–67, 72, 75, 98–99, 118
Public Health England 5–6, 60
purpose 25

Qualitative Research in Sport, Exercise and Health 100–102
Quirk, H. 69–71; Quirk, H. 132–133
Qviström 92

racing 81, 83
Reasoned Action, Theory of 104
reciprocity 2, 5, 27–28, 61; *see also* volunteers and volunteering
recreational running 80–81
Reece, L.J. 15, 16
registration 8, 13
reinforcement 24
Relative Index of Inequality 36
Renfree, G. 46–47, 48–49
Rogerson, M. 116
Rook, G. 115
Royal College of General Practitioners 59, 72
Rozmiarek, M. 104–105, 105
runner typologies 89n2, 97–98
running 79–85, 92–93, 102, 130; as disciplined leisure 81; growth 88n1; mass-participation 80–81; recreational 80–81
running communities 26
running industry 83
running model, challenging traditional 8

St. George's University of London 43–45
Sandstrom, G.M. 54
Sato, M. 102
Scheerder, J. 26
Scientific Reports 113
Scott, H. 25–26, 62–64

self-discipline 94
self-improvement 61
self, sense of 101
self-surveillance 101
serious leisure 92, 94
Sharman, M.J. 28–30, 45, 50, 98, 100
Sheffield Hallam University 35, 71; Advanced Wellbeing Research Centre 49–50, 65–66
Sheffield, University of 35, 71
Shilling, C. 83
Shipway, R. 55, 97
Sinton-Hewitt, Paul 2–3, 7–8, 9, 50
Skirstad, B. 48
Slow Food movement 86–87
slow living 16
slow movements 84, 85–88
slow running 79–80, 84
Smith, B. 23
Smith, G. 80
Smith, R. 36, 36–37
Smith, S.L. 97
sociability 56
social bonding 26
social capital 2, 16, 30–31
social connectedness 2
social context 28
social ecosystem 51
social environment 62
social identity 96–97, 102–103
social identity theory 94
social impacts 2, 131
social inclusion 23
social infrastructure 51, 111
social interaction 1, 2, 8, 15, 26, 61; Colwick parkrun case study 51–56
socialisation 94–95
social isolation 14, 63–64
sociality 103
social media 13
social mission 11
social networks 30–31, 34
social prescribing 72
Sociology of Health & Fitness 68–69
Sofia 106
solidarity 25
South Africa 105–108
speed, preoccupation with 79, 81–82, 83, 85–86
Sport England 11, 12, 35; *Active Lives* 5–6
sports tourism 96
Staffordshire University 62–64
standardisation 9–10

State of UK Public Parks 2016 report 111
Stebbins, R.A. 92, 94, 97
Steele, J. 32–33
Stephenson, A.L. 104
Stevens, M. 66–67
Stevinson, C. 5, 15–16, 27, 27–28, 28,
    30–31, 33, 49, 53, 60–62, 98, 98–99, 118
Stoke Gifford parish council 10
stress 113
Stride, A. 48
subcultures 43
subjectivity change 99
success, understanding 8
support 30
sustainability 16–17, 42, 46, 132

tail runners 82
tail walkers 42–43
target audience 1
Tasmania 65
Taylor, H. 110
technology, role of 71
temporality 56
third places 1–2, 55–56
threats 29
Thrift, N. 53
Tinning, R. 93–94
togetherness 2
trust 2
Turocy, T. 8
Tyrainen, L. 113–114

Ulrich, R. 113
US Department of Health 6

Valentin, S. 66
virtual communities 13
volunteers and volunteering 1, 4, 16,
    42–51, 56–57; barriers 45–46; benefits
    57; centrality 42; Colwick parkrun case
    study 51–56; core teams 42; egoistic
    48–49; episodic 42, 49; flexible approach

46–47, 56; guiding principles 43;
health and wellbeing impacts 49–51,
63; importance 45; motivation 43–45,
46–47, 48–49, 56; non-volunteering
behaviour 45–46; Outreach Ambassadors
69–71; and participation 42–43;
participation opportunities 47–56;
reciprocity 49, 57; recruitment 43, 44,
45; roles 42–43; sense of obligation 43,
44, 49; training 42; unacceptability of
not volunteering 44; women 47–49

Walker, P. 6
Ward Thompson, C. 114–115
Warhurst, R. 14, 96, 100–102
Weir, K. 21–39
wellbeing 2, 5, 27, 49–50, 64–65; *see also*
    health and wellbeing impacts
Wellington, C. 3, 26, 82, 87
West, J. 46–47, 48–49
White, M.P. 113, 121
Whitty, C. 110
whole systems approach 8
Williams, Tom 10, 132
Wilson, E. O. 112
Wilson, K. 81
Wiltshire, G. 15–16, 26–27, 30–31, 42, 53,
    68–69, 84, 118, 119, 121–122, 133, 134
Wimbledon Common Time Trial 9
women: engagement with nature 119–120;
    health and wellbeing impacts 66;
    new exercisers 60; volunteers and
    volunteering 47–49
Worcester parkruns 47
work-life balance 85
World Health Organisation 6, 104;
    *Global Action Plan on Physical Activity
    2018–2030* 23

Xie, H. 26

Zanker, C. 7

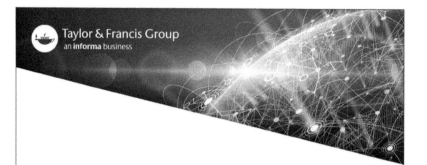

For Product Safety Concerns and Information please contact our EU
representative GPSR@taylorandfrancis.com
Taylor & Francis Verlag GmbH, Kaufingerstraße 24, 80331 München, Germany

www.ingramcontent.com/pod-product-compliance
Ingram Content Group UK Ltd.
Pitfield, Milton Keynes, MK11 3LW, UK
UKHW021455080625
459435UK00012B/519